REV. FRANCIS R. DAVIS
ST. PATRICK'S CHURCH
274 DENISON PKWY. E.
CORNING, NEW YORK 14830-2995

Before the Earth Arose...

Before the Earth Arose...

Articles of redemption and the story of Blessed Maximilian Kolbe

by Jan Dobraczynski
translated by Sr. Mary Leocadia, S.S.N.D.

Franciscan Herald Press
1434 West 51st Street
Chicago, Illinois 60609

Before the Earth Arose... by Jan Dobraczynski, translated by Sr. Mary Leocadia, S.S.N.D. from the Polish *Nim ziemia powstala*..., Instytut Wydawniczy Pax, Warszawa, 1976. Copyright © 1981 by Franciscan Herald Press. All rights reserved. No part of this book may be reproduced, stored in retrieval system, or transmitted, in any form or by any means, electronic, mechanical, photocopying, recording or otherwise, without written permission of the Franciscan Herald Press, 1434 West 51st Street, Chicago, Illinois 60609.

Library of Congress Cataloging in Publication Data

Dobraczyński, Jan, 1910-
    Before the Earth arose....

    Translation of Nim ziemia powstala....
    1. Christian life—Catholic authors—Addresses, essays, lectures. 2. Kolbe, Maximillian, Father, 1894-1941—Addresses, essays, lectures. I. Title.
BX2350.2.D5713   248'.48'2   79-21092
ISBN 0-8199-0783-9

Published with ecclesiastical permission.

MADE IN THE UNITED STATES OF AMERICA

Contents

1. Christ comes again and again	1
2. To be missionaries	2
3. John's baptism and the confession of sins	3
4. Mary already anticipated our anxiety	6
5. What joy to really see Him	8
6. Peace among our own	10
7. Concerning a new dogma	12
8. In the world for the world	13
9. To love one's own child	15
10. Temptation	17
11. The Church in splendor	19
12. To say "yes" to pain	20
13. The elder brother	22
14. With His finger in the sand	24
15. Whoever does not take up his cross....	26
16. Old age, death, Resurrection	28
17. Signs of victory	30
18. No one will snatch them from my hand	32
19. Holiness	34
20. Christ's way of peace	36
21. Oneness—unity in God	37
22. Breath of the Holy Spirit	39
23. The whole truth	42
24. Aid to the hungry	43
25. Once more about hunger	47
26. The public sinner	49
27. John	51
28. Hard Christianity	53
29. God is	55
30. The Samaritan	57
31. The grandeur of heaven	58
32. Thy Kingdom come	60
33. Greed and covetousness	62
34. Anew—for heaven	64

Contents

35.	The peace of Jesus	65
36.	Manhole above us	67
37.	Education or formation of a nation	69
38.	Discretion in love (Lk 14:25-33)	72
39.	With free and easy heart and hands (Lk 15:1-32)	73
40.	No small things	75
41.	The Lazarus of today (Lk 16:19-31)	77
42.	Two conditions	78
43.	To say "thank you"	80
44.	What can each of us do? (Lk 18:1-8)	81
45.	Always find time for prayer	83
46.	Where are these our neighbors? (Lk 19:1-10)	85
47.	Saints eternally alive	87
48.	Death—a grace	88
49.	Hero of our times	90
50.	The great fear (Mt 24:27-31)	91
51.	Hope conquers despair (Lk 1:26-38)	93
52.	A reed (Mt 11:2-11)	95
53.	He was born to witness to love	97
54.	A year of imperceptible change (Jn 1:1-18)	100
55.	To speak of and testify to goodness (Mt 3:13-17)	102
56.	Mother	103
57.	Despite being such as we are (Mt 4:12-23)	105
58.	Purity—chastity—clean of heart (Mt 5:1-12)	106
59.	The light of the world (Mt 5:13-16)	108
60.	Satanic sophisms (Mt 17:1-9)	110
61.	Joy versus sadness (Mt 17:1-9)	111
62.	Romeo and the Samaritan woman (Jn 4:5-42)	113
63.	The hierarchy of reconciliation (Jn 9:1-41)	115
64.	Thoughts about death (Jn 11:3-7)	116
65.	The King on a donkey (Mt 26:14-27)	118
66.	Joy (Mt 28:1-10)	120
67.	Handicapped children (Jn 20:19-31)	123
68.	Victorious banner (Lk 24:13-35)	125
69.	This affects us personally	126

CONTENTS

70.	The Father (Jn 14:1-12)	128
71.	Joseph, the Worker	130
72.	He's always with us (Jn 17:1-11a)	131
73.	Thoughts for Pentecost (Jn 20:19-23), (Jn 3:8)	133
74.	Our saintly mothers	135
75.	The fifth gospel (Mt 7:20-27)	137
76.	The street and the Church	139
77.	Judas (Mt 9:36-10:8)	141
78.	A cross on a neckband	142
79.	A person in need of us	144
80.	Indifference is the worst thing (Mt 11:25-30)	146
81.	Weeds (Mt 13:1-23)	147
82.	The chain letter	149
83.	Examen on manliness	150
84.	Playing with fire	152
85.	Sound the trumpet (Mt 14:22-33)	153
86.	Speaking in silence (Mt 15:21-28)	155
87.	Grandparents, children, and grandchildren	157
88.	To forget oneself	159
89.	Communion of Saints	160
90.	When the pain is greatest	162
91.	Our Christianity must be strong (Mt 20:1-16a)	163
92.	Angels	165
93.	God's share (Mt 21:33-43)	166
94.	To pray for the Pope	167
95.	Missionaries	169
96.	Death and life (Jn 14:1-6)	171
97.	Guidelines for a missionary	172
98.	There must be time for children	174
99.	What then? (Mt 25:14-30)	175
100.	Whatever you have done for the least of these... (Mt 25:31-46)	177
101.	Man, the unknown	179
102.	Before the earth arose	180
103.	Death of Father Tom Rosztworowski	183

104.	A Polish Saint	186
105.	Nicodemus—one of us (An article published in the Spanish weekly *Jesus Christ*)	192
106.	To pay with one's life for the welfare of man	197
107.	God's miser, the story of Blessed Maximilian Kolbe	203
	Introduction	
	The man	205
	The choice	209
	Danger discovered	215
	Misunderstood	218
	Niepokalanów	224
	Mu genzai no Seibo no kishi	226
	In Poland again	240
	The war	245
	At the stake	253
	The Saint	264

1. Christ comes again and again

The prophecy of Isaiah, which the evangelist Luke correlates with the person of John the Baptist, seems to say that when the mountains and hills "will be leveled" and when the crooked ways "will be made straight"—only then will man "behold the salvation of God."

However Jesus came on earth even though the crooked human ways were not straightened, and the inequalities of people were not yet leveled.

With difficulty do the prophecies of God fit within the frames of human history. We count time: before Christ as B.C. and after Christ as A.D. Yet this coming of Christ in the definite epoch of human history had its effects equally in the past. For man, Jesus had to be born and to die on the cross. In God's timelessness all this took place in the moment when the Will of the Most High was expressed and the Mother of Jesus herself was born Immaculate in virtue of the merits of her Divine Son.

The prediction of Isaiah likewise inheres in timelessness. It is hard to say whether it means that the time of improvement of human affairs will actually come. Equally well may we think—either that God's truth will finally plow up the earth and make it better, or that human rebellion will persist to the end of the world. John does not foretell—John calls to witness. He summons the world to conversion, for it is this repentance that will determine whether the graces merited by the life and sufferings of Jesus will be received by all. Human redemption is a precious gift which we received without any merit on our part and we have it within the reach of our hands. But in order to have this precious treasure become a gift for all, the world has to change, get out of the tight circumscription of its own egoism and the "crooked ways" of falsehood.

The essence of the Gospel is this, that its words have a never-changing meaning. John witnessed to the coming Christ. But Christ comes to us at all times and we must be ready for His coming.

2. To be missionaries

Over a hundred years ago when preparations were being made for Vatican Council I and the constitution for the missions was being drawn up, there were cardinals who wondered whether the mission problem wasn't almost too insignificant for the Council Fathers to spend any time on it.

Today we look upon this problem in an entirely different light. The Church has become the mission Church. Pope Paul VI reiterated this emphatically, especially since the beginning of the Jubilee Year. The observance of the centenary of the Little Flower's birthday accentuated the fact that the Carmelite Saint Therese of the Child Jesus was proclaimed the patroness of the missions. She who had never left the confines of Europe had actually spent all her life in her native Lisieux!

What does it mean that the Church of today is a mission Church? The eras of sacralization have come to an end. Knowledge, learning, art, and politics have severed their connection with religion. Secularization of the whole human life followed.

Simultaneously all the people—thanks to the greater spread of culture—became active participants in social and political life. That placed a greater responsibility upon them. Years ago—in the Middle Ages—the Church directed the life of the people. Later on the aristocracy took over this function. But the government, even in communication with other states, cannot assume the whole responsibility for the life of its people today. The future depends upon the attitude and position of each individual human being. Destroying our surroundings, sowing hatred, disregarding the laws of life and innate morality, man becomes the destroyer of the common good of humanity . . . of every person—each one of us! That is why the Holy Father proclaimed this slogan for the New Year 1974: "Peace depends also on you!"

Gone are the days which we call paternalistic—times when the representatives of the Church authoritatively outlined what human life should look like. Today a person decides for himself what his life will be. Therefore, if we want human life to be a truly Christian life, we cannot direct that life by suggestion or demand. In our own vicinity we must act like good missioners who earn the right to speak to people by serving them. We must present the divine truth in a disinterested and discreet manner, helping others and illustrating Christian principles by our own example.

"Let us pray," writes a renowned moral theologian Fr. B. Haring, "that we may be freed from any desire to rule, from a paternalistic stand toward our neighbor. Only then will we be able to ask with confidence to become instruments of the presence of God."

Ancient wise men stood above rulers. The Eastern Magi who came to render homage to the Savior were greater than kings. They were precisely the ones who were deciding what human life should look like.

The Three Magi (for tradition tells us that there were three) understood that with Jesus came a different style of life upon earth. Jesus brought the call for everyone. Every person has his own place and his own work in God's Kingdom.

Our secularized times seem to be turning away from God. And yet by accepting personal responsibility man can come closer to God if he truly desires to find Him. To encourage people to search for God—that is our mission task—ours, the Christians of today.

3. John's baptism and the confession of sins

The baptism that made us Christians is one thing, and John's baptism was quite another thing. By the sacrament of baptism man burdened with the overwhelming original rebellion against God dies, in order to be born again a new man, free and destined for eternal salvation.

The baptism of John was only a prelude to that real baptism, only a preparation for the reception of Christ's teaching. In order to receive this teaching, then as well as now, a person must begin by looking into himself, seeing his own sins and accusing himself before God.

People today do not like confession. They are ready to express their sorrow communally declaring that their life is not what it ought to be. Hence the tendency which appeared among the Catholics of Western Europe to replace confession with general absolution. It is said that this necessity is called for because of the dearth of priests, but it seems that the weightier reason is the dislike of confession.

Confession is neither an easy, nor a pleasant matter. One characteristic thing is that it is easier for a person to go to confession when he has transgressed God's laws in weighty matters. When we have not broken the Fifth, Sixth, or Seventh Commandment we consider ourselves so-called "proper" people and then confession becomes truly difficult. This difficulty is caused by the fact that we have not really broken our friendship with God. We have simply "forgotten" the presence of God for a moment. However, one does not easily forget even for a moment someone that is deeply loved; therefore our conduct proves that we did not really love God that much. It is easier to break with God completely, and after understanding who He is, return to Him, than to not love God sufficiently to arouse the love due to Him within our hearts. The sins of unbridled words, impatience, quarreling, slander, lack of concern about others, lack of moderation in eating and drinking—are "lukewarm" sins—but God, as we know from the Apocalypse, prefers "cold" rather than "lukewarm" souls. The step from "lukewarmness" to disinterested love is a very difficult one.

Confession of sins is not a pleasant matter. Confession is self-accusation. Confession is not meant to excuse us for our sins, nor relieve us of the burden of sinning. By confessing we are disclosing the evil, its motives and source. In confession we are not our own lawyers; we are the prosecuters.

When John baptized people he required that they acknowledge their sins. Therefore John's baptism is comparable to confession. John foretold the coming of Christ—and the Church foretells His new coming—not only traditionally at the beginning of each new liturgical year, but very emphatically on the threshold of the Holy Year.

"Who is announcing this to you?" asked Pope Paul VI in a voice trembling with emotion as he opened the Holy Year for the diocese of Rome, "a poor man, the incarnation of littleness.... I tremble, my brothers and sons, when I speak to you, because I know that I am foretelling things far beyond me, things which I have not witnessed sufficiently, have not served enough, things that ought to be announced by a prophet. I have no written notes before me, such as I usually provide so that my address may be brief and clear. I am simply reading what is in my heart.... Yet I cannot keep it secret, I cannot deny that I am sent. It is not I who speak to you... I am only announcing the words of Christ. I am sent by Christ; I, the successor of St. Peter. Accept me!... The moment has come when I have to demand total dedication and submission from you without reservations...."

Thus speaks the pope. The Holy Year makes great demands on us, Christians, and the moment of decision arrives when we must show the modern world what Christianity really is. By forgiving everyone and helping all men, we will manifest Christ to the world.

In preparation for the fulfillment of this commitment we must begin with the baptism of John—with confession. Jesus who never committed a single sin stepped into the Jordan River to give us an example... that we are to begin to do great things by recognizing our own weaknesses. We must imitate Him.

4. Mary already anticipated our anxiety

"This beginning of signs Jesus worked..." says the evangelist St. John, closing with these words the account of the miracle performed in Cana of Galilee.

For thirty years Jesus lived the ordinary "colorless" human life. He was a child that was no different from other children; became a young man, a carpenter. When Joseph died Jesus took upon himself the care of his Mother and the house. He lived naturally under the eyes of the inhabitants of a small town where everybody knew him.

Until suddenly one day... maybe the same as many another day... there was a wedding celebration—perhaps in the family circle. The hosts ran short of wine. In the East wine is the usual beverage whose consumption does not indicate drunkenness. This shortage will mean trouble for the hosts—will embarrass them now and even affect their future. They are young people just entering upon a new life which they want to begin with dignity. And here—an unkind gossip will repeat for years: those are the people at whose wedding the guests had no wine....

Mary takes notice of this situation and she turns to her Son. Jesus answers her in a manner that seems to be a refusal. He says: "This is not yet my hour." But Mary does not yield. She knows that he has never refused her anything. She does not repeat her request; she simply tells the servants to be ready to do everything that Jesus will direct them to do.

"The salvation of the world began with the Hail Mary," said St. Louis de Montfort. That's right—everything goes back to the moment of the Annunciation. But the salvation activities of Jesus begin with the miracle at this wedding. Mary snatches her Son from his inert waiting. She calls him forth. She asks. She hastens the hour which was to come just as if she had moved the hands of the clock.

Sometimes I think we are wrong in our interpretation of the

role of Mary even when we remember that she is what Pope Leo XIII called, "the Mediatrix to the Mediator." We do not have to beg Mary to intercede for us, just as the hosts at the wedding in Cana did not ask her. Perhaps, concerned as they were about the guests, they did not even notice the impending disaster, and before they could worry about it she had already turned to Jesus.

In the beautiful book of H. Cafferel, *In the Presence of God*, I read not without emotion the words: "Do not think of the prayer of Mary as of something remote in time and place. Let us be bold in approaching her, plunging into her prayer as we thrust ourselves into the dimness of the chapel. She is praying for her countless children, or rather she is praying in their name. A Christian who wants to pray begins his prayer by kneeling down next to his praying Mother."

We do not need to seek Mary to beg her for help. She has already noticed our needs, and is already interceding for us. All we have to do is to kneel down beside her and entrusting our affairs to her pray for what she is praying. For a long time in the life of the Church Mary remained hidden as it were. Does this mean that she was not present in this life? With every century the role of Mary seems to grow. Better and better we now know who she is: the Immaculate Conception, the One assumed into heaven, the Mother of the Church, the Mediatrix of all graces, and the Mediatrix of our prayers. This happens not in order to change something in the eternal plan, but because God wishes us to know her better and understand that she is everlastingly interceding for us, that we may understand from the evident experiences of our era she is our guardian and she alone can show us the way to God's mercy.

At the beginning of the Holy Year let us remind ourselves that the renewal which the Holy Father asks of us has been entrusted into the hands of Mary. And when we consider the effort we are to make let us remember that she has already anticipated our worries; she knows what we lack; she is already pleading for us and has already obtained help for us. We shall attain whatever the Church asks of us if we only join our prayer and effort with her already answered prayer.

5. What joy to really see Him

Let us visualize this: Jesus whom everybody in Nazareth knew for years and who had not impressed anybody as someone unusual, having won recognition and respectful wonder abroad, returns to his native town. During a service in the synagogue, He takes up the Scripture roll and reads the prophetic words—but these prophecies in a very pertinent way speak of Him. Did the inhabitants of Nazareth notice their reality? It seems that it would hit them straight in the eye. But we know that only a few acknowledged the evidence.

The prophecies were signs that would verify the genuine reality of Christ. Such signs we encounter at all times. They are convincing for those who receive them with a gracious heart as something that helps them to believe—and they are unconvincing when one seeks in them evidence excluding all doubts. God wants us to believe Him; hence He does not send signs wholly free from doubts.

In Turin there is to be found the famous Holy Shroud. It has been written about many times. On a long linen cloth the picture of a tortured man, covered with sweat and blood, is imprinted. Evidence of the wounds of the nails, the scourging, the pierced side, the crushed shoulders, the strike on the face, the thorny crown—all of these traces seem to say that it is the imprint of the Body of Christ. Yet in spite of the evidence some of the examiners could conjure up a thousand doubts.

A few years ago there was a celebrated presentation of the Shroud. Cardinal Pelligrini, the archbishop of Turin, was present and the Italian television network broadcast it. The Pope spoke on this occasion and said: "What joy, What a mystery: to see Jesus! To see Him, actually to see.... For us this is a most unusual happiness, because the image on the Shroud which as they say has existed since those times—permits us to contemplate the authentic features of the most holy Face ... satisfies our desire so much alive today, to get to know Him also by sight...."

Way back in 1936 Pope Pius XI said: "Many mysteries still surround this holy souvenir. Nevertheless it is a holy thing, as perhaps nothing else on earth.... Today it can be asserted with full evidence that this is not the work of human hands." Claudel said that the image of the Shroud had for him a meaning "comparable only to a second resurrection."

Scientists are not ceasing to study the Shroud. Many doubts that dealt with the age of the old linen and the sequence of the activities involving the Shroud have been finally removed. We know that in the course of centuries the Shroud was threatened many times; that in the year 70 it was a protection against the Romans, in 1187 against Saladin, in 1532 against fire that destroyed the chapel of Chambery. Pieces of it were given out as gifts.

But of course what was left contains the picture which cannot be viewed without deep emotion. What a Face! Can we imagine Jesus looking any different? Isn't it some sign for our times—so thirsty for visual evidence—that photographic art could bring this Face forth from an old souvenir precisely for us?

"The Spirit of the Lord ... sent Me ..." said the prophecy of Isaiah as read in the synagogue of Nazareth by Jesus, "to announce the year of grace...."

The Jubilee Year is a year of grace. Jubilee years of Jewish antiquity were a presage of the year of Christ's coming. The Holy Year in which we are living should be a year of our return to Jesus, to give witness to Him. The deep bow of the Holy Father over the souvenir of Turin—over one of the signs given to us—has a particular meaning at a time when with our whole life we are to turn to our Savior.

6. Peace among our own

The fundamental point in Christian renewal is, as Pope Paul VI said: "The reign of peace within the Church, among people, in families, in social affairs, between nations."

The Holy Father rightly began with internal peace. Only then, when Catholics themselves become a unity, will they be able to react effectively on others in the spirit of peace.

Let us not fool ourselves thinking that such peace exists. The episode in the gospel about the conflict between Jesus and the inhabitants of Nazareth reminds us that it is most difficult to obtain recognition and a just appraisal among one's own. How often two neighbors, attending church regularly, can be at odds with each other! Two practical Catholics look askance at each other, since one is an advocate of the new liturgy and the other one yearns for the old Latin; one is an adherent of the Church open to all human problems even when these problems are far removed from Christianity, and the other holds that the Church ought to be locked as firmly as a fortress before any contact with the world which threatens it with "contamination." Alas, the acts of the Church are a history of battles between Catholics and Catholics.

The Holy Year program of moral renewal calls for peace, because only peace among people can lead to the establishment of peace between nations. It is a delusion that national treaties will establish peace when there is no peace in men's hearts. The making of peace must begin with peace among one's own people.

There were many widows suffering hunger in the reign of

King Ahab—says Jesus to the Nazareans—and yet the prophet Elias helped only one, the one who believed his words although she was not without faults. However, she acknowledged her faults openly.

In pre-Christian antiquity those who preached the words of God were the prophets. Today the Church is the voice of God. When the Church calls us to peace, we must not let the words go in one ear and out the other with the conviction that they pertain to others. They pertain to each one of us. Everyone ought to convince himself that they have reference to himself also.

St. Thomas taught that in doubts (actually in doubts that cannot be settled by answers in the catechism) everyone ought to maintain a certain freedom, but at the same time show real love in his conduct. These two principles must be exercised simultaneously: freedom and love! Beyond the dogma there is no obligation in the Church to one-way thinking. Imposing certain forms of thought on others was often the reason why people felt frustrated and left the Church. Heretics and saints frequently left for the same reasons. Heretics answered with an outburst; the saints with sanctity, which after some time proved that their way of thinking was right.

Without resigning the right to this privilege of freedom, we must strive all the harder to be more loving and lovable. We must love one another even when our attitudes differ. If I say LOVE, I am not thinking of assuring others and myself by saying: Of course I love him but I do not want to have anything to do with him. To love—that means not to sever a friendly contact with a person. It means to listen to and speak with the person, to trust him and not believe every little gossip at once as a truth, and to try to understand him.

We must begin the Holy Year with peace among ourselves. If we Christians do not become a unity, loving one another reciprocally, let us not begin the Holy Year! The Holy Year must show the world what Christianity really is. We will have nothing to show if we ourselves do not, first-of-all, become Christians.

7. Concerning a new dogma

When Peter beheld the miraculous draft of fish caught in the very same spot where he had been all night without catching anything, he cried out, "Depart from me, O Lord, for I am a sinful man!"

Saying this, he certainly did not want Jesus to leave. It was simply a cry of wonder, of reverence, of shyness, that so great is the God who came down upon earth to live an ordinary human life. Another time when Jesus asks Peter whether he too will go away, Peter cries out in terror, "And where should we go?" No, Peter does not want Jesus to leave. He simply understood how great is the distance between sinful men and the God who created man, and who even now wishes to save man from the effects of his own sins,

The world in which we live grows in deeper knowledge of itself from year to year. Remarkable inventions are discovered practically everyday. The tempo of living is rising—time is flying. In this haste, man is forgetting about God. He is so astounded at his own intellectual achievements that he has ceased to remember the One who has given him this mental capacity.

Even us, so-called believers, remember God less and less. In our daily haste we have almost given up prayer. Who has time to kneel down to pray? Let us look at our children—the children of Christians! If they attend religion classes, most frequently it is because they practically have to: the church is so near, or the priest is an interesting teacher, or the religion classes do not conflict with language classes, modeling, or sports. But just let something in this setup go awry, and we cannot make the effort to rearrange plans for a new schedule—we simply moan and groan about the religion class! Who among the parents on his own initiative ever thinks of having his child go to Confession and Holy Communion at least a few times a year? When religion classes are interrupted for one reason or another, how many parents will personally undertake the important task of imparting the essentials of religious knowledge to their own child?

We are not like Peter who actually cried out, "Depart from me, Lord," but really held on to the person of Jesus with all his might. We say it very softly because we are ashamed of such thoughts: Depart, Lord, because we and our children have no time for You.... We are very sorry, but we feel there are so many more important things to do.... Peter added, "I am a sinful man." We do not say that. We think that lack of time will excuse us from the obligation of explaining away our remissness. We are in too great a hurry—and very often we sin precisely through this haste.

Can we avoid haste? It is true that very often undue hurry is not our fault. In that case all the more should we stretch forth our arms to Jesus, and say to Him, "We have no time; that is why we sin by not caring for the souls entrusted to us. We do not know how to solve this. Come, Lord, help us!"

It is not a simple thing to ask God when we know we are asking Him badly, when haste does not allow us to pray to Him properly. That is exactly why for our times—times when there is such a lack of time—the Church is spreading the knowledge of the efficacy of the mediation of Mary. We believe ever more firmly that all our petitions go, and must go, through her hands. She alone knows how to make our poor petitions real prayers that do not offend her Son. She alone can convert our feverish haste into peaceful fervor.

During this Holy Year we ought to ask Jesus to be with us because we are sinful. We should ask Him through the intercession of his Mother—and the Mother of us all. Let this dogma mature! Let it become one of the fruits of the year 1974-1975!

8. In the world for the world

In his public addresses at the end of the year 1973, Pope Paul VI was constantly emphasizing the slogans of the Holy Year. Among other things he said, "Let us remind ourselves of this great lesson which ought to penetrate the psychology of the modern Christian: to look with greater objectivism on the horizon of the affairs and facts surrounding us, to look with wonder, even with enthusiasm, embracing with reverence, with sympathy, with love the whole face of humankind—even that of a stranger or enemy. But here our troubles begin.... With regard to the world we must maintain our spiritual independence.... We may not be of the world, but we must be for the world, imbuing it with our Christian spirit, giving it a new soul, serving it with our love...."

This reminder is an important thing. Modern Catholics must not commit the error of the modernists at the beginning of the twentieth century. With the desire of bringing Christianity and the world closer together we must not forget that loving the world as it is—even if it is a stranger to us in its moral tenets—we may not accept its standards as our own. Our love must serve the children who gave up our faith, the relatives who relinquished our morality, and neighbors, who from our point of view, are leading improper lives. To cut ourselves off from people whose thinking differs from ours is an unpardonable thing in modern Christianity. However, this does not mean that we have to accept their position, nor share it with them, nor try to find a place for it in Christianity. The movement of so-called modern contestants is often based on the belief that they yield to the temptation of worldly allurements, and having left their Christian principles, blame the Church that it does not follow them, that it is "removing itself from life." The priest who breaks his vow of celibacy, and the lay Christian who is divorced and marries again, are openly in conflict with Christian principles. Nevertheless we must not cease to love him, not refuse him aid when he needs it—yet we must not minimize his outrages by looking for a plausible reason to blame the Church. In his Sermon on the Mount, Jesus said, "Blessed are the poor ... blessed are the hungry ... blessed are the sorrowful ... blessed are the persecuted ... blessed—that is, happy. And so: happy paupers? Are the hungry, the oppressed, happy?

There is no community so ideal in which we do not find the poor, the hungry, the oppressed.... It is our duty to see to it that there be as few of these as possible. But the people who undergo hunger or pain, if they can offer their sufferings with a good intention to Christ—they will be happy. They will be happy because their sacrifice will be the ferment transforming the world, and they themselves—saints. The Beatitudes of the Mount are the call to sanctity. The more saints there are in the Church, the greater the influence of Christianity on the world, and the more the world becomes permeated with the Christian spirit. Hence the success of the Holy Year depends upon this: that the activity of us Christians become more and more like that of the saints.

Saints are not those that flee from this world. They are those who live in the world but offer their burdens for the good of the world: their hunger that of the man next to them—their poverty of possible capabilities, the suffering of loneliness. Saints are those who are in the world for the world, whose standards broaden the circle of Christianity. Everyone of us must imitate them. The imitation of the saints—that is our task during the Holy Year and always.

9. To love one's own child

Reconciliation is the slogan for the Holy Year: Reconciliation in the family, in the Church, among people and between nations.

This is not an easy lesson to learn. Today's world is full of conflicts. War is like fire smoldering in the ashes and ready to burst into flames at the slightest provocation. Peace must be preserved with ceaseless efforts.

But how can the constant threat of war be avoided if there is no peace among people? There are many slights, pretenses, and animosities! A hoodlum attacks a passerby and massacres him. A drunken motorist drives onto the sidewalk and cripples the children playing there. A group of irresponsible teen-agers come upon a girl on a deserted street and attack her. When we read about these things we clench our fists and grow angry. If we could, we would show such a man! Reconciliation? It is easy to speak of reconciliation if we have never witnessed cruelty!

And yet... Jesus says, "Love your neighbor, your enemies do good to them that hate you. It is easy to forgive ideological foes... but harder to do so for the wife of the murdered man, the parents of the crippled children. There are reconciliations that demand heroism—and such a reconciliation cannot be achieved without the help of God.

Jesus says, "Love your enemies, but also: If you love only those who love you where is your reward?" Let us ask ourselves, do we really love those who love us? who loved us?

Do we love our own children? Orphanages are filled with children abandoned by their parents who wanted to arrange their lives differently. There are also children who had to be rescued from their own parents. Not so long ago the British press raised a loud hue and cry about numerous incidents of battery, injury and even killing of children by their parents. Infants had their hands and feet brutally disjointed by their parents. It is estimated that several hundred such incidents occur each year. Are we sure that such atrocities are not perpetrated right here among us?

If you love only those who love you.... A child naturally loves his parents. But if to satisfy their own egoism these parents break up their own home and deprive their child of what is most precious, the family home, will he still love them? Will he love anybody afterwards? Will he not become a hoodlum who without any reason—except that the loss of his parental home might be the real cause—will fall upon an innocent God-fearing pedestrian and massacre him? Or become a drunkard—since forgetfulness of a lost childhood is often sought in whiskey—who drives his car upon the children of other parents?

Everything clicks; the consequences follow one another in orderly fashion. It is not an easy lesson to learn, this requirement of herosim in reconciliation with an evil-doer. But where does the wrong begin? What is the cause, and what are the consequence or result?

Reconciliation during the Holy Year—a sincere conviction that anyone of us could sow evil. If we do not convince ourselves of that, if we do not or will not strive to correct the evil—it will grow and ripen like grain. It is not God's seed alone that brings fruition.

In this Holy Year we must reach down to the very roots of the evil—and only then will reconciliation follow.

10. Temptation

How did the evangelists get to know what the temptation of Christ looked like? Usually they describe what they themselves saw, or what others had seen and told them about. But nobody witnessed the temptation. Jesus himself must have related it to them as He did about the temptation in the Garden of Olives when they were asleep. Evidently it was necessary for them to recognize the essence of a temptation.

The world of the devil and our own nature weakened by the effects of original sin, propel us to evil. But how rarely does this evil appear to us as evil! Usually it comes as a human "need," or simply as something "good."

"Command that these stones be turned into bread," whispers Satan. Is bread anything evil? Can feeding the hungry be anything bad? Jesus does not answer by saying: Man does not need bread. He replies: Not only bread is necessary for man.

The word "bread" embraces everything we need in the realm of materials. Food is not our only necessity. We have to have clothing, housing, and health. If any one of these things is lacking, we are unhappy. Less clearly do we apprehend our need for love, for freedom, for rest, the possibility of mental growth, for silence. Still less do we appreciate the fact that we need God.

The temptation of turning stones into bread is based on the belief that the very process of change is something bad. In the course of our growing needs man might be obliged to turn barren stones into something that will be profitable for human life. The temptation consists in this that the devil will try to convert the matter of "bread" into other things, equally important to man and maybe even more important. But what will all this profit a man if he will have no time to care for his soul? The ancient Jewish Jubilee Year was a year in which there was no work in the fields. The land had a rest, while the people lived on the harvest of previous years. Today that is an impossibility. Our Holy Year must be a time of turning our attention away from the acquisition of clothing and food only, and directing it to affairs whose lack we certainly feel but whose existence we do not even remember.

We must somehow "gain" time for this. We are living a running race at great speed. At the crossroads people cannot wait for the green light and run ahead on the red. They have to be on time to buy their bananas or smoked meat before the others, or they have to "catch"—before the others do—the newly imported clothing, or they have to take their place in line at the rare sweets counter.

Perhaps in this New Year it would be well to resign our place, once or twice, in this rat race for things pleasant, but not essential, and devote the time thus saved to renewal and reconciliation? Instead of running to the forming line or standing at the tail's end, take a look at one's own life? Let us find time for prayer for which we have no time now. Let us convince ourselves that the Holy Year which could change us is flying by every day and has already entered upon its most important period.

11. The Church in splendor

In Fr. Jan Twardowski's enchanting booklet *Zeszyt w kratke* ("Notes in captivity") containing religious talks with children from five to at least eighty years of age, the author tells the story of a little boy who saw everything in church covered with gray dust, as it were. But he was a naughty boy causing his mother much grief and only when he changed for the better, went to confession, and asked pardon of his mother—then he noticed suddenly that everything in the church flashed with colorful brilliance.

How often, we too see everything in a dark color. We say: So what if it is the Holy Year? What of it that it proclaims such beautiful slogans? Who will follow them? The priests will read the bishops' letters from the pulpit, will add their own commentary, and that will be the end. The people will leave the church and forget about what they heard. Where are those whose lives show the influence of the slogans of the Holy Year. There are so many things to take care of: vacations to think about, sending the children to the colonies, forthcoming examinations... Everyone of us has so many problems on his mind. Who remembers the Holy Year?

And so—slowly—the gray dust of worry falls and covers everything in church: the altar, the cross, the confessional, the stained glass windows... Can anything sprout in an atmosphere of discouragement and unbelief?

Did we ourselves assume the work of the Holy Year?

Renewal, reconciliation.... Let us begin with concrete things.

Confession: did we make a careful one, more careful than usual, to purify our soul to its very depth before the activities of the Holy Year? Prayer: did we turn to Her to whom the Holy Father entrusted the Holy Year? Do we repeat daily and earnestly: "I want to do everything with you, O Mary, through you and for you! I know that of myself I can do nothing, but you can do everything that is the will of your Divine Son..." Have we made the slightest gesture toward the man who has a grievance against us (perhaps even justifiable), or against whom we have a grievance (perhaps wholly unjustifiable).

Do we remind the neighborhood—our family, the children, the people around us—for whom we are responsible—that we are living in a year that ought to be a year of witnessing to the faith of Christians and their relationship to that faith? Did we not leave the success of the Holy Year almost entirely to the priest in church? Just as peace in the world is dependent upon each one of us, so also the Holy Year is dependent upon each of us. It will not fall from heaven full-fledged. It will not be the Transfiguration of God whom we shall see in all his glory and might. We must work out this Holy Year in ourselves. We must change our attitude/relationship toward Jesus. We have to determine our own needs and obligations.

After we do this, then one day let us look up at the church. Will not the colors in the stained-glass windows burst forth in radiance, the tabernacle shine in brilliant gold, the cross light up with purple?

12. To say "yes" to pain

On occasion we talk with people and when this talk becomes sincere, full of confidence, sometimes we hear this: I don't understand why that happened to me. I loved that child so; I did so much for him, and he left.... I trusted that man and he betrayed me.... I need good health and here comes this illness... I just do not understand it... others are worse, yet they have loving children, faithful friends, good health....

Do we not ourselves sometimes speak that way or at least think so? In such talk we really blame God but we haven't the courage to say so openly. What God does is not always easy for us to understand. The trouble is as old as the Old Testament. Job could not comprehend why so many disasters fell upon him.

If a tree could reason as man does maybe it too would ask: Why am I spaded around and pruned? It would not understand that the suffering inflicted upon it is for its own good.

Let us go to the hospital and mingle with the crowd of people waiting for some painful treatment. They are afraid of the pain; they moan, complain, ask a hundred times: Doctor, will this hurt me very much? But when the momentary pain passes, what a look of relief is on their faces! Now they are sure that the treatment will help them. Does a painful treatment always help? Does a pruned tree always begin to bear fruit again?

Pain has significance not only then, when it heals our illness. It has its own intrinsic value independent of immediate results. Obviously, the existence of pain does not justify the complacent bearing of it. We are obliged to fight pain—especially the pain of others. We are obliged to heal ourselves. But we also know that we will never be able to eradicate pain completely.

We should be conscious of irremediable pain especially during the Holy Year, for every pain has its own intrinsic value.

Formerly, when manliness was more aspired to in youth than it is today, it was said: Clinch your teeth! When I was a boy, it happened at times that a boy would go to the dentist and have a healthy tooth pulled without an anesthetic just to show that he could bear pain. Of course that was not the wisest test, nor was the motive of that action wise, it was simply a matter of being able to brag about it to others. The point is not that you cause yourself pain. Rather the point is that in pain you preserve the dignity of a man who knows that pain has a value which we can offer to God. We ought to say: Lord God, I know that I deserve every pain, but I also know that through my pain I come closer to you, because every human pain touches you deeply. There are people—many people—who do not know this, who rebel, blaspheme, and fall into despair. If I control my complaints, if I subdue my sorrow within me, maybe you can take my pain for their pain?

To offer your own pain for the pain of others is one of the lessons we ought to learn during this Holy Year. When the

Archangel Gabriel came to Mary and told her about the choice, he also informed her of the honor that was accorded her, as well as the sufferings that awaited her. Thus Mary knew very well what the archangel's question meant. When she answered "yes," she answered with full knowledge and perfect understanding. She chose the honor and the pain. She understood that the pain would be necessary for the human beings who do not know how to suffer.

13. The elder brother

Whom did Christ have in mind in his incomparable story about the prodigal son? Christians, or people living outside the pale of Christianity?

Not infrequently we rationalize: the prodigal son are really those who left. We are the faithful elder brother... only naturally better—not like the one in the Gospel. But how true is that elder brother of the prodigal? He did not have enough courage to leave, but secretly he envied the younger because he knew how to profit by life. He was fortunate enough to taste both this and the other, thought the elder, but I have never experienced anything. But luckily his foot slipped. Let him suffer now! It's coming to him. Let him envy me that I have always been proper! Let him come and humble himself. Let him acknowledge my first-born prerogative.

Meanwhile, we know what happened. The sinner had hardly reached the threshold, and scarcely had he murmured his sorrow when everything was already forgiven of him. In the elder brother anger began to brew. So that one squandered all he could and again returned to favors? And this is what you call justice?

The father did not foster any grievance against his son because he had lived riotously. He knew that later on all the moments of extravagance must be paid for painfully. But that was not the most important thing. Extravagance was an evil thing in the eyes of the father. Whoever loves his father ought to be happy to be able to renounce it for his sake. The younger son did not understand this, but later on comprehended the truth. The elder son renounced it, but in spirit dreamt about those sinful pleasures and envied his younger brother. He was not the least bit better than his brother; in fact he was worse.

Tax collecters, who in their misery entered the service of the rulers, crowded around Jesus; street girls whom misery forced to the sad sale of their own bodies, pressed close to Him. Jesus said to them, "When you will renounce evil and come to Me—everything will be forgiven you at once. You are my sick children." When we have a sick child at home, everything else takes second place. And we rejoice more over the recovery of the sick one than over the fact that the other children were not sick. If only you are sorry—in every church there is a confessional. It is true that your troubles will not disappear. The evangelical manor is the property of both brothers. Worldly riches are the property of all the people. But the elder brother must open the door for you. He must save you from the misery that was perhaps the cause of your sinfulness.

On my desk there is a photograph of a little Negro boy in tears. Someone wrote on the reverse side, "Daily about 100,000 people die of starvation, most of them children...." If we consider ourselves the elder brother of the prodigal son and better than the one in the gospel, we must take part in the feast over the return of the younger brother. We must do everything possible that the return will fulfill the desires of the father. We must open wide the doors of the ancestral home; help our brothers to settle anew in their Father's house. Some will need our material help, others our personal work, and still others our prayer.

The Holy Year calls not only for our reconciliation with others, but it also demands our participation in the reconciliation of others with God ... making it easy for them to achieve this reconciliation. The Holy Year will not accomplish what it ought to, if we who consider ourselves the elder brothers will not contribute our share to this joyful banquet.

14. With His finger in the sand

In the Catholic Church, just as in Judaism, marriage is protected with special care. It constitutes an indissoluble union. In the U.S. in 1972 there was a highly publicized novel by Ann Higgins, *In Search of a Missing IUD,* expressing the painful complaints of both a Catholic and a Jewess against the hard conditions demanded in matrimony by both religions.

In Jewish antiquity there was a law that prescribed the killing of unfaithful wives. "Whoever commits adultery with the wife of his neighbor will be punished by death—both the adulterer and the adulteress," says Ecclesiasticus (20,10) "You will lead both of them beyond the city and stone them there until they die" (Book of the Repeated Law 22,24). In the time of Christ the severe law was not applied. The Romans did not allow the execution of the death sentence without their approval, and their moral level of life dropped very low. How could it be otherwise when the rulers, like Antipas, were brazen adulterers?

In spite of this, the pharisees set up a trap to catch Jesus. Bringing him a woman caught in adultery, they placed before him the alternatives: either he will show mercy and thus contradict the law of Moses, or he will demand the scrupulous execution of the law and set himself up as one far more severe than the standards of his epoch.

Jesus was silent. Bending down he wrote with his finger on the sand. Only after that he said, "Whoever of you is without sin, let him be the first to cast a stone." What he wrote we do not know. Maybe they were only doodlings such as we scribble when we are collecting our thoughts or want to give another time to collect his? Or perhaps Jesus wrote, "You are demanding this woman's death—but you steal; and you kill; and you too commit adultery? There was something in what Jesus wrote that caused the accusers—one after another to leave. Did Jesus minimize the meaning that religion attached to marriage by refusing to condemn the wife who betrayed her husband? We know that the opposite is true. Jesus considered marriage so important an institution that he cancelled the Mosaic law allowing divorce. By forgiving the woman he did not say, "Go, that was not important," but he said, "Go and do not do that again." He forgave the human being, but he did not forgive the sin.

Jesus understood adultery in a much broader sense than many moralists—casuists. For Him the Jews were adulterers when they abandoned God for pagan gods. Marriage is for Jesus the symbol of man's union with God. We do not always give ourselves the benefit of the full meaning of this unusual analogy. We may use the word adultery for anything and everything that is a betrayal of man's union with God. It would be a spurious interpretation of God's law if for one act of adultery a man would suffer death, while for other forbidden deeds, not less heinous, the punishment would not be so great. Furthermore, Jesus is opposed to judging one sinful man by another sinful man. Why would a thief have the right to judge a murderer, or the murderer a swindler?

Jesus, an accomplished psychologist, knew very well that adultery is a sin that instinctively arouses anger and a desire for revenge. Adultery is the daily topic of shameless jokes in taverns and theatres, but the betrayed husband or wife, even if they no longer love, are ready to seek satisfaction for themselves forgetting what heavy responsibilities weigh upon them.

Facing the "letter of the law" there are the guilty and the innocent. Who is not guilty in the eyes of God?

The Holy Year—that's a year in which Jesus writes in the sand more frequently than usual. The wind will wipe out his accusations as soon as we see them. Jesus wants it thus—that they may not remain forever. They are simply to be a reminder and an admonition. When we look for faults in others, he reminds us of our own; when we desire revenge, he admonishes us with mercy.

Let us bend down and see what has been written about us and as quickly as possible go to seek reconciliation with the one whom we are accusing.

15. Whosoever does not take up his cross....

That was a week in which the whole history of humanity converged. In those few days, days of which only a few contemporaries were aware, and whose meaning nobody appreciated, everything was fully realized that concerned man's fate. Man was saved, snatched from the pit of perdition, and once again he could see his goal before him.

We are reliving those days.... But are we really reliving them? Isn't their importance veiled or at least bedimmed by our daily troubles, concern about a journey, food preparations? We celebrate, and rightly so, the anniversaries of great happenings, and during that time mentally review what happened on that occasion. Do we think just as intensely about the events that took place some 1971 years ago (probably, for we are not sure of the date)?

Of all the scenes that took place in those few days let us pause today at one of them. An overworked farmer, Simon, is returning from his field. He was an inhabitant of Cyrene, in modern Libya, where there was a large Jewish colony. For reasons unknown to us he returned to Palestine. Perhaps he returned because he had inherited a piece of family land. The tired man stopped in the crowd that lined the walls of the narrow streets of Jerusalem. Maybe he simply could not get through, and maybe he was driven by curiosity wanting to see the boisterous parade that was leading three men condemned to death by crucifixion.

One of the condemned men could not make it. He was falling time and again, and he was badly wounded. From the evening of the day before, he had been terribly tortured. Striking and kicking him, they had dragged him in from Mr. Olivet last night. He was being interrogated while the beatings continued. There was no sleep for him. He didn't even get a drop of water. In the morning there was another questioning session. Then he was dragged to the Fort of Antonia, afterwards to the palace of Herod, and back again to Pilate. Later on he was cruelly scourged—and this was a torture beyond measure, enough to immobilize a man for a few days. Now they told him to carry his cross. . . .

The guards fearing that the condemned man might die before reaching the place of execution, turned their attention to the heavyset man in the crowd. They grabbed him by the neck and against his will pulled him out of the crowd, placed the cross on his shoulders, and forced him to carry it after the mortally exhausted victim.

At one time Jesus said: ". . . Who does not take up his cross and follow Me—is not worthy of Me." Everything that touches us we call our cross: illness, sorrows, material troubles, misunderstandings. But because God's Providence directs all things, "everything is a grace," as St. Teresa says—this cross is something offered us by God. Suffering serves us as a bitter medicine. Its bitterness is meant to help us. We ought to accept it without resentment. It is adapted to our strength.

Christ says in the Apocalypse, "Be cold or hot! Be devoted to Me with all your heart. Or fight against Me, for maybe the battle will tell you who I really am and the one with whom you are fighting is not Me at all.

But I will spit you out of my mouth if you are lukewarm—if bearing the name of Christian you yield time after time to your weaknesses, desires, cowardice—you give in and do not consider that a fault at all. You explain that my laws are somewhat too severe. You want to reconcile God with mammon—because mammon is not only love of money but also desire of all kinds of ease. You want to have this and that; you close your eyes and ears when I tell you how many people die daily of starvation—yet you constantly claim that you are a Catholic!

Simon of Cyrene at first refused the cross they placed upon his shoulders, but later on he understood the grace that was given him and became a disciple of Jesus.

And we? How do we handle our crosses?

In announcing the Holy Year, the pope placed the cross of Jesus on our shoulders. Are we carrying it, or are we dragging it in anger? Or, perhaps have we thrown it away?

16. Old age, death, resurrection

Not long ago the Holy Father canonized a Spanish nun, Sister Teresa of Jesus, Jornet Ibars, who died in 1897. Saint Teresa was the foundress of the congregation of the Little Sisters, who have as their objective to serve and care for the poor, old and neglected people. In his address that day, Pope Paul VI said, "Maybe there is someone here who will say: a nun again? Another nun glorified? Yes, one more woman raised to the honors of the altar forever! She consecrated herself to the Lord. We visualize her in the ordinary habit of a nun, wholly devoted to prayer, penance, self-denial, engulfed in the current of ecclesiastical life, far removed from worldly affairs—from social problems. No, dear brothers and sons! She is in truth a saint of our times, if we acknowledge that these times are characterized by the aspect of social humanism and are marked by the cult of sacrifice of one man for another man...."

There is no greater modern problem than the problem of man. Man—the inventor of unusual things, and man—so weak that in his weakness he seems to be unnecessary. We wax enthusiastic about the first, and with ever greater impatience think about the second—the helpless child and the powerless old man.

Children are dying of starvation—tens of thousands every day! Children are tortured and killed by their denaturalized parents, as the English press tells us. The French press recently announced the murder of a little eight-year-old girl by her father, a higher officer, scholar, Catholic—who wanted a release from his wife but feared that in the event of a divorce she would take his "beloved" daughter.

The problem of the aged.... Let us take a look around us. As long as grandma was necessary at home, everything was fine. But when she began to weaken, both physically and mentally, the cry arose, "How to get rid of her? Take her any where, as long as it is far away." The lot of grandpas is settled more quickly—they are no good for anything in the house. And what shall we say about the old folks who have no children or whose children have moved away?

The fate of the child and the fate of the old person are the two big problems of our era. The old person is the one approaching death. Youth usually speaks of death lightly and with little concern. Death is something so far away.... For the aged person death is very near... nearer every day. Although nothing is expected from life yet, the human organism will fear the final moment of dying.

We die alone, but in dying we need the presence of another person. Even Jesus in the Garden of Olives wanted to feel that his apostles were near to him.

Do we go with a word of comfort to people who are dying, or do we carefully shun such "unpleasant sights"? Does the Holy Year not remind us about old folks who perhaps are waiting for our visits, our word, and our smile?

And then death.... When we are consigning to the grave someone dear to us and when the officiating priest requests a prayer for the next one about to die, we presume that we shall never again see the person who has disappeared. Never? When the women who did not find the Body of Jesus in the tomb came running to the Apostles with the news, their "words were mere empty gossip and they did not believe them."

Even the Apostles, who were taught by Jesus for years, did not believe. And we? Do we believe that He arose from the dead?

There are many people today who are ready to admire Jesus but consider Him merely as a wonderful man who died and remained alive only in his work! However, the Church speaks otherwise: Jesus actually arose from the dead! This unprecedented miracle really happened. And his resurrection signifies the resurrection of us all. If we do not believe in this, our whole faith is groundless. Aimless also is the observance of the Holy Year.

The Resurrection of Jesus is the key to the history of the world and to the mystery of our own personal existence. If Jesus rose from the dead, then death is not the end of everything; human weakness is only the end of a trial or test; human life is something priceless, and holiness is the energy. By comparison, nuclear energy seems to be something very small indeed.

17. Signs of victory

When it became known that mortal danger threatened Jesus, when he had to hide far from Jerusalem, and when the news reached him that Lazarus was ill and he said he would go to Bethany, the apostle Thomas shouted, "Let us go too, to die together with him." Perhaps in view of this readiness Jesus was very kind to him afterwards in his unbelief. He simply said, "touch my wounds."

Such moments also come in the life of the Church, and in the life of every individual, when everything seems to be heading toward a catastrophe. People dear to us are leaving the faith, our own children shrug their shoulders at what we value as holy, certain forms of religious life—to which we are accustomed—disappear, and we discover in ourselves sins and failings which we had never noticed before.

We feel deeply grieved. We have to overcome doubts, sorrows, loneliness, and a sense of our own helplessness.

But one day it seems to us that Christ is standing before us. No, I'm not talking about any miracle. This Christ is invisible—it is only a thought about him, a feeling of nearness, and Christ shows us his pierced hands and side. The prints of his wounds and of the defeat he suffered! For humanly speaking, these marks looked like a defeat. He seems to say: "Touch them! Convince yourself that they are in truth bloody wounds. And yet, they really brought about a complete turn of affairs. What was well-nigh a defeat became a glorious victory. I arose from the dead, but the wounds remained. The wounds remained as a sign that this is the only real way to conquer."

The Holy Year is passing by in an epoch of Great Indifference. Violent contentions which only a few years ago shook the life of the Church have ceased. Those who were rebelling either left or have fallen into indifference. Just as the press announced recently that in the United States in the last ten years of the total number of those professing Roman Catholicism, the number of practicing Catholics had dropped from 71 to 55 percent. In a beautiful growing suburb of Paris in which many shops and department stores appeared, only one thing was not realized although it had been foreseen in the plans—the building of a church. Evidently no one was interested enough in the erection of it any longer.

Jesus appears to say: "Touch my wounds—the wounds of my Church. They are real and painful. But I suffered them and sanctified them." What is happening in the history of the Church today was foreseen and overcome on the cross. The cross redeemed everything to the very end. The Great Indifference of the second half of the twentieth century was also redeemed on Golgotha.

The cross conquered everything—in advance. The Holy Year is a returning of oneself to the cross, and to victory which has already been accomplished. We were rescued and it is enough for us simply to stretch out our hands to reach the fruits of the victory, and to join his wounds with ours.

And let us observe that ever more frequently in conversation with people one hears: I must somehow make peace with him—or her—for it is the Year of Reconciliation. We must not quarrel during the Holy Year. We must not hate. We have to find another way; the way of love....

These resolutions are still rather diffident and sheepish. And yet they speak of this, that the idea of reconciliation is paving its way among the people. Happily it will continue to pave the way if we understand and begin to feel that the wounds of Jesus are signs of victory.

18. No one will snatch them from my hand

In the last weeks of 1974 the Congregation of the Cult of God issued a document bearing the title Ordo Penitentiae, introducing a certain reform of the forms of the Sacrament of Penance.

The new rite, which will be introduced here only after the enactment of the Polish episcopate, foresees a new form, besides the form of the individual confession almost identical with the present one, and the form of the general absolution adapted to exceptional situations and which demands from those receiving absolution the firm determination to make an individual confession and perform the penance at the first opportunity. This will consist of a communal prayer of penance of many penitents who will afterwards make a private confession and again meet for a prayer of thanksgiving.

The introduction of this new form is related to the change of the name of the Sacrament of Penance to the Sacrament of

Reconciliation. Strictly speaking, this is the name of the sacrament in ancient times. It emphasized the fact that in the sacrament of penance we seek reconciliation not with God alone, but equally with people. It is true that one of the conditions of confession is satisfaction, but absolution precedes satisfaction which in the old way is left to the good will and time of the penitent. Thanks to the new form we will have recurrence to the mercy of God after having first met in a gesture of reconciliation with those whom we have offended.

"For if you forgive people their offenses, your heavenly Father will also forgive you.... With the same judgment that you judge, you will be judged.... When you are going to court with your opponent, make an effort on the way to come to some agreement with him, so that he will not oblige you to see the judge...."

Reconciled with people in the spirit of brotherhood, how much better we are prepared to ask God for forgiveness.

"My sheep... will never be lost; no one will snatch them out of my hand!" Jesus says this with self-assurance and with power, for he does not want to say that we ourselves cannot escape from his hands. Man's free will is always honored. Only if and when we want to remain with him, if we fulfill his will, Jesus will not let us get out of his hand.

The marvelous, prophetical intuition of Pope John XXIII, the decisions of the Second Vatican Council, the proclamation of the Holy Year of 1974–1975, the unusual breakthroughs that occurred in our times, have all given us possibilities adapted to our epoch of fulfilling the will of Christ. The world will not pull us away from Jesus, because the Church of Jesus has found itself in the stream of the world's life. We will find it everywhere, in all the affairs of life, in brotherhood, in peace, and in justice. We do not walk away from Jesus when we go to man. On the contrary, going out to man—the hungry, the needy—we find Jesus.

We shall remain in the hands of Jesus thanks to the help of our Mother, the Blessed Virgin Mary. She strengthens us, encourages us, upholds us in our desire to fulfill the will of God. Her soul ought to be, as Pope Paul VI said, "in every one of us for God's glory." We were placed under her protection in 1946 with the great act of consecration to the Immaculate Heart of Mary by Pope Pius XII. We will not abandon Jesus if we do not leave Mary. This determined will to remain faithful we must strengthen in ourselves.

19. Holiness

We are living too deeply in contemporaneousness to be able to notice the changes in history taking place all around us. Yet what is happening in the acts of the Church today is something incomparable. The Church experienced the Middle Ages, the Renaissance, the Reformation, but all these eras were only phases of one great epoch which started from the very beginning of the life of the Church and ended in the days of the pontificate of John XXIII.

Throughout that whole epoch of almost 2,000 years the Church was deeply involved in earthly affairs. It led people to Christ, but it also had its own ambitious ideas about ruling the world. It protected people, but was also inclined to fight for its own rights.

Up to the times of John XXIII, to the Vatican Council II, to the observance of the Holy Year, the Church has acted above all as the structure of an eternal, everlastingly renewing Institution. It attracted people and "drew them to its own side."

Today we are within the Second Pentecost. The Church is turning to all the people and is offering them the Gospel anew. It does not oppose the secular institutions but offers each one cooperation. Standing within sight of the Great Indifference toward religious ideals, and simultaneously facing the Great Yearning for religion and spirituality, it throws out into the world its invitations to internal renewal, unity of all believers, and dialogue with the whole world.

These are the three objectives of the Church today. But all three aims demand one—holiness.

"In truth, the reality of the mystery of the Church does not wholly consist in the hierarchical structure," said Pope Paul VI, "nor in the liturgy, nor in the sacraments, nor in legitimate regulations. This internal essential Being, the source of sanctifying effectiveness, must be sought in mystic union with Christ."

"Above the hierarchy of power," writes Fr. M. M. Philipon, "stands the hierarchy of love. Above hierarchical structure, the structure of holiness." Therefore, in all the fervent acclamations of the Holy Year is the repeated call to sanctity.

What is holiness? Sanctity? Plainly love, love greater than that which we are ordinarily able to express. Love which begins with the inspiration of God and strengthened by God's grace, expresses itself. Love for every human being, but especially for the suffering. Rising above the commandments, and imbued with the evangelical counsels! "Complete submission to God's holy will," as the constitution *Lumen Gentium* says. "By this will all men know that you are my disciples, if you have love for one another."

But there is a danger that threatens us Christians in the present era. Everybody talks about love nowadays. Love is appreciated everywhere. It is understood that the Church is not necessary for love. On the contrary, many aver that although the Church advocates love, it is at the same time the destroyer of love.

The word "love" does not always mean the same thing. The love to which the Church calls us in this new epoch is simultaneously holiness. It must be sanctity. Opening itself up outwardly to the world, the Church demands of its members ever greater interior coherence and solidarity. We must become better informed Christians. We must be witnesses. Love for others cannot excuse us from the obligation of self-control. If our love is to remain true love, we must strive for sanctity. That's a very big word! But we are living at a critical point of the two epochs, and the epoch just approaching demands such heroic greatness.

20. Christ's way of peace

In the American film "Hospital," which appears on our screens, we have a doctor/director of a large hospital in New York. He is a man psychically drawn up to the nth degree: his marriage is unfortunate, he and his wife constantly quarrel and his children have gotten out of hand morally. To add to the evil, scandalous things are going on in his hospital: incredible neglect is taking place, people are dying due to medical errors and incompetence, and the doctors care only about their pay and personal pleasures. The doctor is so overcome by all this that he sees only one solution—suicide.

A girl saves him from death, and his feelings toward her allow him to regain his poise and energy. He forgets his bad wife and lost children. But the girl poses this problem: if he really loves her, he must leave the hospital with her. The doctor chooses the "duty" of remaining in the hospital and resigns from "love." In the film that seems to be a fine solution. But is it so in reality?

The duties of a man begin with his obligations toward his own family. Granted, the doctor's wife was bad and the children went astray not necessarily because of his attitude toward the family. Certainly there are innocent people (but are they wholly without fault) unhappy in their personal lives who later on "compensate" for their loss by a prodigious effort in some career, especially when that is a social service. But in the case cited we have our doubts—is not the low grade of the medical service in the hospital in a certain measure the result of the director's unconcern? We see how he berates the doctors for using the hospital as a place for finding self-satisfaction only, while he himself in the same way is getting "peace of soul." Doesn't this smack a little of "Kale's ethics"?

"Peace of soul" is a great treasure sought by all men, especially modern man. The film suggests that the doctor found this "peace." In truth, however, is this really "peace"? Perhaps it's only a momentary satisfaction. The girl was a kind of test to prove that he could still attract women. When she leaves, he will find another. And is this his chance to prove that he will now be able to fulfill his "duties" well, as director of the hospital?

Jesus gives true peace and He gives it in a different way. The peace of Christ is not the healing of complexes. A complex is an illness that a person uses as a mask to hide his guilty feeling. Christ demands that we look at our faults openly. A bad wife, delinquent children, whether or not they are our own fault still remain our concern. And peace of soul is not attained when we substitute a bad wife with a better one, or when we close our eyes to our children's conduct, or when we blame others for the bad functioning of an institution entrusted to our care, but only when our conscience will have nothing to accuse us of, and we can offer our pain for the sake of the good cause.

That is Christ's way of giving peace, and that is the peace of Jesus. Too often we want satisfaction and that satisfaction we call peace, just as we call a rapture of feelings, love. Yet the first, as well as the second emotion, is much deeper. We must seek to understand the true meaning of both of these concepts—peace and love.

21. Oneness—unity in God

It happens that in looking over one's own notes written years ago, we stop at an item which speaks of resolutions made at that time. Suddenly, we become aware that those resolutions did not lose any of their actuality. That means that after many years we are in the same place which we were then. Our resolutions have not been realized.

The first reaction that such a discovery awakens is discouragement. So that's the way we are!—we think. Beautiful words in a moment of fervor, and then nothing. ... Everything appears dark and gloomy. We feel disgusted with ourselves.

And yet even in this unpleasant discovery there is a certain joy. Wisely John XXIII kept notes all his life and constantly returned to them anew. We must know what we are like and we must give an account to ourselves as to whether we know how to change at least one thing in our lives. And if we did not change, we ought to meditate on what was the cause of it.

Let us think, was the cause of our failure perhaps the lack of prayer, above all else? We pray, of course—but we pray badly. I do not say little, because prayer cannot be measured by length. Its value does not stem from the number of words we say. We pray badly—we ask hurriedly and impatiently, and rarely do we give thanks. Our prayer is self-centered: Lord, give! Lord, do this! Lord, save! We should ask God, but we ask Him only when the danger is already hanging over our heads. When a marriage is threatened, when we or our children have already fallen sick, when we have suffered a loss, when our children have already left us, when we have encountered human animosity....

For those problems we should have started praying immediately, when we became aware that the trouble existed or was threatening. Oh, long before it comes to us!

We pray badly because we do not join our prayer with the prayer of Jesus, with the prayer of the Blessed Virgin Mary, with the prayers of the saints, with the prayers of other people. We do not pray for the general or common good. We pray only when our good is threatened.

The slogan of reconciliation during the Holy Year reminds us of unity. Reconciliation does not mean only uncovering faults in ourselves. It also means, above all else, discovery of togetherness, oneness, brotherhood. Does it simply mean that we forgive one another and then immediately go our own way? Does it not rather mean to go together now, be near each other, helping one another mutually?

Did not Jesus pray for this: "That all may be one as You, Father, in Me and I in You, that they may be one in Us"?

If only such a unity, such oneness in God would exist, communal prayer would forestall every evil. With this perspective let us look at our old notes. What had we resolved at that time? To curb our tongue in order to not hurt others, to not to tell lies, not even exaggerations, and to not give scandal, even to please others? To tolerate another person? To perform works of kindness and mercy for him? Not to harden our heart, that is, not to treat people unkindly? Not to be self-centered? Not to assess everything by the slogan: What will I get out of this? Not to fear every effort in advance? Rid myself of lack of confidence or trust? Not to fear to be laughed at or ridiculed for doing good beyond measure (John XXIII had to warn himself often against this fear)? Not to fall into discontent or despair?

Not to fall into discouragement! God always allows us to begin anew. As long as we live, it is never too late. We can return to the resolutions of years gone by. But now let us go at these resolutions in a more realistic way. Let us begin by arousing within ourselves a feeling of unity, to feel a "oneness in God" with all people. Then our resolutions will automatically become realized in this unity.

22. Breath of the Holy Spirit

Jesus appears in the midst of his disciples still full of fear after the tragic experiences of the Great Week. By breathing upon them he gives them the Holy Spirit, the promised Spirit-

Comforter, Spirit of Truth, leading to "all truth." Even before the official descent of the Holy Spirit on the newly rising Church took place, they, his nearest and dearest ones, received the Spirit directly from Jesus, that he might be their help in the difficult time of waiting.

For, of course, those must have been very difficult moments that separated the morning of the Ascension from the morning of Pentecost. They were days suspended, as it were, in a vacuum. Jesus departed and left his disciples alone. They were very much more alone than when his body was lying in the tomb. At that time everything collapsed about them and nobody expected anything from them. They could consider the years gone by as nonexistent. They could try to return to what they had been before. Only that now on his departure—he had left them his commission to act. He left directions and commands. They had a task before them as great as the whole wide world. An immense job, and they had no idea of how to go about it.

Only now when the Holy Spirit came down upon their heads in fiery tongues did these lowly people receive power and understanding for carrying out the superhuman task. One would think that in a moment they became giants. But truthfully, with all that they received, they remained the same people no different from what they were before.

The astounding reality of the gifts of the Holy Spirit is that their power appears only in cooperation with man. Their tremendous power lies inactive it seems until we decide to reach out for it. The Church has always had the greatest possibilities available. If they were not always realized it was only because the human effort was not equal to the power of the Spirit. But the whole strength of the Spirit was always in its treasury. Then, in Jerusalem, the Holy Spirit came out as if he were the first to meet the weakness of man. Without waiting for man's initiative, he awakened it himself.

Are we not witnesses of something similar today, after all these ages? The breath of the Holy Spirit is blowing stronger today than ever before. The epochal change taking place today seems to be the direct action of the call of the Spirit of Truth and Sanctity.

On the surface things appear otherwise. In the face of problems shaking the world—the advance of knowledge, demographical crises, economical and moral as well, threats of wars and destruction of man's environment, psychical breakdowns in people and their mad rush to self-destruction expressed in the insanity of alcoholism and narcotics—the changes in the Church may be looked upon as the problems of a small handful of interested people. In reality the situation is entirely different. If we believe, we will notice that this new breath of the Holy Spirit is something extremely important in human life. There have already been several Holy Years in the life of the Church, but no previous Holy Year had a meaning so deep. Other Jubilee Years renewed the Church but no other Holy Year set it up against such formidable horizons. The deeper the world sank into the sea of dangers, the greater were the powers released to save it.

Do we realize the era in which we happen to be living? Do we understand that this jubilee call to reconciliation and to holiness is only the prelude to something much greater, to something that will gain momentum with every year? It was only a handful of people that the Holy Spirit came down upon that early pentecostal morning. Hence, let us not grieve too much over the fact that the call of the Holy Spirit comes today upon a Church considerably reduced in numbers, full of internal contentions and conflicts. If the participation of human power in the work of the Church is necessary, it is not its size that is the measure of its effectiveness. The Holy Spirit and the protection of Mary, the Mother of the Church, are the most important factors. They will be with us if only we take the first step, maybe only half a step. If only we extent a hand, the Holy Spirit will come flying like the wind snatching everything, and will burst into a flame like fire that no one will be able to quench.

23. The whole truth

Not long ago I read a new book, *The Blind Side*, written by the English author well-known to Polish readers, Francis Clifford. The book tells about a missionary who with incredible dedication endeavors to secure sustenance for an African village far removed from any road and condemned to starvation. Finally he secures a plane loaded with supplies, but when the pilot throws the packages down to the village, the missionary watches in terror as the packages break open as they strike the ground, and the priceless food mingles with the sand.

To illustrate the account in the book, the London weekly, *Sunday Times* depicts a shocking photograph of an airplane dropping a consignment of grain for the cattle in a very dry meadow on the plains of Mali. The people rushed to gather the scattered grain, searching for it diligently in the sand. Not for the cattle, but for themselves! A woman with a child on her back dragging herself in search of a handful of grain—that's the picture of degradation into which hunger has plunged the proud nomads.

The situation is bad, and constantly worse. We've already wanted to forget the problem of hunger, but we may not do so. The drought continues, spreads, touches even the terrain which until recently did not suffer from want of rain. Nigeria, the largest exporter of peanuts in the world, will not export even a ton. Ghana, the biggest producer of cocoa will have a harvest this year at least 15 percent less than usual. The coffee harvests on the Coast of the Elephant's Bone have been reduced about one-third. The countries of Western Africa which live on their export of meats, have nothing to send out since 3,500,000 of their cattle died last year. The drought causes the desert to move forward constantly to the south at the speed of thirty miles a year. Meterologists fear that the changes brought about by the drought may bring with them climatic changes and a continued lack of rainfall in the course of decades. The secretary of the

United Nations, Dr. Kurt Waldheim, said, "The threat exists, that whole countries can disappear from the map of the world." The whole strip of middle Africa from the Atlantic to the Red Sea is threatened. Death by starvation threatens 15,000,000 people.

What is worse is that no financial aid can any longer fulfill its assigned task. In the year 1973, 470,000 tons of foodstuffs were delivered to the hungry in the countries of Africa. In 1974, 715,000 tons were needed, but according to Dr. Boerm, the secretary general of FAO, the food reserves are the lowest in thirty years. And help is also needed in India, Pakistan, Bangladesh. So there may not be any grain left for Africa.

"The worst is constantly ahead of us," said UN Secretary Waldheim not long ago. Can we close our eyes and ears to all this? Can we nod in agreement to this that in the Holy Year millions will die of starvation?

The world has entered upon a dramatic period of trouble and hardship in the matter of providing foodstuff. Years of burning grain and hurling coffee into the sea are being avenged. Likewise experiments that brought about the climatic changes are taking their toll. People are dying of hunger.

We should not be allowed to celebrate the Jubilee Year if we will not do our share in the work of providing aid to the dying. "When He comes, the Spirit of Truth will lead you to the whole truth." Is this not the "whole truth"—the truth, that the obligation of showing mercy is the first step on the way to Jesus?

24. Aid to the hungry

We have entered upon the most active time of the year—the year that is at the same time the Holy Year. Spring and summer will bring numerous pilgrimages associated with the cycle of the Holy Year. Without underrating these external forms of devotion, we must always remember that the most important thing is the internal content of the Jubilee: renewal and reconciliation, solidarity, hope, justice and trust.

Rightly the Secretariate of the Committee of the Holy Year, in its Pastoral Document sent to all Episcopal Conferences, write: "Stressing the hallmarks of the Spirit of the Jubilee is the best means to free the Holy Year from even the slightest sign of yielding to any outward show and triumphalism in the celebrations. Above all are to be noted those acts, gestures and interventions in which appears only the absolute "glory" of the Risen Christ."

This same document calls special attention that in the Holy Year, works of charity should loom large. These are the outcome of the very nature of a Jubilee renewal. There can be no talk about reconciliation, brotherliness, or human solidarity, if at the same time hundreds of thousands of people are dying of hunger in many countries.

Somebody sent me a shocking picture that portrays a little hunger-bloated Negro boy crying piteously. On the reverse side of the photograph was written, "Daily about 100,000 people die of hunger—most of them children."

These numbers are true. I placed the photograph on my desk before me because I want to have it permanently in sight. I do not want to forget even for a moment these children dying of hunger.

When I wrote about the hunger suffered by the Africans in Saheli, my words evoked an echo. Responses came by telephone and letters. Help was offered with the assurance that it would not be less than it was when some years before there was an appeal for the hungry people of India, and countless packages were happily received. They wrote, "It is hard to think of this, that being satiated ourselves we do not help others." Unfortunately, not one social institution answered saying it was ready to help in the organizing and transporting of the packages.

In the meantime winter brought new reports of hunger and

dying of starvation. Besides Sahel, where people are dying continuously, Ethiopia was severely hit with a hunger bout. At this time there are some two million people suffering hunger. But again hunger is beginning to plague the inhabitants of India, Pakistan and Bangladesh. Daily about 100,000 people are dying of hunger, most of them children.... Can one live serenely with this knowledge?

Hunger in the modern world did not come about by accident. It is not the result of guiltless failures of the elements. In writing about the hungry in Saheli I mentioned that the catastrophic drought in that territory was caused by the economic demands forced upon the countries of mid-Africa by the European powers, especially France. In the last few weeks the United Nations announced a terrifying report about the constantly increasing, in a catastrophic way, difference on the agricultural level between certain countries of the Third World and the countries well-developed agriculturally. According to the cited report, 1.2 billion people live in a state of misery and starvation—(practically one-third of the total human population) in Asia, Africa and South America. Let us add here that these hunger-stricken countries have four times more children and youth than the highly industrial countries. Therefore, if 1.2 billion people are starving, at least three-fourths of a billion of them must be children and young people starving to death.

This awful plight is not (let us emphasize again) an accidental event. It is plainly the result of the impossibility of making responsible communal investments in agriculture in those countries. If these investments could be accomplished, they would assure those countries sufficient sustenance for all their inhabitants. However, the countries of the Third World (with the exception of countries collecting enormous revenue for the export of oil) lack funds for the necessary investments. Moreover, they are already deeply indebted to the well-developed countries. Since they cannot transform their system of agriculture, they are not able to pay their debts. They fall into deeper indebtedness or pay off some of their debt with the little they have, and with which they could save at least some of their inhabitants from death by starvation. Thus, a vicious circle of misery is formed.

Even if we think that in reality an effective way of feeding the hungry could be found by the respective states or by outside organizations, we may not say, nor even think, that we ourselves are excused from the obligation of caring for those dying of starvation. Every day 100,000 people die of starvation, and most of them are children....

These children do not only die. How truly does Mrs. Alvina de Vos van Steenwijk write (in a widely read article in "Karnetach Dziecka" published by UNICEF) that hunger, constant misery, accompanied by uncertainty, affect them so, "that the child does not know what he can expect. He ceases to trust others, stops trusting himself. He learns to look upon himself and his parents with an eye deprived of recognition, reverence, confidence...." These children, even if they grow up, will not want to learn. They will have no confidence in learning, nor in anything that requires effort. They will become an irresponsible element disheartened from the very beginning, an enemy to the whole world. Hunger not only kills; it demoralizes, and dehumanizes. If the starving people of the world are not rescued from their hunger today, tomorrow maybe they will not have the will or the energy (even if the means were provided) to bring about the transformation of its socio-agricultural problems for the good of the country.

Every day 100,000 people die.... And how many lose their desire to work? How many people are thus awakened to hatred toward those who are satiated? Can we celebrate the Holy Year, if we do not begin doing something for the poor starving people?

It is a principle of Christian life: to carry over the insights of interior experiences into concrete action.

The chief slogan of the Holy Year is reconciliation. Reconciliation with God, reconciliation with another person, reconciliation with the whole human race. Reconciliation with God takes place in the confessional; but satisfaction must be made to the injured person. We must convince ourselves that it is not enough to acknowledge our guilt. We have to compensate likewise for what others have suffered on our account. Let us not say that the people in Africa or in Asia are certainly not hungry on our account! The world is one; humanity is one; everyone who has something is guilty, because the other one does not have it. Our very prodigality, even if it is only throwing bread away, is something that robs those others.

John XXIII, Vatican Council II, the proclamation of the Holy Year—all reminded us that Christianity is for the world and ought to serve the whole world. Therefore, we Christians are always guilty when someone, even if he is in the farthest corner of the globe, suffers hunger.

Let us honor the Holy Year by sending out at least one package for the starving people. Let us not forget that "every day about 100,000 people die of starvation, and most of them are children...."

25. Once more about hunger

In a beautiful booklet about Mother Teresa of Calcutta, Malcom Muggeridge, the author, quotes the words expressed by this apostle of modern times: "Always there exists this danger that we may become simply social workers... if we forget for whom we are doing all this.... In the slums, in the suffering bodies, in the children we see Christ and commune with him.... I always entreat the people to work together with us.... I never talk to them about money.... I write that they should come... more and more... and love people.... We are concerned above all with the lot of the people, the individual person.... To love a human being we must enter into close contact with him.... Every person is Christ for me, and because there is only one Christ, then this person at this moment is the only person for me...."

When we made an appeal for the starving people we received many answers from far and wide. Some were deeply touching, but some voiced the opinion that such an action should be organized, that some institution ought to assume the problem of transportation, and all the rest would only send monetary offerings to its address.

These voices sounded reasonable and I must admit that I myself was of that opinion at first. But when I stopped to consider, I changed my mind. Perhaps, I thought, it may be some sign of God's will that this whole project be realized only through the small individual sacrificial donations.

For years I had worked in the so-called Social Service. Social welfare, or care organized by the government or a self-governing agency with the good offices of trained workmen is no doubt necessary and effective. But there is a danger connected with such an organization—namely, that the private person no longer feels obliged to witness mercy. I pay taxes, he says, so I can demand that there be no children begging on the streets, no beggars dying before my eyes, that homes for the aged be established.

In demanding "organized" action, some such views are generally voiced, as: I am ready to give for the hungry, but let the proper institution provide them the necessary help.... Let that help be sent out by the proper people... Who are the proper people? Officers doing the job for remuneration? Or maybe some idealists upon whom the work would be dumped? Maybe as it was with the first Ladies of Charity, attracted to the work by St. Vincent de Paul, but who soon placed all the duties assumed by themselves upon their servants and from these in time we got the crystallized form of the Charity Sisters?

At present, if we want to help the hungry, we have to buy the food stuff, package it, go to the post office, stand in line.... But it is precisely in this that we find the greatest value of the whole project! We give not only a handful of rice flour or sugar. We also give our effort and our time—ourselves!

Probably in a communal project it would go much further and faster. Much more could be sent. But—let's be Christians! The poor widow's mite is much more valuable than money offered by the wealthy. The words of Christ that this woman "gave more" must be taken literally. A small package sent by each one of us—a package into which we put our effort and time—can compare with the consignment of foodstuff sent by an organization not only in a moral sense. The value of our aid is not measured by quantity. In the last analysis, it is God who gives aid, and He requires of us, above all, an effort of love. In the case of saints, their alms often increased in their very hands. And who knows but what our small packages in the hands of God will not become a greater help and more valuable than those accumulated the organized way. Let us hope that all our trouble will be "worthwhile."

Mother Teresa advocates: Do something beautiful for God! So let us send our package to the poor and hungry—a package made up by us and sent by us. Let it be person to person!

26. The public sinner

In the gospel two sinful women stand before Jesus: a woman caught in the betrayal of her lawful husband, and the public sinner, a woman openly selling her own body.

We know nothing about the first woman. Those who wanted to stone her, left. Jesus says to the woman, "And I will not condemn you." But concerning the prostitute—and many biblical scholars claim she was Mary Magdalen, about whom the Gospel says that she was freed of seven evil spirits (in scripture the number seven signifies fullness—hence it would mean that she was totally possessed) Jesus passes this judgment: "Her sins, and they are numerous, are forgiven her because she has loved much."

The sense of the words seems to say that the public sinner has shown "much love" because her sins were forgiven her. Such a sequence does not exist for Jesus. Whoever knows how to love, who loves disinterestedly, has already been forgiven. The pharisee with whom Jesus dined took on an attitude of "wait and see." He didn't count on anything too much. In his own estimation he did not have many sins, so he was not concerned about their forgiveness. But for Jesus the number of sins is a matter of less importance—of far greater importance is confidence, implicit trust, and love.

The everlasting antinomy which repeats itself endlessly in the Gospel. Two people—two attitudes. The pharisee and the publican. The elder always faithful son and the younger, the prodigal sinner. And always the same assurance that "dearer to me is the repentant sinner bringing his love than the man without sin, but also without love!" I am not afraid, Jesus seems to say, of human sins. Man condemned himself before the ages in the persons of our first parents. I did not give him natural means to overcome the downfall to which he succumbed, but I left him the ability to love. In even the worst of sinners there exists the ability to love. More than that is the need of love! And every love, even though misdirected, is a kind of reflection of my love. If this degraded, but still up to a point true love, will be directed to me, it will purify itself, regain its brightness. Only by way of love do we go to Love. By offering love to a human being disinterestedly, not because it pleases us but because we can help the other, someday in the person of the needy one we will meet Jesus Himself.

We resemble the second woman, the public sinner, because our lives are filled with daily sins which we do not even try to hide. Today's world is full of sin to which we have ceased to pay attention. What are our sins, we say to ourselves, since everybody around us is committing them? And acting thus we invite Jesus. We even expect him to bring us something for our "fidelity"!

The pharisee, the host at the banquet, was in the same position as the woman, a public sinner.

Upon our invitation Jesus comes but only because, thanks to meeting with us, although no thanks to us, he has the opportunity to meet those who do not consider themselves "the faithful," but who love him since they love their fellowman. For them he is with us, and for them, not for us, he has these words, "Your sins are forgiven.... Your faith has saved you...."

And we, we the "most faithful," what will we hear?

If we want to hear the same words, we have to go to learn from those others. Not how to sin obviously, but how to love! If we learn how to love as they love, we shall be saved. Only on this road of love will we find Jesus—we who presume that we have him and do not need to seek him.

Behold the precious moment to discover this sublime truth. The Holy Year is the year of the decisive challenge. Again is repeated the moment when the "publicans" and "street girls" can precede the "faithful" and "right thinking" Christians.

27. John

"Who do men say I am?" asks Jesus. The apostles answer, "Some think you are John the Baptist; others, Elias." Now Elias, the prophet of the eighth century before the birth of Christ, was a personage extraordinarily honored by the Jews, but in view of his antiquity, he is somewhat legendary. John, however, was a contemporary and many people following Jesus had seen him and listened to him. The supposition that Jesus might be the "resurrected John" speaks well of the authority enjoyed by John, the last of the prophets of the Old Testament, who was killed by Herod.

John, like every great saint, perhaps even like every great man, combines in himself two characteristics: solitude and solidarity. He is alone, all alone, grown above the mass of people, sentenced to solitude, admired, but from a distance, sought after to give counsel, yet a man whom no other man could help. However, in spite of his complete isolation, John does not shut himself up within himself. All his life he serves the needs of the people.

Who was John? A prophet, and "more than a prophet." The prophets were announcers of future events. They preached the truths of God correlative with the truths contained in the law. They explained and interpreted the will of God.

Such a prophet was John up to the day of his meeting with Jesus. From that moment prophecies became unnecessary; the promises were fulfilled. Therefore John begins to "diminish," recedes into the shadow, rejoices only with the "joy of the bridegroom." Finally he loses his life. He dies for the truths that Jesus brought. Taking the wife of another was already in reality considered a crying sin, but Jesus raised marital infidelity to the meaning of a symbol of unfaithfulness to God. Marriage is a picture of the union of man with God in the Church. Adultery is a picture of shattering this union.

John dies a martyr to the cause of Christ, the first voluntary martyr, for the very first martyrs were the innocent children of the royal line of David killed in Bethlehem by Herod. John is the last of the prophets of the Old Testament and the first saint of the New Testament.

The life of a saint has its own rhythm repeating itself without variation. The saints are called, some at the beginning, others in the middle, and still others at the end of their life. Everyone of us has the obligation of seeking holiness, but only he becomes a saint whom God designates for sainthood. There is a multitude of saints, that is, saved ones. However, when we say "saint," we have in mind a person whose sanctity God wanted to give us as a model.

The saint acts, one by preaching, another by offering his life for a cause. One is listened to and in order to preserve humility he has to hide himself in his work. Another seemingly works hard for nothing. He is misunderstood, accused, and distrusted on all sides. Everyone suffers and only by suffering fulfills his given task. Everyone must conquer his ego in order to speak of God. The work of the saint is recognized only after his death.

It's almost a rule that in the life of every saint comes a moment when all his life's work stands on the threshold of bankruptcy. What had been the saint's commitment is destroyed by misunderstood circumstances. In the life of every saint there appears to be an event that is like the command of God who told Abraham to offer him his only son—that son who was to be the fulfillment of his hopes and promises. He will become a saint who will obediently raise his hand on Isaac, who for God will be able to resign even the possibility of service for God.

"The least in the Kingdom of God is greater than John," said Jesus. But in saying this, he speaks of John the prophet. The prophets came to an end on the threshold of the Kingdom; John went on further, and became "more than a prophet."

Right after the incomparable holiness of Mary, whose sanctity anticipated her deeds, comes the saintliness of John—not the normal human holiness—but of the highest caliber, the sanctity of him who saw, recognized, and became silent—he offered his silence instead of the blood of the only begotten son.

28. Hard Christianity

Christianity, as an idea, is valued even beyond its own circle. The words of the gospel are cited, the dictates of the councils are spoken of with respect, modern Christian thinkers like Teilhard de Chardin, Charles Dawson, and Hans Urs von Balthasar arouse interest.

The trouble with Christianity begins only at the moment when it presents man with its demands.

Much is written, for instance, about hunger and starvation that touched almost the whole face of the earth. But Christians may not simply write about or speak of this hunger—they must act. However, when they find it hard to prepare a package, or to stand in line at the post office—opposition is voiced. Some propose that the whole business be taken over by an organization; others would want to place all the work on the shoulders of people of good will, because, they explain, all that action is so "work demanding" and gives so little. So much effort to send out such a small package! Does it pay in that situation to be concerned about the whole affair?

Jesus appears to be inhumanly hard when he says, "No one who puts his hand to the plow and looks back is fit for the Kingdom of God." Did I do a lot? Did my effort bring reasonable results? We often ask ourselves these questions. We want to know that we haven't worked in vain. And when it seems to us that our trouble is fruitless or—what's worse—is unappreciated, we feel a certain bitterness.

Satan tempted Jesus saying, "Cast yourself down! God wants man to trust him!" So stop worrying... God will help you. He will send his angels to save you from breaking your bones.

But Jesus answered the devil, "It is not right to tempt the Lord God. Trust in God has nothing in common with the blind casting oneself down into the pit." The devil continues, "Don't believe that any harm will come to you!"

During the war a strange prayer was being circulated in Warsaw. It sounded like this, "I know, O GOD, that as long as I have these words with me nothing evil will befall me." The little card with these words had to be on one's person. That was no prayer. That was superstition. It was proper to pray entirely in another way, "Protect me, O Lord God, from every evil; but whatever you send we want to accept as your holy will which is always, as we believe, directed to our good.

Christian life is like walking between two dangers: between being involved exclusively in human affairs and/or renouncing every earthly activity. The Christian either practically abandons Christianity and plans his life as if Christianity did not exist (and makes himself believe that to act otherwise would be a lack of common sense) or he places everything on God, and when God does not help him (when God did not help man as he desired—for God always helps) he gives up his faith. How often we hear: Since God allowed his child to die... Since God allows famine, misery, human hate, the triumph of falsehood.... I cannot believe!

The duty of a Christian is to act in a human and a Christian way simultaneously, not anticipating the outcome. We should do all in our human power to help the needy, not for our own sake, but because love shown to our neighbor is the way to our love of God. The outcome of our kind action we should leave to God—let us not even desire to see it.

The Holy Year will not change the world simply by the fact that it was proclaimed. That will not make the world better. Only we can make it better if each one of us will put forth an effort by way of renewal and reconciliation; if we join our prayers with the prayer of the Blessed Virgin. But let us not expect to see this change made. If God so wills, He will bless our efforts a hundredfold; he will bring it about—not by a miracle from heaven but by a miracle performed imperceptibly in human hearts—that a change will be made.

Therefore, it is worthwhile to make every effort which has as its aim to aid another person even when it seems to us that our trouble "doesn't pay."

29. God is

The Church of our times is a mission Church. The Holy Year is a mission year. And we ought to be missionaries—every one of us.

Today's people go to church much less frequently than formerly. They do not listen to religious instructions. They marry outside the Church and get divorced. They do not send their children to religion classes, and if they do send them it is without conviction; the children sensing this, play truant.

This is not always a deliberate discarding of religion. Simply, people today are so busy that they do not have time to remember even more important things than mere daily affairs. However, they are not happy about this either. They feel that they are missing something. Not knowing how to free themselves from moral problems they try to be deaf to them. Then follows ever greater haste—squandered hours in talk, whiskey, and narcotics. The radio is blaring for the sake of blaring; the television set is on all day without any interest as to what is being shown.

Must people be so busy that they cannot find time for themselves, to think about the purpose of life and their own moral status? Sometimes that is so. But much more frequently haste has entered their blood, as it were. People hurry along although they themselves do not know why. They postpone thinking for "later on," which too often becomes a "holy never."

The harvest is great, but what can we, the missioners of the life of today, accomplish against the pressures of the general haste and deafening noise? We have to stress, above all, the importance of time for thinking—for others and for ourselves. Preaching the Truth is wholly useless if the person to whom we want to speak of the Truth cannot hear what we are saying in the noisy surroundings. The time spent in thinking about our moral responsibility is certainly a time of more intensive concentration than time given to vacation plans or foreign tours; however, if we find time for these excursions we ought to find time to meditate about our spiritual needs. Modern man not only needs to know about God; more important is it for him to remember God. The Christian who does not read or hear anything about God commits a sin of neglect—a sin against the first commandment, for he sets up his "idolized" affairs ahead of the debt he owes to God. But no less does he sin when engrossed in his haste he cannot offer God a period of quiet meditation. Sometimes we hear a person say facetiously: "I have no time even to commit a sin, I am too busy."

But one can sin by that very thing; being too busy to have time for God. In a certain locality beyond the border I saw a banner hanging on a wall with the inscription: "Let us remember—God is!"

It is necessary for us to have such a reminder within ourselves always in order to step out of the stream of noise and haste at least for a moment and find God in prayerful thought.

30. The Samaritan

To understand the story Jesus told about the Good Samaritan properly, it is necessary to view it in the light of those times and circumstances.

Bandits fell upon and wounded a man, no doubt a Jew, a Judean. A priest was going by that way and then a levite (that is someone belonging to God's dedicated people, comparable perhaps to a modern monk) passed by the wounded man unconcernedly occupied only with his own affairs. Only a Samaritan, seeing him, stopped and took care of the victim.

The Samaritans were a mixed tribe. The early Jewish people on the middle plains of Palestine mixed with the people from the depths of Asia. The religion of Moses merged with their pagan beliefs. The faithful Judeans considered the Samaritans as "unclean," as heretics with whom they were to avoid contact. When the Jews from Galilee went to Judea to celebrate their feast days they went out of their way to bypass Samaria.

And here this "unclean" Samaritan showed mercy to the faithful Jew!

No doubt it has happened to us, and maybe more than once,

that in times of need we received help not from one from whom we expected it—not from "our own," not from a Christian—but from a foreigner, from an unbeliever.

Jesus foresaw such a situation. Christianity is a school of love, but not everyone that considers himself a Christian has profited by the lessons taught in this school. Yet this mercy shown to a fellowman is the real proof of our love of God. We cannot love God without loving our neighbor.

There are people who do not know God, maybe even deny his existence, but still love people and wish to help them. And Jesus says, "Do as they do." For him true love is more important than words without love.

But the situation could have been just the reverse: the wounded man could have been the Samaritan, the "unclean heretic." What then? Would we, the faithful, having found him on the road, have helped him?

Sometimes we say that we would help this person but he is so unapproachable! I would help this or that one, but he has his own friends, let them help him! He is suffering—so what? That's his own fault; he was impossible, and unbearable. Why should I help someone so far away when certainly there are people nearby in greater need (but having acknowledged the necessity we do not seek those "nearby"—it satisfies us that we are exonerated from not aiding those "far away"). Why, he's a thief, a sneak, a bluffer! Am I to aid a thief? a sneak? a bluffer? a swindler?

Jesus said, "Do just what this 'unclean' Samaritan did." But what would he say if this same Samaritan were lying wounded on the road?

31. The grandeur of heaven

Non-Christians sometimes say, "Jesus Christ condemned all human drudgery. He praised Mary who simply sat at his feet and listened to his words, and reproved the hard working Martha." However, that view results from not taking the gospel as a whole but forming conclusions from fragmentary excerpts.

Who was Mary in the episode of the two sisters? Some biblical scholars take her for the same person as Mary Magdalen, the public sinner. From the gospel of St. John we know that the friend of Jesus, Lazarus of Bethany, had two sisters, Mary and Martha, and it was "Mary who anointed the feet of Jesus with fragrant oil and wiped them with her hair" (Lk 11:2).

Let us recall once more the motive of the two brothers which intertwines itself many times through the gospel and which is most striking in the story of the prodigal son. The older brother who had never left his father returns tired from the field and finds the house ablaze with lights, music and song, and a banquet being served joyously to celebrate the return of his brother who had squandered all he possessed, but now was instantly forgiven. The older brother says, (how similar to Martha) "So I, father, have worked in the sweat of my brow while he who cheated you sits next to you at the banquet?"

Mary had left home and sinned. Afterwards she acknowledged her faults, threw herself at the feet of Jesus and received absolution. Her feeling of gratitude made her so loving that in her love she was ready to forget everything. Her transport of love did not permit her to waste a single moment that she could spend with Jesus.

Those souls are always nearer and dearer to the Heart of Jesus—former public sinners, lost but found later on, returning full of more thankfulness and love than their brothers and sisters who had never gone astray. That does not mean that Jesus does not love the others: the young man who had always kept the commandments of God, or the faithful Martha. He loves them even when having escaped the taint of sin they retain what Jesus detests: worry. Instead of joining their effort to a joyous hope, they add it to their uneasiness. They serve God faithfully but only as if everything depended exclusively on their effort, on their intelligence, and on the success of their endeavors.

"Martha, Martha," says Jesus, "you work for Me; that's fine! But while you work you do not stop worrying. In her transport of love and trust, Mary has forgotten everything. She is blessed because she has found Me again. I will not deprive her of this joy. That's her moment. A time will come when she too will work, and worry, and suffer. That's the lot of man on earth. In this moment, however, a most unusual and important thing has happened: a human person has understood my love for you people and this discovery has enraptured her. I am waiting for just such a moment in each one of you. I yearn for it. If you would be able to be so devoted to Me as Mary is at this moment—all the troubles of the world would come to an end in one breathless instant. But this will never be. Your love will continue to live through its many crises. In that very moment, when it bursts forth in a flame, you can be at ease about the world. I will not let it perish. Nothing will happen to it while this close relationship exists between man and Me, while this state of your great happiness and my joy lasts. Heaven—that's exactly just such a flashy extending into eternity!"

32. Thy Kingdom come

Some thirty years ago during the uprising in Warsaw many people believed steadfastly that by engaging in battle with the cruel occupant they were not only going to throw off the yoke of slavery, but above all they would bring about the sanctification of the country in the spirit of God's justice. These people praying during the years of occupancy, repeating the words "Thy Kingdom come" thought only about the kingdom that would be realized all around them. Some of them when dying in the barricades later on experienced, for the second time in the war, a terrible disillusionment: the enemy proved to be stronger than their idea!

Those whose lot it was to survive came to understand with time that they had reasoned incorrectly. One does not fight for the Kingdom of God not even in the most just of just wars. To our human impatience it seems that a battle will resolve any problem. The real thing looks different. The existence of Poland could and had to be saved with blood and sword. But to do so called for a human effort of an entirely different order. And if our ideal is the ideal of God's truth we still need, besides effort, the grace of God.

In pre-war years Catholics, not only exclusively Poles, saw the affairs of a Christian life in a simple way, somewhat similar to the way the Christians of the Middle Ages saw them. Already then the world was becoming different. The postwar years marked a "long jump" in changes. The war taught people many things. Human knowledge moved forward by leaps and bounds. Brotherhoods came into being that never existed before. In many respects people became more mature.

At the same time, however, many people gave up their religion, and very often because the teaching of religion was not made applicable to the changes in the trend of thought. Then it followed that the necessity of professing one's religion in the contemporary world became a difficult problem. The world creates tempting mirages whose quick realization demands easy solutions. Although wise in many respects, man cannot always detect how dangerous are easy moral solutions. Suddenly modern man discovered his body. Instead of directing it, he allows his instincts to dominate it. Sex is the enormous motor in man that has to be controlled, but which today thoughtlessly rouses and sways him.

The modern Catholic must reassure himself that daily prayer in the words of Jesus "Thy Kingdom Come" has not lost its reality. But the realization of the petition must be attained in a different way from what we imagined. It is not by forcing something upon the world but by convincing the world of the beauty of this Kingdom. We, Christians, living in the main stream of the world, have to strive to uphold our ideals. We have to live a life of witness. We must be the first in doing good, and stay far away from every evil. An Italian Catholic who lost the referendum in the matter of divorce, must remain faithful to the decree of indissolubility in spite of the slight rift in the law that could change it. West German Catholics must remain faithful to the decree forbidding abortion, although the new regulation there allows a convenient artificial possibility of preventing conception.

A Catholic must remember that Sunday is still a holy day, with its obligation of attending Holy Mass, even though we have planned an excursion, or some social activity. The modern Christian must assume the additional trouble of seeking and finding suitable solutions which will always allow him to fulfill his obligations to his religion without excluding him from the community in which he lives. One must know how to choose between the attractions of contemporary life and its pitfalls. He must always be true to himself even when that is not easy.

33. Greed and covetousness

We frequently say of ourselves, "I am not that greedy." Others have beautiful homes, rich furniture, and an automobile. I do not desire luxuries. I only want to have peace. I just want the assurance of freedom from worrying about the next day. I might not have much, but I want to know that the little I have will last me a whole lifetime. Is that asking too much? I am certainly not greedy. I am concerned only about peace and the possibility of a peaceful occupation. Is it bad to want to work well?"

Once upon a time, we remember, there came to Jesus a young man who had never broken the commandments of God. Jesus looked at him with love. Yet the young man acknowledged that "something was missing." Then Jesus said to him, "Give away what you have and come follow Me." This advice seemed too hard to the young man. He went away, and Jesus looked after him with sadness.

Would we call that young man greedy or avaricious? He possessed riches, that's true, but he did not make bad use of them. He lived an honorable life. He did not kill; he did not steal; he did not commit adultery. He did not desire what others possessed. Maybe because he had enough he never broke the commandments of God, he was never hungry for bread; nor did he ever experience any angry covetousness. Having possessions, he had peace. This peace saved him from wrong doing.

Yet Jesus told him to get rid of what he had—to get rid of the peace that possession gives.

Also, when another man came to Jesus asking Him to command his brother to share justly the inheritance left by their parents, Jesus sent him away almost angrily. He said, "Beware of any kind of greed." Have we no right to what our father and mother left us? Wasn't the request of the man justifiable?

When does greed actually begin? Is it when we want to assure ourselves of something for tomorrow? When we want to leave something for the children? This situation seems to be somewhat similar to the distress of Martha. Jesus does not condemn possessions, nor common sense. He censures only our uneasiness and worry—our inordinate desire to play safe, to protect ourselves—at any cost—from all future troubles. We must learn to possess as if we did not possess, not attaching our heart to our possessions. We ought to think about how to serve others with what we have, and not about how to acquire more. As long as there are hungry people on earth—something will always be "wanting" in us as it was in that young man. And sometimes, for our good, God wants us to lose what in our estimation (but only in our own estimation) insures our future, so that we may live on what God places in our hand every day.

I will serve God, but I want to live without daily troubles—that prayer of petition is not pleasing to Jesus. To accept daily frustrations, and disregard troubles, to renounce security and accept whatever comes with absolute trust, that means to be the disciple who chose "the better part."

When we are worried about tomorrow and this worry does not permit us to listen to God's words, that's when greed begins.

34. Anew—for heaven

More than a hundred years ago, when the pope proclaimed the dogma of the Immaculate Conception of the Blessed Virgin Mary, that dogma was the answer to the accepted teaching of that time, which certain exponents of it promulgated, and that by his own efforts alone man is able to attain every perfection. The dogma recalled to mind that all man can attain is the combination of his effort with grace and that the only person, truly perfect on the human level, was Mary, the Mother of God, "full of grace."

After the last war the context of teaching was completely reversed. More and more frequently, in place of the blind trust in the personal powers of man, there appeared feelings of impotence, fear and despair. Two powers in particular seemed to suppress man with their ruthlessness: sex, the all-powerful drive of the senses which seems to direct the whole human life, and the threat of death. Man, according to some scholars, trembling before death must surrender himself completely to sensuality.

As though in answer to these fears there appeared another dogma: the dogma of the Assumption of Mary with body and soul. Against the ideal of the all-powerful sex urge was presented the ideal of purity; facing the threat of death—the joyful consciousness that death is merely the threshold of another, better life, which each one of us can enter in our whole being, that means, with body and soul.

"Do not be afraid," says Jesus. My Father and yours wants to give you heaven, and this heaven already exists—is waiting for you. However, you must earn it, work for it. Heaven—like all of God's acts—requires also your input. God does not want to grant you happiness which would not also be the result of your merit. Would you be truly happy if you would receive heaven entirely free? The most precious gift is when the giver calls upon the receiver for cooperation; the greatest happiness is when we not only receive but also give. It is said that marriage is the mysterious picture of the relationship of God to man. In marriage people choose each other mutually; they offer their love to each other. God wants our love and heaven is the meeting of God's love with man's love. It is not a reward for something not even for a virtuous life, it is love which has rediscovered love. That is why heaven needs the whole human being and why Mary went to heaven with soul and body, just as we too will enter it.

Since She is now there, She knows as no one else does man's road to despair from fears and the slavery of sensuality to happiness, peace and joy.

"The more absolutely She will rule," wrote Blessed Maximilian Kolbe four years before his death in the Auschwitz concentration camp, "so much the more will even errors result in greater good. From morning till evening, how many errors there are! Resolutions are made and we go our own way.... Even if something is done not as it should be, as is necessary, let's make an act of sorrow, give ourselves to the Immaculata and be entirely at ease knowing that the Immaculate Virgin will convert it all to a greater good.... When our holy Father, St. Francis, was dying, he said: Let us begin, brothers, anew. We must always begin anew, in spite of our weaknesses, miseries...."

35. The peace of Jesus

An American diplomat circles the earth and wherever he finds a fierce battle going on, by means of negotiations he brings about an amnesty. There are some who call him a "creator of peace."

But can peace brought about by the American diplomat be a lasting peace? Isn't it only a momentary compromise? Of course even such a momentary peace is valuable since it creates the possibility of substituting it for another, better peace. But if it should remain only a temporary compromise, the conflicts would break out again, sooner or later.

Jesus said: "My peace I give you," but he also said, "I have not brought peace but division." The peace of Jesus is not a compromise. It is the peace of Jesus Himself, the true peace, which is not obtained by means of diplomatic travels, diplomatic talks and various auctions. It is peace based on certain principles and if they are not accepted and preserved, there will be nothing but division. Jesus does not promise peace "at any price," a momentary patching of a situation without resolving the problem completely.

The peace of Jesus is based on the precept: Do not kill. It means that it is forbidden to kill a man, forbidden to dishonor human life, forbidden to indulge in any kind of hatred. If we safeguard our so-called rights with hate, in the eyes of Jesus those rights are no longer right. Man is obliged to protect human life always and everywhere, the right to life, and justice which makes life possible. War is not a monster of and in itself; it is the practical development of hatred. Hatred begins in the heart and ends on the battle field.

The peace of Jesus is not peace "at any cost," it is peace for which a big price must be paid. It is a troublesome peace. It cannot be obtained by hazy promises. It is often painful, since the battle for this peace often begins among those dearest to us. Not long ago we viewed a distressingly interesting film about the tragedy in a child's life whose father was a drunkard. There are many tragedies in the homes of parents whose children abandoned the principles inculcated in childhood. Perhaps never before have conflicts between generations been so sharp as at present.

In the years of World War I when Europe was painfully covered with bloody battlefields, Mary turned to the three little children of Fatima in Portugal. Through them she called upon the Church to spread the cult of her Immaculate Heart and to entrust mankind torn apart by all the wars to the care of this Heart. Twenty-five years later the pope complied with this request during World War II, much worse than the first. Then he pleaded: "O Mother of Mercy, obtain peace for us from God.... O Queen of peace, pray for us.... Give peace to the fighting world in the spirit of justice and the love of Christ!"

We must constantly pray for this peace; this troublesome peace so hard to win must be sought incessantly. The Holy Year is also a year of seeking the peace of Jesus.

"I have brought peace to the world," says Jesus, and all I desire is that people will get to know this love, because it is this love alone that can create true peace. But before this love can burst into a flame I will have to suffer, and my whole human nature trembles in anticipation of the suffering. In the perspective of intense effort and suffering you tremble also. But do not be afraid. My sacrifice has already brought victory."

36. Manhole above us

Not too long ago I had an occasion of visiting the silver mines of Kutna Hora. I walked along the dark narrow corridors excavated in the rock so low that I had to stoop in order not to strike the ceiling with my head. Water was trickling down the rough rocky walls with a soft murmur, the little lamp was giving forth a weak gleam.

This corridor of an ancient mine reminded me of my sojourn some thirty years back through the canals of Warsaw, and of the thoughts that went drumming through my head, especially during the tragic return by means of the canals from Mokotowo to Midtown.

In the dark canal we walked in single file. It was impossible to bypass anyone, and impossible to turn back. No one knew where we were, or how long our march would continue. Hours went by and we were still walking. At times we would stop and stand still for a whole hour. People mortally exhausted just dropped helplessly into the water.

Then it dawned on me that this underground march is very much like our life. Somewhere there is an end and an exit to the light of day. But before we reach this exit, hardships, dangers and tremendous efforts await us. Therefore, we have to be ready to endure as much as possible with great courage and patience. We must muster our will, and believe in the light awaiting us. Not only was it necessary to believe that such an exit exists; it was also necessary to arouse self-confidence in being able to reach it. Periodically, a blind fear would grip a person. We passed by bodies of people who had fallen and did not rise again. Who would have strength enough to continue to the end? was the thundering question in every mind. Would anyone be able to reach it?

"Will many people be saved?" someone asks Jesus fearfully. Jesus does not give an answer to this question. He says something else, "Gather your strength and go. You have a 'narrow gate before you,' in reality countless obstacles to encounter." At another time and place, speaking about the rich, Jesus said that they are like elephants that can squeeze through the eye of the needle. We do not know whether he spoke of the town's gate called by that name, or whether he meant a simple needle's eye. In this second sense, of course, it would never happen. But Jesus added, "What is impossible for people, is possible with God." God knows how to lead an elephant through the eye of a needle. God can do anything... everything. If we believe in God we have the right to trust that everything he desires will be accomplished.

Actually Jesus gives this answer to the question, will many people be saved? Everything is possible for God. It is possible for

God to save many people. It is possible for God to save everybody.

Everybody? In a world where there is so much evil, hatred, injustice, falsehood, crime?

One moment of sincere contrition saves the blackest spirits—you have it—says the Spanish poet Zorilla in his beautiful miracle play about Don Juan Tenorio. God made man an extraordinary gift, the gift of the Sacrifice of His own Son, a priceless treasure. One word of supplication to Jesus will suffice, one thought, and all the evil will be blotted out.... One thought.... "Collect all the sinners of the whole wide world," says Jesus in a vision to Sister Faustina, "and sink them in the depths of My Mercy." Do we remember this? Do we remember the cry of the good thief on the cross and the answer of Jesus?

Why ask, will many people be saved? Why ask, will I be saved? God wants to save all men. The saving "manhole" is just ahead of us!

37. Education or formation of a nation

Polish Romanticism of the nineteenth century created some magnificent poetry of that period. But combined with romanticism Messianism spread the well-nigh blasphemous idea: "Poland—the Christ of the Nations." The archbishop of Warsaw at the time of the January uprising is today one of the candidates for sainthood—Sigismund Szczesny Felinski wrote in his memoirs, "My spirit had to blush for that blindness of the pride of the accepted apotheosis of the Polish nation.... However much my people suffered as victims of cruel misrule, they did not go to martyrdom willingly, nor without sin, as our Savior did." Many long years of suffering had to follow to make the Polish Catholics understand that the way to Divine Truth is founded not in the boastful external likeness to Christ, but in a humble imitation of his holy life.

Thirty-five years ago, the day before the most disastrous of wars, there appeared again among the Polish Catholics fanciful dreams about the unique role of our nation. They were beautiful concoctions, but how unrealistic! Polish life of those days was far from the ideals of Christian morality. A little nun, a "Magdalen" (the popular name for the sisters of the Congregation of our Mother of Mercy), Sister Faustina, promoter of the cult of the Mercy of God foreseeing from the early 1930s the approaching war prayed fervently for Poland. In 1937 (a year before her death) she noted in her memoirs, "I often pray for Poland, but I see God's great displeasure with our country because it is ungrateful...."

How easily we are inclined to believe that we are better people than others. I don't do anything wrong, we say. But what good do we do? What do we do that is good for our environment? To do good is to sanctify something, to surrender or renounce something. Whoever gives from an abundance not even feeling its loss—gives nothing. Whoever gives from the little he has—gives much. And that's all that counts.

Perhaps today when everybody's greatest lack is time, the most precious gift is the gift of time?

The scholastic year has just begun, the children have returned to school or preschool. Today everyone in Poland understands the great problem of educating the young. The value of education seems to be appreciated by all. Everybody also values highly the health of the young generation. There are no parents who would not be concerned about good nourishment for their children, of providing vitamins and reassuring them of a rest in fresh air. Children are healthier and stronger than ever before.

But besides education and health there is still, and this is the most important, the matter of formation, or good breeding. Of what benefit is it that a child acquires knowledge and enjoys good health if he is not brought up properly, and is not fully a human being? If he will not have the heart, free will, character and understanding of good behavior? And yet the matter of upbringing is of least importance in the estimation of today's parents. Learning, or teaching is left to the school; concern about health—to the colonies and camps. Upbringing cannot be delegated to just anybody.

Formation is a matter of daily and constant vigilance and example. There are hours for study and months for rest. Good breeding must be carried on incessantly. The formation of good habits takes place at the table (who cares about the conduct of a child at the table today, and yet from this small beginning follow great things) in the streetcar, in the woods, on the street, at home and with strangers. The heaps of rubbish children leave behind them makes me shudder. But did the parents think enough to teach children respect and order? They must be given an example of good breeding. We suffer from the thoughtless roar of transistor radios the young people are playing everywhere, on the streets, in the gardens and the otherwise peaceful woods. But did their parents bring them up in the appreciation of peace and quiet?

Only he can effectively train another who himself constantly remembers how to behave properly and gives an example by his own conduct. Whoever himself does not appreciate quiet, his child will be an even greater foe of quietness. A good example often produces some fruit. A bad example, alas, always bears bad fruit in great abundance. When parents do not stress good order, their children will be notorious destroyers of their surroundings.

In order to train children well, we need time, and this necessary time must be found. Training cannot be relegated to others. It is true that others can and should help parents in this character development. However this does not mean "cranky aunts" who will correct the young wherever they meet them. It means people who always act so that their conduct can be an inspiration and a model for imitation. If we are to form a new generation, we must all help to train them, everywhere, in every place. If everyone of us will always watch himself so that his conduct is proper, a whole new generation will be brought up properly. We are not a different nation than the previous one. Only the formation of early good habits in the young people will, or can make us a better nation than others.

38. Discretion in love (Lk 14:25–33)

So I am to hate those dearest to me?

Obviously not. Jesus uses here specifically a dramatic form of antithesis, understood perfectly well by his hearers who do not protest remembering how often he spoke of love for man.

Thirty-five years ago many of us were leaving for war; we were leaving our dearest ones. It was a matter of protecting the whole fatherland. But a contemporaneous war threatens those who remain more than those that go to the front. We left our beloved ones with the feeling that they were remaining in danger. We did not know when we would see them again, or if we would ever see them. Five years later we were leaving again for the uprising. There were those who left earlier to their special party, to a secret conspiracy. Does this mean that we stopped loving? Or rather, did we choose a love that was broader, greater, embracing within itself also that which was our dearest love.

In the love of God is embraced every love. We often repeat that loving our fellowman we are already on the way to the love of God. But we must also be able to say that loving God, loving him in truth, that means not just in words, but if necessary sacrificing everything for this love, we are likewise loving men in this same love.

"In our religion we need strong souls," says the foundress of the gray Ursulines, Mother Julia Ursula Ledochowska, "souls that are brave, self-forgetting, ready for every sacrifice, for every kind of labor...."

We imagine at times that loving our own we serve them best by our words and our presence. I love the child, we say, so we have to be near him, helping him. But this child is already grown-up, has his own life, and his own plans. Love among people does not always create harmony. It seems to us that since we love others and they love us, out of love they ought to agree with us. Those others think: I love my parents and I sense their love, but does that mean that everlastingly I have to be subservient to their will and submit to them in all matters? Tastes change as well as customs, conditions, and relationships. We do not want a love imposed upon us as a burden.

The love of God for people is marked by a wonderful discretion. Nobody loves us as God does, yet God does not impose his love upon us. He, the Almighty One, patiently waits for our first move. He is always ready to forgive us our indifference. He permits us to neglect his love for the love of a human person. Only sometimes he shows us, just as dramatically as did the words of Jesus, the true hierarchy of love, which is at the same time the only hierarchy of true love.

Such should be our love for our dearest ones: we ought to move aside and wait patiently for the moment when we are needed. Impose nothing and demand nothing. Wait and pray. Assuming such a position we do not stop loving them. We love them fully—in God.

39. With free and easy heart and hands (Lk 15:1–32)

In an animated cartoon for children, when one of the chicks is lost in the woods the motherhen locks the rest of her children in the chicken coop and runs to look for the lost one. That is usually our reaction: the first gesture is to make safe what we still possess.

And yet Jesus says distinctly, "If any one of you lose one

With Free and Easy Heart and Hands (Lk 15:1-32)

(sheep) . . . does he not leave the ninety-nine in the desert and go for the lost one. . . ."

What do these words mean? First of all they speak of the unusual love of Jesus for people. The most loving of mothers divides her love among her children. She loves the lost one, but she is also concerned about those who remain with her. The love of Jesus in view of the loss seems to forget about everything. Jesus seems to want man in his love to forget about everything. He pardons Mary, the sinner, when in a transport of love she forgot about the obligations of a hostess. He promises heaven to the bandit on the cross when in his transport of reverence he forgot about his own pain. He joyfully greets the prodigal son who, returning to his father, forgets about his own shame. Let the older brothers of the prodigal son be offended!

Simultaneously, however, Jesus demands love. Would he who is ready to go out in the night to seek the lost one, allow the remaining sheep to get lost during his search? Would he who loves the lost one love those less who did not leave him? Does he not love Martha just because he allows Mary to neglect duties of a hostess? When his Church sets to seek and restore unity among the children of God, would He, Jesus, allow that Church to perish?

Yet that is precisely what is being said. There are Catholics who blame John XXIII, Paul VI, the Second Vatican Council, of undertaking the task of securing oneness while provoking to rebellion those whose faith is tied up firmly with the old forms of the Church, e.g., the Latin Mass.

That liturgy was only a form in which the life of the Church was already cooling off for a long time. Today that form must undergo a change for the sheep have been lost and their rescue demands different forms of action. Such is the evangelical sense of the renewal carried on in the Church. Such, too, is the sense of the Holy Year.

Not only the universal Church; every Christian home has its own sheep that has been lost. If we truly love, we must leave all our affairs, all plans, likewise our irritations, pretenses, attachments as well as our troubles and worries—everything that binds us—with a serene heart and open hands to look for the lost ones. That does not mean that we must yield to evil. We must save also the lost sheep from themselves.

"The difference between 'today' and 'yesterday' rests on this," said Mother Ursula Ledochowska already in 1930, "'yesterday' the sheep grazed only in the pastures ... 'today' they are rolling down the precipices or climbing upon the steepest rocks. Therefore, we too must leave the quiet lanes of work in order to go after them and pull them up or down, here and there, like a true shepherd...."

40. No small things

There was a time when you could throw away some little thing, a leftover or core. Nature itself would liquidate the impurities. There were not many people in comparison to the size of the earth. Today, when every second two people arrive on earth (roughly about 78 million annually) if everyone throws refuse on the ground, our environment in a very short time would become irreparably damaged. The same is true with noise. Some time ago when Father Stolarczyk and Dr. Chalubinski were roaming over the Tatra Mountains they took with them the mountaineers' music band, and when they parked anywhere for a while they chopped fir trees for a watch fire. They were all alone on the extensive mountain range. Today it is high time to silence with ever greater effectiveness the thousands of transistor radios disturbing the silence of the mountains, the peace along the seashore, and in general, the quiet in all public places. Everything begins with small things. A child whose parents allow him to break branches and trample on the grass will grow up to be a destroyer of nature. What we call "hoodlumism" today and lack of culture will eventually become the crime of despoilation of everything essential for human living.

Money does not seem to be a threat in the hands of an individual person. It is assumed that whoever has money has the right to use it as he pleases. That is the origin of prodigality, of the need for luxuries, of the lack of responsibility. Money is spent for the sake of spending it, and afterwards the purchased objects are misused. A person begins to forget that money has a social function, and its possession carries with it obligation toward others. In a certain instant wealth can become a crime which deprives others of their freedom or condemns them to a death of starvation. Whoever has become addicted to luxury has needs that constantly increase. He becomes more and more reckless in accumulating his wealth. Then, like the governor in the Gospel fearing poverty, he becomes guilty of cheating.

It is not always easy to detect the moment in which apparently small matters change into things of great moral weight. Hence it is important to act properly in small things in order to know how to act well in great matters. In this same way children should be taught, and trained. How important is the lesson taught by Saint Therese about the necessity of denying ourselves in the very smallest things.

Little things even in insignificant matters may grow into big things. Undertaking the work of bringing aid to countries suffering hunger and starvation we did not expect too great a result. In the meantime, the contributions offered by the people from Poland went up into a fund of millions. Whole transports of nourishing foodstuffs and medicines were bought with this money and sent to Africa. It is harder to estimate the number of individual packages that were sent, but that is not small either.

We can be happy about the response. But we must not forget that it is only a drop in the ocean of necessities. People are not ceasing to die of starvation. Let us remember that!

41. The Lazarus of today (Lk 16:19-31)

Certain evangelical pictures are so vivid that having them before our eyes we fail to notice their symbolic significance. Lazarus in the parable of Jesus is a beggar covered with sores, lying on the doorstep of the mansion of a rich man, and only dogs come and lick his wounds. We think to ourselves that we would notice such a man at once and would immediately hurry to aid him.

Today's Lazarus looks entirely different. Someone asks, "Come visit me." This someone is a lonely person, depressed by her lonesomeness, convinced that the whole world has abandoned her. We promise, "Of course, naturally, we'll come." Perhaps at that very moment we had the best of intentions, but afterwards, day after day goes by. The lonely person waits for a sign of the promised remembrance from the other one. Lazarus! In vain!

Someone comes or telephones. That bore again! we think with irritation. That person does not know how to come to the point, he babbles on and on from one theme to another. We listen to him standing on one foot, then on the other. We are not interested in what he is saying and at first somewhat delicately, then more bluntly we begin to let him know that his words do not concern us. But he keeps on talking. Who knows, maybe he, himself noticed our behavior, but maybe his talk with us is the only possibility he has of talking himself out. Maybe nobody wants to listen to him. In the end we conjecture some little lie in order to get rid of the bore. He walks away. He was also Lazarus.

Recently there was an English film on television about a little girl who came home to her parents from a boarding school. But her parents were divorced and each one of them is leading a life so demanding that they have no time to notice their daughter. The abandoned child seeks in vain for some contact with them. This little girl; she is a little Lazarus.

Somebody asks us to intercede for him. We promise, however

that for which he asks is a troublesome problem. We procrastinate; put off the intercession from day to day. We say to ourselves, "maybe there will be an opportunity." But the opportunity does not comes, and time flies. Eventually we forget about the matter, and Lazarus is still waiting for the fulfillment of the promise we had given.

Somebody lifts his hand high as we drive in our car. Maybe this is a deserted road, maybe it is raining, maybe it's a woman with a child. But we do not stop. The one in need of a lift may have wet clothing and will dirty up the car. The police may call us to task on a kidnapping charge. If we take someone in, maybe we will have to take him all the way to his home. So many troubles can arise.... We give a hand sign expressing our deep regret for our denial, and ride on ahead leaving Lazarus on the road.

Perhaps somebody asks us for a loan. It would not cause us any trouble. However we know that the petitioner is not a reliable debtor. In truth, he repays but never on the promised terms, and he has to be reminded of his debt. So in order to avoid future trouble we excuse ourselves with some fictitious reason. And yet, maybe that loan was really necessary for that not-so-reliable person—Lazarus?

There is always some Lazarus pretty close to our doors. How do we act toward him?

42. Two conditions

A few months ago Pope Paul VI in a general audience touched upon a theme which, as he called it himself, is one of the most complicated, and simultaneously, one of the most important in the life of the modern Christian.

Today's world seems to be constantly drifting away from God. Living its own autonomous life, it has no respect for religious obligations, good enough if it tolerates them.

What should the role of Christians be in this world? Once it was said: Run away from the world! Hide yourself, perchance in the desert! Today, especially since the time of Pope John XXIII and the last Council, the outlook is different.

Today, "we can look with sympathy on humanity which studies, works, suffers and constantly goes forward; more than that it calls us to cooperate in the worldly development of our epoch as citizens who desire to join their effort with the efforts of all for the realization of the common good...."

How should a Christian act toward such a formulated expression of ideas? Is he free to throw himself forward into the affairs of the world, and accept them as his own?

Yes, but under two conditions.

First of all, a Christian can and must stand in the mainstream of the affairs of the world but he should not allow himself to be swallowed up completely by the affairs of material development. Working for the advancement of the material life he should at the same time work for the deepening of his own spiritual life. He may not resign from Holy Mass, prayers, sacraments, or deprive himself of a moment of self-examination. "The more," says the pope, "the Christian will be able to preserve the character of a free and poor man in the worldly kingdom, so much more authentic will be his religious character and more effective his activity...."

The Christian must work harder than others; he cannot let himself be outdone in his participation in temporal affairs and beyond that he must conserve time and energy for eternal matters.

Second: the time has passed when the general public opinion so-called "good thinking" determined the conduct of a person. Today's public opinion is often far removed from the Christian outlook. This opinion recognizes divorce and premarital sex, agrees with abortion, often advocates the need of hating one another, looks with a tolerant eye on drunkenness.... The true Christian cannot let such an opinion terrorize him; while still living in the world he has to keep to his own criteria of proper conduct. "We are obliged," says the pope, "to exercise our own moral judgment, alert and ceaseless. Temptations and occasions of sin... today are equally as aggressive as hidden. One must know how to escape these in preserving one's own virtue."

"In this way exercising such self-discipline we will be able to live in our world not allowing evil to overcome us but conquering evil with good, remaining always faithful to Christ Crucified; on the other hand, leading an honorable and praiseworthy life in the wise perfectibility of the present hour."

43. To say "thank you"

Suddenly the telephone rang. I picked up the receiver. Nobody answered. A mistake? Maybe a bad connection?

Let us recall what we were doing at the moment the telephone rang. Were we saying something that should not be said? Were we thinking about something we should not think about? If so, in that case, was it only an accident that the telephone rang? It is said that there are no miracles. Obviously miracles do not happen to liberate man from activity. But in reality miracles are happening incessantly every moment.

Let us look from a certain perspective at our own life. There were moments of pain, unbearable it seemed to us, moments of terrible disasters, great despair, and deep disgust with ourselves. But afterwards, after weeks or years, it was evident that all of that was necessary, for thanks to those sufferings we escaped something much worse.

I remember an incident that happened in Starowka at the time of the insurrection but in the very first days when the border was not yet strongly bombarded. People were still living in their homes. A certain mother realized that a child of hers was sick. The woman was close to despair. The child could not stay in the same room because of the other children present. The only thing left to do was to move into the corridor. She said, "Oh, how cruel God is! He has afflicted me with so many things and now this sickness...." A few hours later the first bombs fell on the city. The room was destroyed. But the woman and the child were saved because they were in the corridor.

An accident? And the history of the Japanese Marytown? Having come to Nagasaki Father Kolbe tried his utmost to buy a place for the building of a monastery. He did not have much money, so it wasn't easy for him to find a suitable site. Eventually he wrote, "We have bought a big place.... It is really the slope of a hill. On May 16, 1931, a Saturday and also the feast of the Blessed Virgin Mary, Queen of the Apostles, we transferred everything to the Japanese Marytown or Mugenzai no Sono which literally means Garden of the Immaculata...."

The place was large but off the beaten path. The construction of the monastery met with thousands of hardships and troubles. But in 1945 when the atom bomb fell on Nagasaki, Marytown was saved just because the top of the hill kept it out of the line of sight of radiation heat and fallout!

So many times each one of us has escaped danger. Did we ever think later on that God wanted us to be saved? That by allowing us to escape some catastrophe healthy and sound, he did this to give us another chance, one more opportunity to take stock of ourselves?

Do we know how to be grateful to God for that?

Today a person does very little for another person. Likewise is there very little gratitude. The word "thanks" belongs together with "please" and "sorry," words disappearing from our language.

Do we have an occasion to say, "I thank you," to God?

44. What can each of us do? (Lk 18:1–8)

From time to time disturbing articles about the future of the world appear in the press. The population of our planet is increasing with frightening rapidity and in the opinion of many scholars, growth is greater than the amount of life-sustaining resources. Industry too is developing with lightning speed, but its creators often forget that its uncontrolled development threatens the natural source of supply with destruction. Inconsiderate exploitation of the earth leads to disaster, a picture of which is the drought on the plains of Saheli.

Disturbed by such reports people are beginning to listen to the counsels of those who hold that the only remedy for this evil is by radically curtailing the birthrate by all means possible, often not even thoroughly verified. These people complain about the position the Church holds that the only morally tenable view is to take advantage of the naturally infertile days and self-control.

No doubt the Catholic is in a difficult situation. On the one hand, worldly propaganda predicts dire consequences following an uncontrolled birthrate, on the other, this same propaganda is conducive to the arousing of sexual instincts. The modern world has both awakened and increased the problems of sex, demanding at one and the same time that human sex deny its natural objective which is the begetting of descendants. Under the stress of both tendencies, the Catholic begins to weaken in his outlook and often he is of the opinion that the Church is too absolute in its demands, that the Church must yield to the use of all kinds of methods of limiting descendants.

Jesus had foreseen this temptation when he asked, "Will the Son of Man find faith upon the earth when He comes?" If we believe that God exists, if we know that this God is love and mercy, we must trust that the fate of the world is in the hands of God's Providence. This does not mean that no catastrophe can ever touch us. If man hastens toward his own destruction of his own free will, that destruction will come. God does not want to save man in spite of man's desire. The earth still has gigantic possibilities of nourishing its inhabitants. The main problem is still not the global amount of food supplies, but the justice in sharing it, avoiding criminal waste, such as squandering an enormous amount of money on warfare, setting a limit on those who are supplied beyond measure (and who actually get sick on overeating) in favor of those who suffer want.

But what can we, little people, do to make the world better? The world will be more just if every person acts better. Everyone of us can contribute to the realization of this justice if we help feed the hungry by fighting prodigality (and that waste means not only war material but also wasting bread by throwing it away, as we see it in garbage cans, ruining good clothing, breaking furniture in a drunken brawl, tearing down tree branches, trampling on lawns, cluttering up premises) by overcoming our egoism, giving up a surplus, especially if the people next to us have a need, by trying to avoid luxury, and in a word, by sharing.

Each one of us Christians is contributing to fairness and justice by trusting and not allowing ourselves to be overcome either in word or in thought by doubts about the Church's teaching of God's word. To be a missionary, and today we must all be missionaries, that means to have control over our thoughts and words.

45. Always find time for prayer

How often do we say, "I have no time to pray."? In the morning a person is in a hurry, in the evening he is exhausted, and during the day there is not a moment for recollection. Such is today's life in constant haste!

Is life really like that, or do we make it such? No matter how it is, a Christian must not stop praying. The more activly we live, the more we must pray. Rightly did Mother Ursula Ledocjowska teach her sisters, "The more absorbing the work is, the deeper the foundation of prayer must be."

Although we are constantly driven by haste, we nevertheless lose a considerable amount of time in worthless thinking, at times in no thinking at all, on trains, streetcars, in assembly lines, and walking the streets. Our haste is spaced by long periods of such emptiness existing.

Prayer does not always have to be said on our knees in church, and in solitude. One of the most important benefits of the spiritual life is to learn how to pray at every moment in our thoughts.

This is not easy. The science of recollection is a great art. In order to be able to pray mentally one must drive everything out of the mind that is useless thinking.

Naturally, this does not mean that we may not have any orderly thoughts in our mind, but how often do we relive in our thoughts long periods of some frustration or anger. "He told me... he dared to tell me...." And so in the streetcar, on the street, at work... wherever it could be much more profitable to breathe a short prayer: "O Lord, help the man that injured me. Do not punish him for that as you did not punish me for the many times I did harm to others."

How often for quarters of hours do we not indulge in vain thoughts like: "How do I look? What did they think of me? Did they like me?" Instead of such thoughts how much better to think: "O God, I am nothing. If you permitted some good to be done through me I am glad of it, but I want to remember that you did it and I was only the awkward tool in your hand.

In the old-time handbooks of the spiritual life this was called: ejaculatory prayer, or aspirations. Today the words make us smile. But the fact remains that it pertains to a prayer for every moment, a prayer that deafens our thoughts about self. We need to answer vigorously to our interior searchings and sorrows.

A person who in God's presence reverts to his own self-assured merits does not pray, but only vainly puts on airs and graces. In truth he does not turn to God but rather to himself. He stands, as it were, in front of a mirror: "Oh, how smart I am, how good I am, how beautiful I am...." We must remember that the real enemy lives in our very selves. In moral theology it is called "the human spirit." It means: to seek self-satisfaction everywhere.

Prayer—that is to acknowledge our powerlessness and then ask for good things for ourselves and for others. For such a prayer we can always find time.

46. Where are these our neighbors? (Lk 19:1–10)

As the measured years of our life flow on, we have more and more of our near and dear ones "on the other side." Formerly we went to the cemetery out of necessity or curiosity, but today we go as if it were to the home of our friends.

What is happening to those whom we loved? We do not see them. The cemetery is certainly not their home. It does not seem to us that they are where their bodies lie turning to dust. Their remains are only a remembrance of them. And yet we feel that they are perhaps very near to us. We sense their proximity although we cannot see them.

For a Christian the world of the deceased is a world of real beings.

Thanks to our faith we know that the saints are concerned about us. The word "saints" here embraces not only the saints canonized officially, raised to the altars by the Church to be our models. In the broad sense of the word, the saints are all the saved souls. Remaining in close contact with God they are also in contact with us. They are not angels, as some Catholic pressmen sometimes speak of them. The guardian angels are pure spirits who by God's command care for us here on earth. But up there in heaven the saints surpass the angels—reaching a degree of intimacy with God to which the angels are not entitled.

We know that the saints are with us; although we do not see them they accompany our life. They intercede for us, and petition for us.

It is possible that some of our neighbors are damned. Damnation, that awful mystery of man's free will which refused obedience and remains in this refusal. It seems that a part of the punishment which they suffer consists in this that they see our life. That could be, judging by the stories of Jesus about the rich man and Lazarus, the beggar. When the saints see our life they influence it by making it easier for us to avoid evil; the condemned can only see it—how the evil sown by them continues to realize itself.

But what happens to the people in purgatory, who have to serve a temporary punishment? In the other world there is no time, but purgatory appears to be a state which equally falls under the laws of our earthly time measure. It is often said: that someone is suffering "purgatory on earth" and who knows but that some spiritual predisposition does not make it possible for us to begin our purgatorial punishment in this life. The essence of purgatory is the acceptance of suffering as something absolutely necessary, something that we ourselves want because only in this way can we be purified.

The people detained in purgatory are already saved. Having this knowledge they remain at a distance from God. Do they see our life? We are inclined to judge (but this is only my own private opinion) that they do not, and that is part of their punishment. They remain in gloom, always subject to their time.

We can aid them. We must be ready to help them. The Holy Year gives us great opportunities by offering us the privilege of easily gaining the jubilee indulgences. An indulgence offered for the deceased reduces their punishment and brings them closer to us. We go to meet our deceased friends not by burning a light on their graves but by praying for them.

In France, in Montligeon, there is a Church of the Blessed Mother of God, Redemptrix of the Souls in Purgatory. From there I brought this beautiful prayer with me: "O Virgin Mary, most worthy of all honor, have pity on the souls condemned to a time of purgation far from God and from you, our merciful

Mother. Break their chains, free them from the dungeon in which they moan. Take them under your protection, and especially have mercy on the most abandoned souls. We beg you, O Mary, unite us all in heaven that we may remain forever at the side of your Son, our Lord Jesus Christ."

47. Saints eternally alive

The cult of St. Therese of the Child Jesus encompassed the whole world with unusual swiftness. She died in 1897, was beatified in 1926, and proclaimed a saint of the whole Church and patroness of the missions in 1927. In 1973 the entire Church solemnly observed the centenary of her birth.

In spite of the admirers of "sweetness" whose efforts in the course of years, as Bernanos testified, tended to "kill" the cult of St. Therese, this devotion survived, spread, and brought to light the true characteristics of this saint of gallant stature, deep understanding of theological truths representing holiness in an unusual way as demanded by the needs of our times.

The cult of St. Therese also blossomed in Poland. St. Therese's books are sought by Catholic readers. In 1971 the Discalced Carmelites published the two volumes of "Writings of St. Therese."

The growing devotion to St. Therese awakened a desire in many of her admirers among us to find some reference to Poland among the published words of the saint. We sought in vain. Therese was not too well acquainted with the world (with the exception of her pilgrimage to Rome, she never left France, not even her native Normandy), had little interest in public affairs (about which she certainly had to hear a great deal in the house of her uncle whose passion was politics and who used to write articles for the local press), never mentioned Poland—with one exception, however.

In the convent at Lisieux there was a Sister Stanislas. In 1897 the elderly nun was celebrating the fiftieth anniversary of her religious vows. To honor this golden jubilee Therese composed a playlet about St. Stanislaus Kostka. The little drama does not have any literary value, on a level with all the rest of Therese's artistic productions. But as always it contains interesting formulation and betrays the thoughts of the author.

Two statements in the playlet are worthy of citation. St. Stanislaus was asked by his companion, "Do you love Mary? Please tell me about her." He answered, "About the most blessed Virgin? What can I tell you about her? Why she is my Mother." Praying to Mary, St. Stanislaus said, "I have one desire so great that if it were not fulfilled I would not experience happiness in heaven. My dear Mother, please tell me if the blessed in heaven can continue to work for the salvation of souls. If I could not work there for the glory of Jesus I would rather remain in exile and continue to fight for Him...."

Both statements apply equally well to Stanislaus and to Therese. The cult of St. Stanislaus also suffered from the admirers of sweetness but is now recovering its proper form. It is worth finding out what Fr. Joseph Majka wrote about the saint. When the sugar coating is blown away, St. Stanislaus also appears to us as the saint for our times.

Now, as never before, we need young saints, full of resolute willpower, able to show us how to control the senses, the inclination to cheap exhibits, and lack of understanding and ideals.

For God there are no dead, there are always the living: those who fight with evil and conquer it.

48. Death—a grace

The Church looks askance at all prophetic announcements. God does not want us to know the future beyond what we can legitimately decipher from reasoned premises and conclusions. Especially panicky forebodings of dire disasters that are to befall the world, never received the stamp of approval by the Church. Even when the propagators were saints, or protagonists of miraculous events acknowledged by the Church, complete freedom was left to the Christians to believe those forecasts or not.

Lucia, the oldest of the Fatima children, announced various frightening future events. Pope John XXIII and Pope Paul VI forbade her to spread them. The Church takes responsibility only for that part of the apparition which speaks of the mercy of God, of the intercession of Mary with the Heart of her Son, of the call to penance, and of safeguarding from evil.

God demands confidence from us. We are to believe that he is always standing beside us guarding the world. No evil will befall us without his will, which means that even if we suffer something painful it will rebound to our good. "Everything is a grace," said St. Therese, "everything that is done for our good, in the sense of eternal good."

The predictions of Jesus have an entirely different character from purely human forebodings of impending evil. Jesus points to certain signs foretelling the future, but as some theologians correctly observed, they are signs that were in evidence from the very beginning of Christianity. The era of the coming of the end of the world began with the moment of Christ's death. This era has existed for centuries and may continue for centuries. God wants us to be ready for the coming of the last moment. The day of the Lord will come unexpectedly, like a thief in the night.

Death arouses fear in us. We are afraid of dying and we fear the unknown that will open up before us.

Actually we ought to get rid of all fears. Death is also a grace. It will come for us at the most propitious moment. A person dies when his life's record shows the most assets, or has the least liabilities. The One who is waiting on the threshold of our agony is Jesus, who loves us and is most merciful. We ought to die with the feeling the prodigal son had when he returned to his father's house. We should also remember that no matter what evil we have committed, God loves us and wants to forgive us. There is a truth not emphasized enough, that God loves sinners even more, we might say, than the righteous. The child that comes home with a note of deserved approval makes us happy, but in this joy there is much self-satisfaction. The child who comes with a note of disapproval, perhaps after a punishment but full of sorrow and a sincere desire to do better touches us deeply. And although we know that his embarrassment will be our embarrassment, his hard efforts to improve will be our hardships too, we rejoice all the more because we understand that it was a lesson that helped.

To learn how to look upon approaching death without blind fear is also a lesson to be learned by all of us during the Holy Year.

49. Hero of our times

Among the arguments that testify concerning the validity of the gospel, I personally find the best to be the argument of the psychological integrity of its heroes. What genuinely honest people they were! Not some fabricated types, but ordinary people, and convincing by their very reality. There has never been an artist to depict such people.

Still more could be said that the people of the gospel, being people of their epoch are likewise people of all epochs. It is true that in certain ages there prevailed the skeptical/cynical type of the sadducees, in others the pharisaic type leaning toward pride and cruelty. Man always remains the same, but the times evoke certain human elements and display them openly.

To which evangelical personality is modern man most similar? Looking for the model we should perhaps stretch out to the "thief" hanging on the cross on the right side of Jesus.

Who were the criminal companions of Christ? Most probably

members of the robber band of Barabbas. Their chief won an unexpected freedom but they had to undergo death. The name Barabbas (bar rabbas: son of the rabbi) seems to testify that he came of the pharisees, perhaps their extreme wing, from the movement of the siccarists, so-called cutthroats. That was a group of patriotic partisans who in the course of constant killing were transformed into bandits. We see this apparition often in our times: planting bombs, and hijacking planes.

In the face of death this bandit acknowledged his defeat. Having begun the battle for the good of his countrymen he came to be the fear of his brethren. Now a sense of guilt and the justice of the cruel punishment dawned upon him. The Romans were enemies but the punishment they meted out was simply an act of justice.

At his side was another suffering Man about whom the bandit had heard worked for the good of the people. He never changed his way of action. For this he suffered torment and cruel ridicule. Above his head it was written that he is King and they derided his Kingship. The Man received all the insults without a word. In spite of the ridicule he certainly acted like the King. In his attitude there was such a wondrous dignity that the bandit, a mere man, who lost everything, asked, "Remember me when you come into your Kingdom...."

And at once he was saved. Sooner than the apostles and disciples ... he preceded them all—the bloody bandit, because he acknowledged his fault and believed in the Kingdom whose King was the Man hanging on the cross next to him.

Man today seems to be so far away from God. Yet at the same time, he is so very near to Him.

50. The great fear (Mt 24:37-44)

Traveling for several weeks through western Europe, I had the feeling that this whole area is so prosperous and yet at the same time afflicted with mortal fear. In Italy, where the atmosphere seems to be most tense, Italians said to me, "We are living in the fear that tomorrow may bring some catastrophe which with one stroke will sweep away all our possessions."

Prices are going up day by day. Unemployment is increasing. The ruin of our natural surroundings is growing. Political unrest is getting stronger and taking on the form of terror, kidnapping, and bombing attacks. The number of mentally unbalanced men ready to kill for any reason whatsoever is on the increase. Prosperity thus threatened begets a wave of uncontrolled egoism.

In the course of the last few years in all of western Europe there was a tremendous drop in the number of births. Natural conception gave way to contraception. Even before the war W. Majdanski wrote that the ideal of the western civilization is becoming the model: Mr., Mrs., and mongrel. When the number of children diminishes, the number of pet animals increases. Western Europe models itself upon the United States of America where in 1973 two billion dollars was spent on food for cats and dogs, and only 425 million on sustenance for children.

Naturally there followed an unusual drop in the number of religious practices. At the same time superstition and fortune-telling became popular. Thirty-five percent of the people in the West consult their horoscope daily. Seventy percent of these people take these reports seriously. The houses of men and women fortune tellers are bombarded by those seeking advice or reassurance.

The famous American film *The Exorcist* appears in Europe. Crowds form lines to see it and experience a thrill which in many cases turns into hysteria. The film portrays the preternatural possession of a twelve-year-old girl. If for some people it is the disclosure of the work of Satan whose existence they had practically forgotten, for the great majority of viewers it is only an uneasy fear-arousing sensation.

The tension through which the Western world is living does not mean that these convulsions are the end of the world. This is not the first time that a great moral crisis has shaken the human race, although it seems greater to us than any previous one, does not have to be the last one. But Jesus advised us to be alert and he predicted that it would come rather unexpectedly. In a world immersed in unrest, we Christians have much to do. Our work must be a mission. We must show the world our faith purified, free from errors and weaknesses. We must testify to it with our lives. We must spread it not only around ourselves but also reach out into the depths. If we are to be more creative, we must also become more saintly.

Such are the invocations of our Holy Father. Such were the slogans of the Holy Year 1974-1975.

But we must never forget that we are not alone. Jesus is with us—the same Jesus who will be born for us anew. The time of advent reminds us constantly of the mystery of waiting, of hope, and of love!

51. Hope conquers despair (Lk 1:26-38)

Some 120 years ago Pope Pius IX announced the dogma of the Immaculate Conception of the Blessed Virgin Mary. The proclaimed dogma was the final definitive statement of the truth well-known to Catholics for a long time. Already, in the middle of the fifteenth century, faith in the Immaculate Conception was spreading and deepening in the Church. The Council of Trent was close to proclaiming the dogma. Four years after its proclamation, in 1858 in Lourdes, little Bernadette Soubirous saw the mysterious Lady who spoke these words unintelligible to the little girl, "I am the Immaculate Conception."

For many years the popes had the custom of beginning activities decisive in the life of the Church on the feast of the Immaculate Conception. On December 8, Vatican Councils I and II were opened. From this choice of day came the understanding of the name given by Vatican Council II: that the Mother of God is the Mother of the Church—its Patroness and Model. Vatican Council II and the Holy Year, and the great work of evangelizing the world, have a chance of realizing their commitments only through the intercession of Mary. She alone is free from sin which weighs on all mankind. She alone can lead us to her Son.

At the beginning of the Holy Year Pope Paul VI issued a pastoral letter explaining what the cult of the most holy Virgin should look like in our present time. This cult should above all be biblical, i.e., based on excerpts from Holy Scripture, which "from Genesis to Revelation refer in no uncertain terms to her who is the Mother and co-worker of the Redeemer." On this occasion the pope expressed the opinion that "the Christian of our times should profit by the use of the Bible as a fundamental book of prayer and dip into it for inspiration and for unparalleled models."

It is necessary that the cult of Mary be liturgical, i.e., incorporated into the liturgical cycle. It may not be cut off from the liturgy, nor may it be mixed in with it. And so, for instance, the Pope in fervently promoting the recitation of the rosary calls our attention to the impropriety of reciting the rosary during the Holy Mass.

The cult should also have an ecumenical character because the problem of uniting all Christians is at this moment most dominant in the Church. We must ask for this union through Mary. "We have the greatest confidence," said the Pope, "that the honor paid to Mary, the humble Handmaid of the Lord, will become not a hindrance but a help and the point of meeting on the way to the union of all who believe in Jesus...."

Finally the cult must have an anthropological character. The changed feminine role in human society makes it difficult for some to accept Mary of Nazareth as a model since the horizons of her life, as they say, seem to be very narrow in comparison with the horizons of the activity of modern man. The Pope reminds us that "the Blessed Virgin was always given as a model by the Church not because of the kind of life she led," but because of her perfection in walking in the footsteps of Jesus. Mary can be considered, "a mirror reflecting all the hopes of man in our epoch," she is not, "a picture of a woman passively submissive, but of a woman fearlessly proclaiming that God is the One who lifts up the downtrodden and humble, and overthrows the thrones of the rulers of the world."

Pope Paul VI assures us that, "For modern man, torn between despair and hope, afflicted with a sense of his own limitations, and at the same time tossed about with limitless aspirations, for a man with a troubled soul and a broken heart, with a mind tortured by the mystery of death, crushed by loneliness and a feeling of spiritual depression—for this man the Blessed Virgin Mary, pondered upon in the light of her earthly life and its meaning which she possesses in the Kingdom of God, may become a benevolent vision and uplifting word, the victory of hope over despair, a feeling of belonging over loneliness... a vision of life overcoming death."

52. A reed (Mt 11:2–11)

Whom did you come out to see? asks Jesus speaking of John, a reed shaken by the wind?

"Man is a reed," wrote Pascal, "but a thinking reed. He is weak and easily broken, but he can think."

Man has an intellect, he has a will, and he has received grace. The intellect and will together with grace constitute a power that defies the natural brittleness of the reed. Therefore, speaking of John, Jesus sets him up as the counterpart of the broken reed.

Not long ago the English *Sunday Times* stated that statistically only 29 percent of the people in Great Britain believe in a personal God. This of course pertains only to the Anglican community which possessing no dogmas, likewise does not possess a sufficiently strong discipline of faith. But sad to say we notice this abandoning of faith also in Catholic communities, not only in France but even in Italy and Spain. We must accept the fact that religion is on the wane.

This happens for a number of reasons, one of which we'll mention here and perhaps the main one: contemporary civilization creates a wonderful mirage of happiness and convenience. Neither one is unreal, but based on the truth that the higher the civilization the more necessary for man is a higher standard of morality. However in practice, the very opposite is true;... it is taken for granted that higher civilization exempts man from moral obligations. Profiting by the good things of the rapidly advancing civilization and simultaneously deprived of moral standards, man becomes an unsafe destroyer whose conduct can often be a real threat to his environment.

Many people agree with the existence of the above mentioned truth, but do not consider the moral life to be the outcome of a religious life. However practice makes it evident that morality not rooted in religion is hardly concrete and does not enjoy enough sanction. Man shrugs his shoulders: why should he be honest? Why not betray his wife? Without external sanction man seeks sanction within himself. Is the good that a man determines for himself always a truly good thing? Do we not cover up our comfort, sometimes unconsciously with the term "good"?

Religious sanction has such a beneficial influence on morality because it demands of man a decisive firm stand in the face of objective standards and tells him to overcome his weaknesses.

Toward the end of her life, St. Teresa of Avila was traveling through Spain in order to establish a new convent of reformed Carmelites in Burges. It was a Spanish winter with a drenching rain and falling snow. Rivers were swelling. While crossing the river Arlonzon the wagon bearing the Sisters got stuck in the middle of the stream. The elderly sickly Mother Foundress had to step into the icy water and while alighting hurt her foot. She reached the shore barely alive. She complained to the Lord Jesus thus, "And this too had to happen to me?" The voice of Jesus answered her, "Teresa, that's how I always treat my friends." "Oh, my God!" she cried, "so that's why you have so few!" Afterwards he added, "God treats his friends harshly not because he wants to hurt them, after all he treated his own Son the same way...."

In the face of moral desires that our faith demands, we must be as strong as John was. By nature we are like a reed, but with grace we can become the antithesis of reeds.

53. He was born to witness to love

The French Catholic press electrified the public with the news about the suicide of the Brazilian Dominican Tito.

The Dominican had been arrested under the pretext of revolutionary activity. In the years 1969–1970 he suffered unthinkable tortures inflicted by the wild imagination of the political police. The successful kidnapping of a Western diplomat by the Brazilian partisans resulted in naming and setting free a group of prisoners. Thus Tito gained his freedom and found refuge in France.

But now he could not live after what he had gone through. Four years after attaining freedom, the Dominican committed suicide.

He was hardly responsible for his act of self-destruction. He had fallen into a state of deepest psychic depression. The guilt and responsibility for his death falls on others.

We older folks remember how a similar situation looked in the period of occupation. It happened that a person having survived the tortures of the Gestapo found himself in freedom. How quickly such a person regained his equilibrium. But the occupation continued and the released man knew that he could be arrested and tortured again. That was not a departure to live in a free country. In spite of this people were regaining their serenity of soul and often returned to their conspiratorial work.

To what can we ascribe this? Perhaps to the specific atmosphere that reigned in the community. Little is said about this atmosphere, and little is written. It was an atmosphere of brotherhood and sacrifice. That at times it happened otherwise only confirms the rule. Never had help been given another person more quickly. For a person released from the claws of the Gestapo everybody wanted to do something.

Did the Dominican Tito find such an atmosphere when he arrived in France? Alas, we are living in an era of terrifying egoism. A rat-race for profit and pleasure has taken the human mind away from the sufferings of others. So much is written about people dying of starvation and how small the witnessing to their hunger! Our world of such great possibilities is also the world of suffering people, of the lonely, and the despairing. Who remembers them? I know a person who lives in the conviction that she is the victim of hateful gossip in her environment. Strictly speaking there is no such hatred. Nobody is persecuting the poor old lady, but neither is there any person who cares about her life. Is it any wonder then that she has fallen into such despondency?

Great human affairs are usually expressed through the concrete actions of individuals. When we speak of hunger we must see a hungry person. When speaking of a neglected person we have to see a person slumped in deep despair. Alas, it happens that we speak of great affairs but the only concrete solution, as far as we can see, is our own person.

It would be unfair to blame the French community alone for the tragic death of the Brazilian Dominican Tito. If Tito, after gaining his freedom, had come to Poland would we have been able to contribute to the rehabilitation of his inhumanly tortured psyche? Would we have known how to surround him with such love and sincerity that he would understand that the evil he suffered does not preclude the goodness of God?

God called all men to freedom. He offered us the world which can be transformed into evil or good. When man ruins the earth God permits him to suffer the consequences of his wrong doing. But God does not hurry with his punishment. He wants man to understand and to change himself. God does not want to condemn anyone. He loves even those who torture others. It would be a very simple matter for God with his almighty power to correct every evil. He wants the good to correct the bad. If people have been a man's executioners, others by their conduct ought to level off that evil. In the world there is an incessant ongoing process of equalization. The good done by one person levels off the bad perpetrated by another person.

Jesus came upon earth to show us how this work of equalization should look. He did not descend to earth as the God of vengeance. He was born as man, subject to human fate, temptations, and suffering. He was brought forth on a cold night in a stony cave because there was no house for him. He lay in a hard crib for there was no cradle for him.

He wanted to show that God does not want to save us without us. Evidently we ourselves will not overcome our wrong doing with our own goodness. We are much stronger in evil than in good. But Jesus has opened up for us a source of such powers with which we can overcome every evil. All we have to do is ask for help that we do not fall into the false conviction that we of ourselves can conquer every evil. Uniting our nothingness with God's almightiness we can do everything.

In the age when man convinced himself that with all his ambitions he constantly stands in the face of unknown and always threatening powers of nature—Jesus being born a weak human child tells us about the necessity of trusting God. But it may not be an effortless trust. We must work as much as we possibly can. When we trust, our work will be the work of God.

Jesus was born to tell the people about the love of God for

mankind. Not only to tell, He witnessed to this love with his whole life ... from his birth in the stable to his death on the cross.

And our duty as Christians is to witness to this love of God. We who have received so much have to reciprocate. Our life must be a replica of the love of God. "When I am kind," St. Therese of the Child Jesus would say, "then Jesus himself works through me; the more I am united with him, the more I love my sisters...." Loving mankind in this way, giving him in our love the love of Jesus, we save him from despair. Tortures are not necessary for a man to fall into despair. Let us just look around us. There are people next to us on the brink of despair. If we do not show them a kind heart who knows what they will do.

On the birthday of Jesus we must look around very carefully. Maybe there is a person near us who is waiting for our help. Of ourselves alone we cannot give him much. But with Jesus, we can save him.

54. A year of imperceptible change (Jn 1:1–18)

The beginning of the year 1975 opened up a new phase of the Holy Year, and the most important one.

Up to that time it was a time of preparing the whole Church in the spirit of renewal and reconciliation. Now the center of activity is transferred to Rome. In the year 1975 the Eternal City attracted tens of thousands of pilgrims and likewise tens of millions of tourists. The former sought in the Roman churches a renewal of spirit which will enable them to evangelize the world better, the latter viewed the sights of Rome, the beautiful jubilee celebrations, and listened to sensational reports of what they believe is taking place behind the Bronze Door. Those who were fortunate enough to find ourselves in Rome that year went as pilgrims for prayer, for interior renewal, for strengthening in ourselves the will to do good.

No doubt there were less pilgrims than sightseers who are not thinking of experiencing a change in their lives. And maybe more than one of those looked askance upon all the festivity thinking that the Holy Year is something "outdated" and "not of our day," something without meaning; that in the face of progressive and revolutionary events taking place in the world, the Church is only a "marginal" institution whose life hardly interests anybody.

As though anticipating this view we read: "And the Word was in the world... but the world knew Him not. He came unto his own but his own received Him not..."

How many people noticed the birth of Jesus? Great worldly events were taking place when in a small country, in an obscure town which nobody knew except those in immediate surroundings, a Child was born. The Child will become a Man—but will always remain in the narrow confines of his own. Those "pagans" who will come to see Jesus in the last days of his life will be like the curious tourists coming to Rome in 1975 to see the celebrations of the Holy Year. Jesus had then said plainly, "The seed must die in the ground in order to bring forth fruit...."

The Holy Year ended together with the year 1975, and perhaps many still think that it was a somewhat pretentious manifestation of the life of the Church. They say, "And what did the celebration give? What did it change? What did it achieve?"

But something did sprout. In those who really live the Holy Year awakens the power "to become the children of God." They understand their sonship and want to be faithful to it. How many of them are there? Maybe not too many. As the Church began its work with a tiny group of apostles, so it may begin its renewal with hundreds or thousands. However, the renewal will embrace everything. For we are not building on our own possibilities. We are building on Him who having come unnoticed does not cease to give us "grace after grace."

55. To speak of and testify to goodness (Mt 3:13–17)

Jesus the Son of God came upon earth as a real man. Man grows and matures and Jesus took upon himself the whole evolutionary process of human maturity. After thirty years of a hidden life, having reached the fullness of spiritual and physical development, he began to teach. From beginning to end he was subject to human weaknesses and temptations, but in contrast to all other people, he never succumbed to any temptation.

Why then did he receive baptism which signifies purification?

Jesus came upon earth to bring an exceptional revolutionary teaching. All the religions of the world imagined their God to be an all-powerful monarch demanding attention and honor and indiscriminately punishing every disobedience. This God did not come down to man, man had to bow before him on his knees. Even the religion of the Old Testament was above all the teaching about a God demanding honor. Words about the love of God would appear in it, but were hardly noticed. The contemporaries of Jesus who were exponents of the Jewish religion, be they pharisees teaching their own narrow views of the laws of purity, or essenes fleeing from life, or zealots waiting for the Messiah to avenge in a bloody manner the wrongs suffered by the chosen people, all of them knew only the terrible God of power and punishment.

Jesus throughout the span of his whole life will speak of a God of incredible goodness. His God desires the happiness and good of every man. He wants it so much that he becomes Man himself, suffers for the people and undergoes a human death of martyrdom for them. In the teaching of Jesus, God is a Father, the father of the prodigal son who promptly forgets all the misdeeds and ingratitude in order to be able to forgive and overwhelm his son with joyful love.

This God loves without limit and desires only our love. What we do for him does not count, what counts is that we offer him ourselves and our work. If we answer God's love with our love we need not worry about the success of our work.

However God demands one thing, the good will of our emotions. We are to love him not because "of compulsion, duty, or fear." God waits for our love; He waits patiently until we understand his goodness and that consciousness will release the emotion of love. Hence we must get to know his goodness to be able to love him.

Will we ever get to know his goodness if we think that the love of God is our due? To appreciate God's goodness we must be conscious of our faults and failings. We must convince ourselves that we do not love, since we do not know how to love. We ought to say, "Lord, we are sorry for our sins and, O God, give us the strength we do not have."

That is exactly what the baptism of John signifies.

Jesus never committed a sin. But he wanted to show what the position of man must be if he wants to know God's goodness. Therefore, Jesus asked John to baptize him.

In his teaching and with his whole life Jesus spoke the love of the heavenly Father. Is it not also our obligation not only to speak of God but to witness with our life his goodness? If the world to which we are to bring Jesus is to understand God's goodness, what kind of people do we have to be, the "evangelists" of the twentieth century?

56. Mother

A woman came to me to ask for some advice. I had known her some twenty years ago. Within the course of those years she had become a widow, but had brought up a daughter, witnessed her marriage, bequeathed everything she had to her, and generously allowed this daughter with her husband and children to live in her own home. Today when the mother is already old, the daughter with her husband is making life miserable for her by turning off her light, and depriving her of access to water. The objective of such conduct is clearly to drive an old person out of the house and to force the mother to seek shelter in some institution. And when the woman dared to complain, the daughter accused her of disturbing the peace at home because she sings the Little Hours and recites the rosary aloud.

People are forsaking their faith. We feel bad when our nearest and dearest ones give it up. If they are our children we ought to look for the cause in ourselves. Evidently we did not present the truths of God to them in a proper way. If they leave the faith in a deep conviction that faith is not giving them anything, but in its place they have their own code of moral conduct, that can be a certain relief for us. Their conviction, although erroneous in our estimation, is sincere and sincerity begets respect. God looks differently upon those who do not believe because they do not know how to believe. Faith must come from conscious conviction. It must be free from compulsion. Dialogue with unbelievers, which the Church invites us to do, is dialoguing with those who do not know how to believe.

But a person who for the sake of acquiring a residence accuses her own elderly mother, whom she owes everything, of disturbing the peace by reciting her rosary aloud, cannot inspire respect in believers or unbelievers. That is simply the height of selfishness without one iota of feeling.

And yet, sad to say, self-interest is not as rare as it seems to us. Sometimes it takes on a different aspect. The Church implores Christian parents to send their children to religious instructions. One can understand how parents, bereft of faith themselves, are reluctant to do so, but even there, I would think, they ought to let the children choose for themselves. However, often so-called Christian parents resign from the obligation of providing religious training for their children just because they do not want to take on the additional trouble of seeing to it that their children really attend these instructions. They are ingenious in justifying their action by claiming, "this learning is of no worth," "it's cold in church," "the children are simply wasting time," "they do not get anything out of it," "the priest doesn't know how to instruct them, or interest them."

Some of the dear old grandmas are deeply distressed by this situation. Mothers who brought up their children religiously look with sorrow upon the indifference with which their daughters are now bringing up their children. The parents' generation is tired—that's true. But if they are to be considered religious people, then at least for the sake of the mother who brought them up, they ought to be concerned about the religious education of their own children. At least for the sake of the mother!

57. Despite being such as we are (Mt 4:12–23)

Jesus is calling us to work in spreading the Kingdom of God. He called not only the apostles, and they, as the Gospel says followed him immediately. He also calls every one of us Christians. Not too long ago Pope Paul VI said, "Evangelization needs people. . . . Why are they so few?" Today when thoughtful reflections upon the lay priesthood make it possible for us to understand that every Christian, every baptized person, bears within himself the call to mission, to the apostolate, to the honor and dignity as well as the responsibility of spreading the Gospel, why is it that evangelization is progressing only at the price of great hardships and efforts? This is surely the call of every secular Catholic who wants to be truly faithful. Evangelization, the Kingdom of God, and the Church need souls. Men and women who will set up for themselves a formula, a program, the joy of their life. . . ."

Each one of us has the task set before him of witnessing to his faith.

But I cannot do that!, we say. I believe . . . but to testify? Our faith demands truth . . . and I tell lies, we say. Maybe they are not big deliberate lies. . . . But I tell lies constantly: out of politeness, to find an excuse, not to refuse openly, to make life easier for myself. . . . Faith requires that I help the other person. This one is dying of hunger. What did I do for him? I do not say that I didn't want to help him. I even had the best of intentions. I promised myself: I'll do this.... I'll go to him.... I'll send that.... What happened to those promises? What was actually realized in action?

We are not only sinful. We are weak, lacking in perseverance. The more frequently we take a good look at ourselves, the more miserable we appear to be. We considered ourselves brave, but we are cowards. We thought we were smart, but we are feeble. How many of us having reached old age are beginning to discover an unlimited amount of mistakes committed in our lives? Now we can say to ourselves, "It could have been different... but this way... we have wasted our lives."

That is all true. Yet even such as we are, we are constantly called to mission work. Jesus called the weakest, the most miserable ones to himself. Such were the apostles. People without talent, without science. People very human, weak, and sinful. But he sent them such as they were into the world. And they spread Christianity throughout the whole known world. It would be very pleasant to offer Jesus wisdom, courage, health, skill and ability to convince others. But if he wants us to be apostles that do not know how to speak and convince, do not possess courage, are not in good health, we must give him our nothingness.

It is hard to understand this, we can only feel it, but the more we are dependent upon him for everything, the less we can do by our own efforts, the more we receive from him, the more we give, thanks be to him for this.

58. Purity—chastity—clean of heart (Mt 5:1–12)

February 2 was the day of the presentation of the Infant Jesus in the temple. The day of blessing candles which symbolize the offering of man to God. On February 2 of the Holy Year 1975 the Holy Father accepted the renewal of the vows of all religious men and women of the whole world made in their name by the representatives of their congregations.

One of the three religious vows is the vow of chastity. Chastity in the traditional meaning is tied up with virginity. Monks and nuns making their vows express their desire to remain in the unmarried state. Hence, at times some people far removed from Christianity get the idea that for Catholicism, marriage is the end of purity.

Jesus said, "Blessed are the clean of heart." The definition of "clean heart" reaches into the very depths of the problem of purity or chastity. To speak of chastity simply in the biological sense would be too narrow a view of the virtue, for Jesus himself adds, "Whoever looks at a woman with lust has already committed adultery with her in his heart."

Impurity begins in the heart, in thought, in desire, in the imagination, and in the will. The modern world does not appreciate purity. A few years ago when I was beyond the border, I spoke with vehemence about a certain very popular pornographic film, because of its so-called "documentary" values, even lightminded Catholics in name laughed at it. Afterwards, they said, "That's not the way these things are spoken of nowadays." "And how are they spoken of?" I asked. "By showing everything openly? By displaying every intimacy? By discarding what even my generation called shame?"

"We are not living in the Victorian Age," I once heard. The "Victorian Age," the age of the English Queen Victoria, was an epoch in which great discretion was practiced in the matter of dealing with the two sexes. It was a time in which a girl of marriageable age was not supposed to know what matrimonial life was like. The man was allowed to live a riotous premarital life under the conditions; however, that was all done secretly. In reality it was a public secret about which everybody knew, except that everybody pretended they didn't. Thus it was an age of fraud and deception. Then at a certain moment the women declared loudly that they knew what their husbands did before the wedding and that they wanted to do the same. With that moment sexual morality was degraded in England and in many other countries.

Happily we are not living in the "Victorian Age." We have no reason to cover up with silence the important affairs of life. But that does not mean that we should belittle purity. The teaching of the Church has not changed in this regard. The Christian is obliged to observe purity of body and soul before marriage and chastity of soul after vow and vows.

It is true that it is not easy to observe purity, living in the world where it is considered right to free oneself as soon as possible from chastity, as if from some unnecessary shackles. In the name of a so-called "explanation of the situation," or in the name of "perfect honesty," as it were, films, television, theater, books, photography, paintings—all supply the mind and imagination of man today with pictures which distress and must truly distress us, because we are creatures whose reason is not always strong enough to rule over the demand of the senses. Thought ignites desire and desire arouses the will to a realization of the thought.

To live in the world, and not allow the imagination to be sullied, that is the big problem for Christians today. To not let oneself be convinced that courage is based on seeing every picture, and that since others look at it, I too must look. Purity is born in the heart, in the choice we make in ourselves, and in the conscious decision fortified by prayer. We will not change the world, except by beginning with ourselves. The purity of the world begins in the heart of each one of us.

59. The light of the world (Mt 5:13–16)

According to provisional accounts, in 1974 ten million children, from ages one to five, died of starvation. Hunger is spreading. The food supplies which the starving countries could have bought have dwindled, and the prices have gone up. For many fields there will be no grain seeds to plant.

For warfare in the year 1973 (I cite the Parisian *Express*) the world spent the inestimable sum of $207 billions. One tenth of that amount would suffice to bring sustenance and fertilizers to the 40 poorest countries of the world. America's newest bomber airplane costs $76 million.

The satiated world has gone over on a "better" diet. We eat more and more meat. To produce one kg of meat we need five kg of grain or 20 kg of vegetables. When we eat more and more meat the people in the world lack bread.

B. Jay Forrester of Massachusetts announced that the only way to prevent the spread of starvation would be to allow weaker beings to die out. Thus was the first vote cast demanding that the starving give way to the satiated.

A child in the United States receives fifty times as much as a child in India or Pakistan. One well-nourished child, answered some voices, is condemning three others to a death of starvation in the year 2000. This is horrible!

You are the salt of the earth.... Who? We, the people who have to direct the fate of all on earth wisely. You are the light of the world.... Who? We, Christians, who have to conduct ourselves in such a way that all who see our good works will honor our Father in heaven.

The world, this grand world of constant technical progress, is not directing itself with wisdom. Starvation did not fall down from some terrible cosmic disaster. It was born of hundreds of years of egoism, of living at the expense of others, of community and colonial profits.

And we Christians, are we the light of the world?

Lent is approaching—a time of the annual examination of conscience.

In this Holy Year our self-examination ought to be even more scrupulous. We must ask ourselves, "How and in what measure did we help the hungry? What and how much did we sacrifice?

How much did we squander that should have been set aside for the needy; how much money did we spend on superfluous luxuries?"

Lent is also a time of penance. Let us quit pretending, let us stop protecting ourselves with dispensations saying, "these are different times." Let us organize our life. Let us decide, what can we deprive ourselves of today when life is not yet demanding too much self-denial of us.

60. Satanic sophism (Mt 17:1-9)

"I have it as an assured fact that the devil can never, nor will God ever allow him to find a soul not trusting self in anything and deeply established in faith.... If such a soul should notice the slightest hesitancy about any one of the articles of faith ... such a doubt would certainly be the beginning of the temptation by the devil...."

So wrote St. Teresa of Avila 400 years ago.

The world stopped believing in Satan, made a laughing stock of him (with which the devil is undoubtedly greatly pleased) and when it suddenly became aware of him, it saw him in the horror of Blatty's stories and in *The Exorcist* on the screen. It saw him only as a terrifying spectacle yet with a kind of thrill. From such a devil one quickly returns to the pleasures of life.

Satan is not a funny scarecrow nor a horrible apparition whose very picture paralyzes the will. His activity is different. Hidden in our thoughts he suggests all kinds of "doubts." We are sick.... Why did a good God send this illness? Our marriage is incompatible.... Why did God who calls himself LOVE not forewarn our emotions from this error? We suffered some material losses ... why did God not protect our property? People are hungry.... why doesn't God command the stones to turn into bread? Satan—that's the thousand "why's" which plague us—not that we might find an answer but only to accuse God of not being a bureau of protection.

God did not descend to earth and live an ordinary human life just to protect us from losses and disappointments. He told us to pray for protection from the greatest of all evils—and he protects us but in a different way.

Let us look at our own life. How often have we really placed our trust in God? How often did we say firmly, in spite of all contrary suggestions: this illness, this loss is sent by God, so it cannot be bad; somehow it must be necessary for us. How? Maybe we do not know just now—at the moment. But evidently we needed this experience. Let it be as God wills. As often as we say this, so often we will notice that the illness passes or becomes less serious than it at first appeared to be. The loss is not nearly so hard to bear or some benefit ensues therefrom. And even if we have to live through some real pain to the end we learn later on that this painful experience was necessary to open our eyes to some very important matters. . . .

Satan did not know who Jesus really was—God or man—and therefore suggested doubts to him too as he is accustomed to do to ordinary people. They sounded like this: does human pain hurt you? Does your own pain disturb you? Free yourself from the disturbance! Perform a few miracles which will gain you renown and honor.

Jesus refused these satanic sophisms. Being God he went forward accepting human pain in order to fulfill the will of God and thus save man.

61. Joy versus sadness (Mt 17:1–9)

Recently the Secretariat of the Polish Episcopate made a joyful announcement about priestly vocations in Poland. The number of seminarians is not ceasing to grow. In 1971 it was

4,088 (991 of these in religious orders): in 1972 the number was 4,130 (1,073); in 1973, 4,174 (1,139); in 1974, 4,216 (1,125). In the first class year of studies, 1971, there were 700 seminarians; 824 in 1972; 942 in 1973; 1,006 in 1974. The number of ordained priests was 480 in 1971; 604 in 1972; 557 in 1973; and 638 in 1974.

The largest number of students is being educated in the diocesan seminaries: Tarnowo—260; Katowice—251: Krakow—219; Wroclaw—195; Warsaw—191. So much joy! When the whole world is experiencing a great crisis in vocations, we have no such crisis! How grateful we should be to God for this!

There are also other joys. Recently I received a letter that touched me deeply. A group of people from Auschwitz informed me that, in 1974, they provided for the hungry and needy by sending 63 parcels of medicines to Africa, seven parcels of foodstuffs to India, nine parcels of medicines and used clothing to Brazil. If in every city the size of Auschwitz there would be found such a group of self-sacrificing people, our aid to the needy, and to those starving to death, would take on an impressive dimension. Again, all we can do is thank God for this burst of generosity.

Such reports call forth a wonderfully happy reaction. The modern world easily falls into sadness. The economic crisis in the world is beginning to be felt everywhere, the ghost of starvation spreading over Asia and Africa, anomalies in nature—all of this is conducive to depression and creates uneasiness. Today's world does not know how to be happy. It knows only hilarity... to throw itself heedlessly into all kinds of amusements that have the character of stupefying narcotics.

This sadness grips our hearts. We too are full of sorrow and uneasiness. But we must fight this deadness. So often preparing for confession we say to ourselves, What should I confess? There is nothing in my life that constitutes sin.... What about our sadness? Sadness without a concrete cause is a denial of confidence. Since God is, and we know that he is love and goodness, we ought to look forward into the future with the greatest confidence and trust in spite of all evil forebodings.

If we will try to acquire this confidence, God will help us. Suddenly like lightning on a cloudy day, the insights will come that I have enumerated above. God knows our weakness, our fearfulness, our tendency to succumb to some "probable future uneasiness." To lift up the hearts of his three dearest apostles he appeared to them in the glory of his Transfiguration.

He helps, but he also demands from us a faith expressed in a freewill battle with sadness.

62. Romeo and the Samaritan woman (Jn 4:5–42)

Polish television portrayed Shakespeare's immortal tragedy *Romeo and Juliet*. It was a very good show thanks to the excellent actors, and above all, the actress playing the part of Juliet. At the same time it must be said that the director allowed himself a most improper license. He deprived the tragedy of the final conclusion in which the two warring families are reconciled over the dead bodies of their children so tragically deprived of life.

In spite of all his realism, Shakespeare was a thoroughly Christian writer. He portrayed the love of Romeo and Juliet conflicted to the hatred of the adults. The director, minimizing the spiteful quarrel between the Capulets and the Montagues, placed the emphasis on the sensual love of the young couple. He did not notice, or did not want to notice, that the intensity of emotions and the impatience of this love between the youths is the tragic result of their parents' opposition.

The age of Shakespeare, the Renaissance, was an era similar to ours with its great changes, profound upheavals, early maturity, and feverish impatience. Romeo and Juliet fit our era: the bodies of children, through the neglect of their elders, are given over as prey to their newly awakened and unbridled sensations. But Shakespeare's epoch was closely knit with traditional customs, something we cannot say about our times today. And, although the traditional ties are broken, we have not a few so-called "love" suicides today.

The truth of the matter, then as now, is that these suicides are a protest against the depreciation of love. Then, its foe was the conventional marriage arranged by the parents. Today, it is physical unions called "love" which precede true love. There is no time today to experience love based on the appreciation of common ideals, strong enough to make sacrifices. Before young people understand what mutual sympathy means, they have already become lovers. Hence the feeling of disillusion and the everlasting search for new loves which never have a chance to become "true love."

"You spoke rightly," Jesus said to the Samaritan woman, "because you have already had five husbands and the one with whom you are now living is not your husband."

Jesus was not thinking of a formal matrimonial contract. Divorces, although condemned by Jesus, existed among the ancient Jews, but they never became a plague as happened in the Roman-Greek civilizations. Saying "husband," Jesus was saying "love." So many times you looked for it—and now you did not find it either. You could not find it seeking it in such a way.

Although such was the life of the Samaritan woman, Jesus bent over her mercifully. He came upon this earth to save people, not to condemn them.

The Duke of Verona says at the end of the tragedy to Capulet and Montague:

> Look Montagues! Look Capulets! What a
> scourging meets your hatreds!
>
> Heaven chose Love as the instrument
> to kill the joy of your life....

Shakespeare sees in the death of the young people the

punishment of God. Jesus by love saves the whole world from punishment.

63. The hierarchy of reconciliation (Jn 9:1–41)

We have spoken of this a few times already, but it is necessary to say it once more. "World peace," as Pope Paul VI said in his New Year oration of 1975, "cannot be something ready made. It must be continuously created; it is the outcome of an uncertain balance the continuance of which can be assured only by steady progression...."

Peace on earth is not at all that certain. In spite of the desire of millions, even billions, there are people who are ready to disrupt it. When, on the one side good sense leads to understanding, on the other side greed and imposition of one's will on others threaten severe conflicts.

For that very reason the motto of the Holy Year is—reconciliation. Calling for everybody to be reconciled with everyone else—individuals and nations—the Church is conducting a great work of peace. Wars do not begin on the boundaries; they originate in the hearts of men.

But in reconciliation a certain hierarchy prevails. It is easy to be reconciled with a person whom we will never see, about whom we only know that he exists. It is harder, much harder, with somebody standing near us. Therefore, it is essential that reconciliation begin with those nearest to us—our very own. Before reconciliation can take place with people outside the Church, Christians must become reconciled with one another.

Is this necessary? Evidently it is since in the last days of 1974 Pope Paul VI issued an apostolic appeal for reconciliation in the Church. "There is a vital need," he wrote, "that everyone in the Church, bishops, priests, religious and lay people take an active part in the common effort at perfect reconciliation.

(Let everybody show himself a submissive son of the Lord....) Let all, in conformity with their position and dignity... create such a climate that an effective reconciliation can be attained.... For our reconciliation is born of the sacrifice of Christ who voluntarily underwent death for us—the cross, like a main flagstaff of the Church beneath which it directs the whole world, ought to become the inspiration of our common affairs that they be truly Christian. They ought all be based on a personal denial of self. This self-effacement serves to reach out to others in a brotherly way—allowing for an appreciation of the abilities of every person and giving everyone the opportunity of bringing in his contribution to the Church community...."

Everyone is necessary in the Church; each one has the right to fulfill his role. Must we be reminded? Alas, some Catholics know how to ruin the reputation of others, to cast slanders, or suggest by a meaningful silence that those about whom they do not want to talk are "bad" Catholics, while they consider themselves "good" ones.

Before we begin to speak to the world about reconciliation, let us take a good look and see if we are reconciled among ourselves. And let us not begin to use big words about reconciliation and peace if we have not renounced pride with regard to another Christian.

Before we begin to count the losses in the Church, let us first see whether by our conduct we have not driven someone out of the Church.

64. Thoughts about death (Jn 11:3–7)

Not long ago I saw the film *Jeremiah Johnson*. Considering its final utterance, this horrible and brutal film is nevertheless morally a Christian film.

The theater was filled to capacity. A crowd of maturing adolescents predominated. At the very beginning, the film depicts a man traveling through an American desert. It is winter; the hero is inexperienced, and he is almost dying of hunger and freezing from the cold. Despairingly he tries to get some food, and to start a fire with his frozen fingers. When he finally gets it going, a huge ball of snow falls from the tree and extinguishes the fire.

Every misfortune of the hero was greeted by the viewers with outbursts of laughter. The young people were practically delirious with laughter seeing how the hungry man was trying to catch a fish with his frozen hands.

I must say that this wild laughter aroused an awful resentment in me. Then when the hero found another trapper frozen to death in the snow—the laughter subsided. Could only the picture of death force the thoughtless crowd to a semblance of respect?

Films of cowboys, battles, and crimes have accustomed the audiences of today to the sight of people being killed. A gunshot or the hurl of a knife, and a man falls . . . that's the end. Corpses fall even in comedies. But a slow and expected death, that's something not generally seen.

Some day a "trailing shadow" will slide through every human life. At that moment the person will understand that he must die. Before that time he thought lightly of death. Now he knows that something mysterious, and painful is awaiting him, and that something will be the end of his present existence—the end, or the threshold.

We Christians believe that after death we fall into the hands of God. This God is Goodness itself and Mercy. Crossing over the threshold of death we are like the prodigal son at the moment when he stepped within the gate of his father's domain. If we return with the same feelings of sorrow, repentance and confidence in the mercy of God the Father, we can return peacefully.

But to enter within the gate of mercy we have to cross the dark threshold which arouses subconscious fear. On the threshold we will feel alone, absolutely alone. "O God, why have you abandoned me?" the dying Christ complained. Even he was not free from the feeling of aloneness that accompanies agony. For this final moment we must evoke all our reserves of courage and trust. The more conscious we will be of our dying, the more we will need to possess this courage.

Why, we could ask, does God allow this fear if right beyond the threshold he is waiting for us with his mercy?

It seems this fear is necessary to rid us of our lightminded sense of self-confidence. Whatever we have done, it seems to us, we are leaving the threshold of death with empty hands. We must make ourselves understand this. Even if over our grave they will speak of our merits, we must know that only in a small way have we cooperated with the graces and talents received. Death must not be just another gesture whereby we pride ourselves in our own estimation.

At least in the face of a picture of ordinary death, the provocative laughter ceases. Those who do not take anything seriously must finally realize that the effective falling due to bullets or knives on the screen is in real life dying.

Before Jesus brought Lazarus back to life he allowed him to die. Before he will resurrect us, he will let us die. To be able to appreciate the enormity of God's mercy we must exert our best effort in trusting that divine mercy.

65. The King on a donkey (Mt 26:14–27)

In the interesting, yet greatly controversial film of A. Wajda, *Pilate and Others,* Pilate asks Jesus, more or less in these words, "Is it true that you came to the city on a donkey at the head of a big parade?" Jesus answers, "No, hegemony, I have no donkey and I came to the city in the company of only one man...."

This perversion of the historic fact as it is written in the Gospel undoubtedly aims to prove that the activity of Jesus in the light of those days was as small a matter as the entrance of two single travelers into the city on a certain day. For that matter, the whole film is developed in the convention of portraying Jesus to the world, either busy about other affairs, or perhaps indifferent to all things.

But beside this complete indifference we, too, in today's world, have a great interest in Jesus. However, it is a search for a different kind of Jesus from the one we know in the Gospels and from tradition, a new Jesus, a would-be most "modern" Jesus. Following this tendency, historic truth is sacrificed, and new situations are created to enhance his problem.

Saint Paul wrote, "When a different Jesus is preached to you, one whom we did not preach...or...a gospel which is different from the one you received, you accept this quietly" (2 Cor. 11:4)

For Jesus did come riding into Jerusalem upon a donkey and was greeted with an ovation by the milling crowds of pilgrims on the streets of the city.

Rev. J. F. Six writes in his very recent booklet *Jesus*—"The procession begins. Jesus is riding on a donkey. Some are spreading their garments on the ground, others, branches.... In reality Jesus simply joined the procession of pilgrims and became its leader.... The meaning of the procession is important. Everything begins well in Jerusalem, just as everything began well in Galilee—with enthusiasm. Both in Galilee and in Jerusalem wild messianic hopes make the people drunk with joy, the pilgrims and the Judeans alike... and Jesus graciously makes a concession in favor of this messianism, imperfect as it is, yet truly sincere,... however... simultaneously... he opposes this feverish messianism with the messianism of peace.... He wants to be king of the poor...."

Jesus joins the procession in which the participants announce the messiah—leader and victor. Jesus is not that kind of messiah and never will be. He is the Savior of all, the conqueror of sin not of the enemies of Israel. This is only a momentary superficial concurrence. In the next few days there will be a division. These very same people who are acclaiming honor to Jesus of Nazareth will cry out to the Roman procurator to crucify him. Then again, after a few weeks these same people will begin to return to the teachings of Jesus. They will begin to return when a feeling of lonesomeness for the Jesus whom they saw will awaken within their souls.

Jesus is with everyone who seeks him in his own way—often a seemingly queer kind of road. He does not even quench a naive kind of enthusiasm. Patiently he waits for the moment when man resigns himself of his vision in order to see the Truth.

66. Joy (Mt 28:1–10)

We are living in times of stress and strain. Life brings short periods of joy, it is true, but it is not the overwhelming joy that reaches deep down into the heart and makes us sure we will always be returning to it.

And such, exactly such, should be the joy of the Resurrection.

Jesus arose from the dead. We repeat these words in every "credo." But when it comes to looking at this fact with the eyes of a cool observer we feel something akin to unreality.

For decades the Church has been placing greater emphasis on the humanity of Jesus. The first centuries of Christianity seemed to overlook the ordinary human life of Jesus, emphasizing instead that it was an unusual life replete with miracles. Continuing in the Apocrypha, they imagined the miracles about which the Gospels are silent. Today we try to see Jesus as a true man, as though he were one of us, subject in everything, except sin, to the laws of life—so ordinary that he would be unrecognizable in a mass of people.

And this ordinary human being whom we could pass without noticing if we had lived in his time, has risen from the dead.

We know the absolute positiveness of death. We pray at the graves so that those lying there might enjoy another, happy life. But can we comprehend that we will see them again?

Jesus performed many miracles: he cured the sick, and expelled evil spirits. But today we know how to explain away miracles. We know there are many mysteries still hidden in man. Death is still a threshold beyond which our hypotheses do not reach. It is the threshold of the unknown.

But Jesus brought them back to life and later, he, himself arose from the dead.

Those who do not believe will try to explain the history of the Resurrection by a general illusion, an imaginary death, a delusion perpetrated by the Apostles.

Yet belief in this wondrous fact has lasted for ages. Thousands of people agreed to sacrifice their lives for this faith. And it is impossible to speak of Jesus by passing over the fact of his Resurrection in silence. Jesus is revealed as the wisest, the most beautiful being, but without resurrection he is only a shadow of himself. Nothing else can explain the fact that he lives and his work has existed for twenty centuries. In human history there is no dearth of wonderful individuals. But of not one of these is it said that he arose from the dead. No one saw them after death. And their cause did not come to life in the course of centuries. If today, in the midst of the unusual epoch of changes, discoveries and achievements of human intelligence, there is a renewed interest in this Man who centuries ago, in a far removed province of a great but long nonexistent empire, due to the cowardice of a local official of a central power, suffered death, and afterwards as his followers claimed, arose from the dead, that is truly an apparition worthy of consideration. Only the cause of someone who has risen from the dead rises again in hopes. Therefore, might we not say that the cause which does not cease to rise from the dead is the testimony to the resurrection of that person?

In any case, we Christians must make this clear to ourselves:

just how alien is the fact of the resurrection to the intelligence of the twentieth and close to the twenty-first century, for without accepting this fact we cannot acclaim our Jesus. There can be no evasion here. No assurance that the Resurrection of Jesus was only spiritual, beyond history, mystical. We must convince ourselves that our faith demands an acceptance of the fact that at one time in history something occurred that transcends not only our knowledge but even our imagination.

The word "mystic" can have various meanings. It is said with respect that a mystic is a person having experienced a spiritual contact with God. It is said disdainfully that mysticism refers to a position not grounded on human reason alone. True mysticism must be based on a real fact. One cannot speak mystically with God if he does not accept that this God, having become man for us, really came back from the dead.

"If Jesus did not rise again, our faith is vain," says St. Paul. God could certainly have redeemed us in some other way. But if he wanted to save mankind by the life, death, and Resurrection of Jesus, we can be assured that his solution was the best way. It was the right way opened up to man. God wanted to show us how much he loved man, even such as he is and such as he can be made to be. Jesus passed through the world saying things which we can never fully appreciate, so far do they surpass us. Finally, he performed a miracle the world had not seen; he crossed the threshold of death and promptly returned to life again. He proved by his return that beyond this threshold is to be found the mercy of God about which he spoke so many times.

To speak of Jesus and not tell about the resurrection is to disown the proof which no mere human being is able to give! Jesus could have left us with only his teachings, and we would have been rich. But death would have continued to be a threshold of uncertainty. Having stepped over it and returned, Jesus gave us the sign that the doorstep of death is the gate to the home of the Father of the prodigal sons.

Resurrection is the greatest of graces! It is the miraculous loving answer to suffering and death! Jesus will return to earth for us! He gave sense to a life which seemed so absurd.

If Jesus had not risen, what meaning would the words spoken to the thief hanging on the cross next to Jesus have?

But if Jesus arose from the dead, those words have meaning for everyone of us. And when we fully comprehend this, an overwhelming joy must permeate us. Such a joy as the sorrowing women felt when they came to the tomb with despair in their hearts and suddenly heard the words: "He is risen as he said."

67. Handicapped children (Jn 20:10–31)

In the last few weeks some disturbing voices were heard in the press. Someone wrote that handicapped children are so unhappy and cost so much that, plainly speaking, it would be a "humanitarian thing" to pass the sentence of death upon them.

That such opinions were ever voiced is not too surprising. The ghost of overpopulation and of starvation is hanging more and more threateningly over our world. Even if we do not feel it, we hear about it often enough. In truth, the majority of educated people claim that the means of feeding all the people exists, that the only thing necessary is to cut off the production of military arms, to curtail prodigality, to secure the cooperation of all in the just sharing of goods, and above all a different, better attitude toward all men. However, these arguments do not reach many people since they call for effort and denials. It is easier to not deny oneself, and to pretend that the only solution of the trouble is the removal of the weakest.

Are handicapped children really unahppy? Those who have dedicated their lives to them, the Sisters of Fisher, Samaria, and similar groups caring for children's homes, claim that they are not. When these children are lovingly cared for, they can learn to forget about their handicap. Do they cost so terribly much?

Certainly less than alcoholism, and the consequences it costs the community (furthermore, drunkenness is a major cause of the children's sad condition). The drunkard destroying an expensive piece of furniture or china, the umemployed drunkard, the drunkard who kills people by driving onto the sidewalk, can never pay off his debt to the community. He goes to prison for a short period of time, comes out, drinks again, and again destroys property. Nobody ever mentioned the necessity of liquidating drunkards. But words about liquidating handicapped children have been uttered.

The struggle with drunkenness is a hard battle because to conduct it successfully it is necessary to start with oneself and those dearest to us... while the perspective of removing the handicapped appears to be a relatively easy disposal of the problem.

We, Christians, must not forget that every person is the property of God. If a person is weak or sick, if he causes us some trouble, let us consider whether or not that trouble has some meaning for us.

The weakness of a child develops parental love. A sick child is the school of sorrow in the life of those who have lost the fundamental social feeling. A child is the joy and pride of his parents. But when the child begins to cause trouble with rebellious actions (a frequent occurrence today), the parents begin to express regret for having children. Whoever understands what a child's hopeless illness is, will look differently upon the rebellion of children and will not withdraw his love for them. Parents train and educate their children, but children also educate their parents.

How unmerciful God is!—some people say as they look upon retarded children. God is very merciful, since he causes every pain permitted by him to open up the heart of man and renew in him a sense of responsibility. On the body of our humanity are wounds like unto those on the Body of Christ. When they are touched, their healing significance is discovered. For their selfless dedication in caring for retarded children, the Sisters have received this privilege. But Jesus desires our faith also. He wants us to believe, even though we do not deal with retarded children.

68. Victorious banner (Lk 24:13–35)

It happens that exhaustion makes us feel like the two men who were going to Emmaus in the evening of the day of the Resurrection.

We were building our life on certain expectancies. Hope told us not to notice hardships and obstacles. Maybe even in our consuming enthusiasm it seemed to us that what we were aiming at was already here, closer and easier to reach, and even a little different than it was in reality—more appropriate for us, and more to our satisfaction.

But something happened that undercut our hopes. The stroke fell like a lightning flash from Golgotha. We realized that what we were waiting for will never happen.

We ceased being fighters for the cause. This does not mean that we made peace with reality. But now we only moan and groan. Everything appears dark. Pessimism has covered our horizon. It would be best to die and not see it, we think and say. We speak more frequently about death. We think of it as an escape. We begin to explain it to ourselves; it cannot be so bad since, thanks to death, we can save our dreams.

And suddenly a shock. One of those unusual meetings which everyone of us has had, at least once in our life. A meeting in which by means of words, actions, or gestures of the person, we suddenly recognize the Crucified. It is not true that we have never met Jesus. We have met him many a time, in a person who asked us for something; in the one who told us words of truth—maybe even bitter and painful; in someone who suddenly, not knowing why, stretched out his hand to us; in the most forthright opinion expressed by someone we considered foolish; in the sudden conversion of those whom we looked upon as lost....

Too bad for us if we did not make the discovery as did the two disciples at Emmaus. Jesus does not always want to reveal himself against our will. If our pessimism and our complaints hide the truth from us, he may go away unrecognized.

But if we recognize him, let us not try to grab him by his cloak. Let us not demand that he stay with us. Let us do as those two did, immediately, on the run, let us return to our life. He does not want to hear our groanings. Instead he desires our activity. We are to continue to fulfill his will: we are to witness to him in the world where he remains hidden and is ostensibly the loser.

Whatever our hope was, it continues to exist. Maybe we will have to correct our wishes in the spirit of a greater self-forgetfulness. Maybe we will have to look for our good also beyond our tangible good.

The good that we must do for others always exists. It is always waiting for us. People are always hungry, suffering, and in need of our compassionate act and our witness.

And death is not an escape from an evil life. It is the goal—the winning post. The runner does not leave the track to cross diagonally across the field to get to the goal sooner. He runs the race to the end, and he runs until he sees before him the banner of victory pinned on by the judge.

69. This affects us personally

Before the beginning of the 1975 Season of Lent, Pope Paul VI delivered an oration in which he once more reminded us: "The present Jubilee Year demands of us the witness of full solidarity with the people with whom Jesus wanted to be identified in a special way. Thus we will show our brothers and sisters in a most significant way that this Year is "holy" for all people...."

Who are the people about whom the Pope speaks? Thus Paul VI also clarifies: "Not one of the disciples can possibly be ignorant of the fact that Jesus identified himself with the poor. To the end of time the poor will be with Jesus...."

After years of hope for welfare, comfort, abundance, and the easy life, we have hard years. Not everybody in the world feels these hardships in the same manner. Where some need only to limit themselves somewhat, others suffer hunger unto starvation.

For the love of God let us not forget, that in the starving countries people belonging to our human family are dying daily! Hunger in the lands of the Sahel, in India, in Pakistan, and Bangladesh, has not disappeared. It has instead become greater since the price of grain went up and there is now less grain on the market of the world. In the monthly *Etudes* in early 1975 it was stated, "An inhabitant of Bangladesh whose sustenance consists mainly of vegetables annually consumes 230 kg of plant products. But a resident of the United States being fed mainly on beef consumes 950 kg (of which only 80 kg are agricultural products no matter in what form he eats them—all the rest, over 800 kg is given to the feeding of slaughter animals). It was said that the "holy cows" of India were making the people poor by their very existence. How much more do the well-fed slaughter cattle use up for their food, which could save millions of people from starvation!

When the rich world eats too well and too much, the poor world goes hungry and dies of starvation. The problem of these disproportions was not such a burning question as long as there was enough grain for all. Today, when the world reserves of grain supplies have dropped so low that there might not be enough seed for planting, the rich are overeating what belongs to the poor. They are stealing from the poor by their overabundant eating.

"Do you not understand," said Pope Paul VI to the participants of the last Roman Conference, "that this pertains to you—to each one of you personally?"

Do we not understand that this also pertains to each one of us personally?

While we are beginning to plan our summer tours, our travels, and our vacations, should we not ask ourselves these questions: What have we done up to this moment for the hungry? What do we intend to do for them?

70. The Father (Jn 14:1–12)

The teaching of Jesus constantly grips us with its newly discovered aspects. We may read the Gospel hundreds of times and yet we will always find something unexpected, something hitherto unperceived. The simplicity of the Gospel is only superficial. In literary critiques, they speak of certain writings which have a so-called "second bottom," that is, an addition, or the real contents, deeply hidden. The Gospel is a literary product with countless "bottoms." It should be said perhaps that it is a production accessible to all, for by its childlike simplicity it has a "bottom" for every reader. The Gospel is certainly directed to the needs of everyone. But the Gospel must be lived if we are to discover the "bottom" meant for us.

One of the thrilling evangelical truths is the word used by Jesus to describe God, the Father.

For the ancient Jews the concept God, or the Father, was not altogether foreign. However, he was a strict Father, demanding, angry, inclined to punish. He was also a Father who jealously guarded his son Israel and promised to protect him only.

The Father of Jesus is someone entirely different. Jesus did not have an earthly father. Joseph fulfilled the role. Joseph is a true model of a human father. His whole life is one long service performed for the persons entrusted to him: his beloved Virgin-Wife and his foster son. Joseph cares for them, teaches, helps, protects, and supports with his work; while at the same time he is uninterruptedly attuned to the inner rhythm of the home and is himself subject to this rhythm.

But of course the Father in heaven is an infinitely perfect father! He also directs, teaches, serves, cares for us, gifts us with the world and helps us to mold this world. He loves man with a love that must call forth a thrill of delight. It will suffice to recall the picture of the father of the prodigal son. This father forgives everything, forgets everything.

The "father" image of Joseph helps Jesus to form his image of God the Father. But the perfection of the fatherhood of Joseph is only an echo of the perfection of God's Fatherhood which only the Son of God really knows.

Whoever recognizes Jesus, already knows the Father, for they are One. Jesus not only speaks of the Father; every act of Jesus is an act of the Father. The life of Jesus is the revelation of the eternal fatherly activity of God.

The modern world knows the meaning of totalitarianism. I do not speak here of political totalitarianism. I am speaking of the tendency of modern man to impose his will and his practical outlook upon others. Such totalitarianism is "educational" and leads to a real battle between the generations.

The Fatherhood about which Jesus speaks is the very opposite of totalitarianism. God does not impose his will on anyone. Gently, in a fatherly way, he tries to make peace with man. He implores, convinces, eternally offers love. He does not force. He does not set any limits to his love, for any nation or group of people, the Church, Christianity or community of believers. Every person is a child of God the Father. And even as a person moves away from God by the effect of the mysterious law of love he is drawn to God, he is wanted by Him.

71. Joseph, the worker

"Being practically seventy-years of age," wrote Angelo Roncalli in his diary, serving at the time as papal nuncio in France, "not much can be expected from the future. There is no use in fostering illusions but time to become accustomed to think about the end.... After my return from Paris I will pick up my usual life without ambition, in a wholehearted fidelity to my obligations... in union with Jesus... with Mary... with St. Joseph, my beloved companion, my model and my protector...."

Little do we know of the Saint whose silent figure we met in the stable. The Gospel recorded his thoughts but did not report a single word voiced by Joseph. We do not hear his voice. Yet "to other saints," says St. Teresa of Avila, "God gave the grace of helping us in one or other need; to him, the honored Saint, he gave the power of helping us in everything...." Thus Teresa contributed to the spread of the cult of St. Joseph; she also promoted the work of building the first church under the name of the silent Saint.

Growing together with the centuries, the cult of Mary was slowly extricated from the shadows of the figure of her husband Joseph. Pope Pius IX confirmed the teaching about St. Joseph's special protection over the Church. Pope Leo XIII wrote in his encyclical "Quamquam pluries" that St. Joseph has, "a feeling of responsibility toward all the Christians who are entrusted to him in a special way" and over whom "he exercises a fatherly control." Pope John XXIII inserted the name of St. Joseph in the canon of the Holy Mass. Previous to that, in 1955, Pope Pius XII had established the first of May as the feast of St. Joseph, the Worker.

Jesus came upon earth and was brought up in the home of a poor carpenter. He wanted to sanctify the hardships, the human work, the life dependent on the wages earned by the work of human hands. He was not the modern "intellectualist" scorning physical effort. He took over the work schedule of his foster father and was faithful to this schedule up to the moment when he began his teaching activity. And even then he surrounded himself with workers like himself.

All those who labor for a living and by this labor secure the means of supporting their family, have their exemplar in St. Joseph. The litany calls him the model of those who create, mold or produce. "Exemplar Opificum." Every healthy and numerous family has its protector in St. Joseph, in the industrious father who covers up the hardship of his toil with a smile and seems to drop out of sight in his protective role.

Today when so many needs oppress us that we ourselves do not know what to ask for, the satisfaction of which need is most urgent, Joseph seems to be very near to us. Because he knows better than we do ourselves what we need, just as a good father knows better than his children do themselves what is necessary for them. We can pray for Joseph without telling him what we are asking for. He himself will take our work in his hands, our daily toil, our family chores, our educational needs, our concern about the young generation, and will tell us himself what we are to do.

72. He is always with us (Jn 17:1–11a)

Somehow I always have the conviction that the span of time between Ascension and Pentecost must have been a very hard period for the infant Church.

The Apostles were not self-assertive, independent people. Weak, cowardly, and not overly bright, they obediently followed Jesus. They were easily discouraged when left alone. They broke down completely in spirit when Jesus was imprisoned and suffered death. There is nothing to tell us that the time they spent with the Risen Savior made them more self-assured than they were before. The incredible miracle of the return of their Master from the dead did not change them.

From our perspective the ascent of Jesus to heaven is a fact of wondrous glory. But for his disciples the departure of Jesus from their life, after a moment of rapture, must have become again a time of renewed fears and a feeling of lonesomeness.

It was necessary for Mary to be with them continuously during these ten days. She knew how to be with Jesus even when he was away from her. When the Apostles lost their sense of security she remained hopeful and stalwart.

What is Christianity? The way to Jesus. We are to get to know and love him. Whoever loves me, Jesus will say, fulfills my commands. But he does not wait for this to happen. He loves us before we have shown him our love. Jesus gives himself to us in the Eucharist as unloving as we are, weak, cowardly, with so little understanding.

The season of the annual Easter Holy Communion of obligation is coming to an end. Once a year around Eastertime.... Once? Would we agree to meet someone we really love only one time during the year? The Apostles could hardly live ten days without Jesus. We who can approach him daily, are we to wait some three hundred sixty-five days?

Holy Communion, we'll say, is not the visible, tangible Jesus. That is true. Our senses are silent, our feelings remain cold. We do not see, we do not feel, very often we cannot concentrate enough to express any gratitude. And yet we know who He is whom we can meet. If we believe, then we must believe in His presence. If we are convinced that it is He, we can expect all things from Him.

Jesus is not disclosing himself to us. He wants faith. He is not looking for transient feelings. He desires lasting hope. Confidence and faith are already love.

In every church there is a power that is able to transform our weakness into strength. Do we reach out for it? But maybe we say to ourselves, Let's wait for a better moment. . . ? Who knows whether there will ever be such a moment? For we are at our best then, when we know that we are bad. And he knows us well, just as we are. And yet for just such as we are, he asks the Father.

73. Thoughts for Pentecost (Jn 20: 19–23), (Jn 3:8)

It is blowing over us like the wind. You hear the sound it makes, but you do not know where it comes from or where it goes. We do not see it, we only hear the rustle of the swaying trees and the hum of the gently waving grass. . . .

Who is it? Who is he? Let us try to find our own answer to the question. We can imagine the Father in human form. The Son was seen when he came down to earth by people who passed their witness on to the next generation. But, Him we envision as a dove or a flame suspended over a bowed head.

Theology calls him the Love of the Father for the Son and of the Son for the Father. He is spoken of as the "soul of the Church." We honor him too little, remember him too rarely, perhaps because the concepts "Love" and "soul" are too impersonal for us.

He is certainly Someone. Jesus calls him the Counselor who will remain with us forever. This Conselor will come from the Father in the name of the Son. The Risen Savior breathed upon the Apostles saying, "Receive the Holy Spirit." That was like a first descent—internal. Afterwards, the second had to come the external, at dawn on Pentecost Sunday.

Jesus departed, but he did not leave us orphans. He came again, this time unperceived. We can see him only when we love him.

The departure of Jesus to heaven on Ascension Day was not the end of some "era of Jesus," and Pentecost Sunday is not the beginning of an "era of the Holy Spirit." Jesus returned to us hidden in the Holy Eucharist. We can always find him. The Christian life is the way to Jesus. Everything, the Church, its structure, the hierarchy, devotions, sacraments; all this serves but one purpose: to lead us to Jesus. Paris is worth a Mass, cynically announced the French king ready to pay everybody for his crown. It could have been said in reply that the whole of Christendom does not measure up to the value of one Holy Mass, and the Mass, the moment of Transubstantiation.

Everything converges in Jesus. Since everything leads to this union with him, it follows naturally that "everything" that leads to Jesus is the work of the Divine Person whom we call the Holy Spirit.

The world did not come to Jesus. The world broke away from God and chose its own glory, but seeking one's own glory is surrendering to Satan. It was Jesus who came to the people. He conquered sin with his own blood. He canceled the signature written by man. He opened heaven to everyone.

However, this "great possibility" requires our agreement or consent. Jesus will not enter a second time among people to teach and call them. The One he is sending for us is the Holy Spirit.

The Holy Spirit is the invisible God, always active among us. He did not appear "instead of" Jesus. The Most Holy Trinity always works together as a unity. The Father is always with the Son; the Holy Spirit always with the Father and the Son. But it can be said that what Jesus accomplished has become for us a convenient, predestined treasure from which the Holy Spirit teaches us to draw. In this sense we may speak of the "era of the Holy Spirit"—the time in which he is active above all.

Mankind was saved and redeemed on the cross. But in order to make the work of salvation effective for each individual person, there follows a long history, and in this history the deciding figure is the Holy Spirit. It is he who in human ways ceaselessly activates the work of the Son, through the Church, through Christianity, and also in still another way, by his own inspiration directly approaching individual people. The treasure earned by Jesus is not the property of only the baptized. It is a gift to all. The sacrifice of Golgotha was equally offered for believers and unbelievers ... and the Holy Spirit addresses himself to all.

The Father is the Creator, but in his creation he asks the people to imitate him by creating with him. The Son is the Redeemer, but by redeeming mankind with his blood he calls upon the people to "fulfill" with their action what in reality does not need to be fulfilled, but which ought to be fulfilled to preserve the freedom of the human will. The Holy Spirit in the "fulfillment" of the work of God, for he finishes this work in man and in history, by his grace bringing to fruition all human cooperation. The Holy Spirit is in Mary, and in the work of Incarnation, Co-Redemption, Mediation. His activity is evident in the work of the saints. He is in every good human act. The activity of the Holy Spirit encompasses us like the air we breathe. Hundreds of times daily, we meet him. Every day we hear his voice. Do we say "yes," or "no" to him?

Unsuccessfully we try to touch the intangible one. His inaccessibility is the measure of his universality. The Son incorporates the oneness of our human nature; the Holy Spirit, the changeableness of humanity. Jesus calls everybody to himself; the Holy Spirit goes to each one individually. He blows over us like the wind. We do not see him, but we hear the rustle of the swaying trees and the soft hum of the gentle grass. We do not see him, yet our miserable human words are trying to interpret him....

74. Our saintly mothers

The Holy Year of 1975 was also Women's Year. For us Poles, it had a tremendous meaning. In the history of our nation women have played a greater role than anywhere else.

Not long ago I read words that made a deep impression upon

me. On the feast of All Saints someone wrote that this is a day of both the canonized and the uncanonized saints and among them, above all, "our holy mothers."

If we are looking for the roots of everything really great in history, if we are seeking the sources of the action and inspiration of every big idea, of every remarkable act, we will always find at its source, a mother.

Let us look into the lives of heroes, of victorious generals, of upright rulers, of genial reformers, creators, discoverers, and saints. The one who trained these people, enkindled in their hearts the fire of magnanimity, was their mother.

In the history of Poland rarely do we find women "fatally" corrupted with egoism. As a rule, mothers bring up their children with complete self-sacrifice, fighting with whole-hearted dedication for their life and health, getting their descendants accustomed to serving high ideals, and then humbly disappearing in the shadow of their sons. The tragic years of the war saw mothers who—at the sight of the gas bombs—pushed their children away from themselves hoping in this way to save their own lives. I do not know of a single incident in which a Polish mother did this. Today there are mothers who allow their unborn children to be killed. There are others who are given to the abuse of alcohol, tobacco, and narcotics, under the pretext of prevention, of pain-killing medicines or the extreme use of cosmetic practices that endanger the life and health of their descendants. In these follies there is great thoughtlessness, a passive submission to the wave of this current "style," an unhealthy ferment, haste, fear of every pain, and seeking one's own pleasure at any cost.

It must also be acknowledged that the great majority of girls having once crossed the threshold of youthful folly become mothers deeply devoted to their children. I am convinced that we are not threatened by an extinction of the tradition of our incomparable Polish mothers.

Our saintly mothers.... For a child the mother is everything! Afterwards he grows up, goes into the world, makes little of his parents and the home he outgrew. But the age of reason catches up with him, and he looks roundabout himself, his parents who are no longer living, and he discovers alas, too late, who she was who long ago, some sixty or seventy years, brought him into the world and later on sacrificed herself unstintingly to pass on to him her faith and her love. Yes, we get to know our mothers only when they are no longer alive. We rediscover them in our best moments . . . in ourselves.

We need to pray for our mothers. But we also need to seek the intercession of our mothers—our holy mothers.

75. The fifth gospel (Mt 7:21-27)

There was a time when you would meet people questioning the reality of the life of Jesus. But from the middle of the last century, it is almost impossible to disbelieve: countless articles and other things continually testify to the fact that Jesus really lived.

People's interest in the figure of Jesus is at present so great that every scholarly discovery concerning his person is becoming a veritable sensation.

Such a sensation occurred in 1945 in the Egyptian library of manuscripts in the Coptic language belonging to the first centuries after Christ. Among the discovered writings was found a so-called "Gospel of Thomas," an apocryphal document known for the last few decades of years to biblical scholars but only in fragments. Now the entire apocrypha have been translated into French and in the press some articles appeared which gave rise to the claim that the "Gospel of Thomas" is neither more nor less than the very earliest first account of the gospel from which, after some revisions, derived the four canonical Gospels.

The sensational news has little to do with the scholarly aspect. The "Gospel of Thomas" does not contain an account of the life of Jesus but is simply a compilation of 114 of his words. A brief introduction assures the reader that these are the "secret" words entrusted to Thomas Dydimus. This "secrecy" betrays the fact that the document has a gnostic character. Gnosticism was the heretical doctrine separating the faithful into the "secret initiates" (gifted with secret knowledge about God) and the ordinary believers. Gnosticism cropped up more than once in the history of Christianity. Even, however poor in content the text of the pageant "Jesus Superstar," it incorporates the constantly recurring refrain of dispute between Jesus and his disciples. They say, "You do not understand anything!" and he answers, "You do not understand anything!" But it can be said about the words of Jesus what a certain woman said of the words of Pope John XXIII, "I understand everything that he says!"

From among the 114 words of the "Gospel of Thomas," eighty are plainly an alteration of the words used in the Gospels. The rest have a definitely heretical character.

In the Fourth Century the Church determined which writings and sayings of Jesus, (repeated and sometimes misconstrued by the people) are really authentic. In this way the Canon was established as the index of revealed writings. The Church never claimed that outside the Canon no true words of Jesus can be found, however it does not honor those words with the stamp of guaranteed truth. Let us not forget that the apocrypha were literary productions on the canvas of Christ's life and their authors could also create words befitting the figure of their hero.

Neither the "Gospel of Thomas," nor any other of the apocrypha is the Fifth Gospel. If anybody should want to use the term "Fifth Gospel," he might use it to describe or in reference to the Shroud of Turin.

This stupendous document is miraculous evidence, to the extent to which we give it our attention, reaffirms all, even the slightest details of the Passion of Christ mentioned in the Gospels. Subdued are the voices of the doubters in the authenticity of the Shroud. The pronouncements of Popes Pius XI and Paul VI ring out ever more categorically. The books of Vignan, Barbet, Hynk, Cristofari, Ricci confirm us in the conviction that we have in our hands the true linen in which the body of our Savior was wrapped and that the face which looked upon us from the photograph of the Shroud is the face of the Man about Whom the Gospel speaks.

76. The street and the Church

Someone said to me: I was walking along the street on the last Good Friday. The street was filled with hustle and bustle. Women were crowding in front of stores to which some attractive wares had been brought. Every little while angry retorts burst forth among them. They were ready to fight for their place in the long line and looked angrily at those standing in front of them.

Groups of inebriated men were walking the sidewalks. Their drunken faces seemed to be more repulsive than ever before. I had the impression that everyone of them was just looking for an opportunity to start a fight or drunken brawl.

At this very same time in the churches, Good Friday services were being held. Christ was dying again on the cross. I stepped in but I could not pray. Anger swelled within me. I thought with bitterness of those drunkards and bickering women.

And as I stood there filled with indignation I suddenly came to myself. I am like the evangelical pharisee eyeing the poor publican standing next to him. "Oh how much better I am than that one," thought the pharisee. I pray, while that one, even though he enters the church for a minute, will leave immediately and go over to that crowd of drunkards and fussing women. He will become one of them.

And maybe, the pharisee thought, if the majority of people

are like those on the street, how high I must stand in the eyes of God. I can be assured of God's protection and salvation.

But is it God's will that I think only of my own salvation? Did Jesus die only for me?

The renewal which has taken place in our times in the Church was born of the consciousness and conviction that the Church has become the asylum of a small number of believers who prayed within its walls for their own salvation. In the meantime outside the Church there were ever growing masses of people. Surely the Church is not only for the elect, for the "well-meaning," and for the "pious pharisees"! It is for all people! Even for those who do not go to church.

There are Catholics who feel sad in the renewed Church. They miss the atmosphere of quiet and recollection. They miss the Latin Mass which used to isolate them, as it were, from the nonpraying crowd. And it may be true that the post-conciliar Church has become a bit noisy, full of discordant voices in which all speak and may speak, for everyone is now allowed to speak in his own tongue. And yet, although this way may not be pleasing to us, the older brothers of the prodigal son, such a Church is open to all. In it there is room for all human searchings and all human weaknesses, for only by searching in the Church can we find our true way, and only by bringing our weakness to the Church can it be healed.

If we hate the world which irritates us by being what it is, we shall never contribute anything to bring it closer to Christ. In vain then we will cry: "Lord! Lord!" Jesus died for all mankind and wants to save all. He is looking for the sick and infirm, not for those who consider themselves healthy. And only in so far as we are able to love the former will we fulfill his will and save—also ourselves.

77. Judas (Mt 9:36–10:8)

From one viewpoint the Apostles are a symbol of the twelve tribes of Israel that constituted the chosen people; from another, they are the institution of the Church of Christ which turns to the whole human race and wants to embrace all mankind.

In the midst of the Apostles is the traitor Judas. Who was he? A whole literature of its own has grown around this figure. Besides those who condemned him, were those who tried to exonerate him and explain him. For them, Judas was the "most intelligent of the Apostles," the "defender of a healthy reason," "by his deed he wanted to convince himself who Jesus really is," "wanted to force Jesus to act." Judas was the "agent of the temple." And maybe really the "agent of the pharisees" who sought contact and understanding with Jesus?

This last concept is tied up with the whole theory promoted by certain circles of contemporary Jewish scholars. These learned men are trying to prove that the real opponents of Jesus were only the priest-sadducees, not the pharisees. The teaching of the pharisees did not differ from the teaching of Jesus; therefore, there could not have been any essential conflict between them and the Master from Nazareth. The only conflict was that Jesus stubbornly insisted on being God, while the pharisees were ready to acknowledge him as the messiah, but only a human messiah.

Hence Judas would be in the circle of the Apostles as the one who took a great interest in the human character of the activity of Jesus. This human character was overthrown when Jesus announced to his disciples that death was awaiting him. At that moment Judas left—had to leave. He could serve a human ruler and he could serve an almighty God, but he could not serve someone who, being God, hid his almighty power. Whoever Judas was, it is certain that it was in the plans of Jesus to die as a weak man in order to arise from the dead as God. The apostles could break down before the overwhelming strength of their enemies, but somewhere in the depths of their hearts they preserved their faith and the promise of Jesus. Judas alone lost this faith.

The cross is inseparably united with the Resurrection. In the life of every Christian, every one of us, we find the cross and darkness. Everything seems to contradict that which it was so easy to believe in the sunny days! If at such a time we say: "That's the end, nothing will change any more," we will become like Judas. The Body of Jesus will be sealed in the tomb and we will go forth like Judas into the night.

We must be with Jesus at the cross frequently ... whether we want to or not. And those who were hanging there beside him had to be with him. But the problem did not end there, nor could it end there. Jesus left the tomb—he arose from the dead! History without the Resurrection is history without an ending.

A gospel that would end on the cross would be only the gospel of Judas. It would be a gospel of frustration and unbelief even if it would speak beautifully of Jesus. The cross does not finish, but rather, begins the history of the Church in which Jesus is again risen from the dead.

78. A cross on a neckband (Mt 10:26–33)

A few months ago I was traveling through southern France. For the night we stopped in a small town at a little hotel that was practically empty at the time. In the hotel restaurant three people waited on us: the proprietress, her daughter, and son. Each one of them had a decorative cross of a rather large size around the neck.

The next day was Sunday, so I asked the daughter serving us at the table, "At what time will Mass be offered in the local church?" She frowned and went with my question to her brother. I heard him as he answered, "How should I know? I don't go to church!" Then the girl turned to her mother. I saw the two of them scanning the pages of the local paper. Not finding what they were looking for, the mother left the hotel. In ten minutes she returned with the information that Mass will be offered at ten o'clock.

The beautiful little crosses around the neck were only ornamental.

If Jesus is calling upon his own to acknowledge him before people, he does not mean such a declaration. Christianity is not measured by the number of little crosses on the neckbands of boys and girls.

Some years ago a certain Polish columnist recalled that the ancient cross is the forerunner of today's gallows. Wearing a little cross around one's neck is like carrying silver or gold gallows around. This sign means something and obligates one to something.

The external profession of Judaism by the house of King Herod the Great did not prevent the royal family from committing every kind of possible crime. In the family of the Idumean kings licentiousness went hand-in-hand with murder. The daughter of the son of Herod, Arystobul (strangled by order of his own father) was Herodias. She was married to her uncle Herod-Philip, but another uncle, Herod-Antypas, took her as his wife.

John the Baptist reproved Herod-Antypas for this, although it was apparent that for such criticism he would be put to death. The last prophet of the Old Testament could not be silent.

It is equally true that in the Roman world conditions were no better. Roman peace established by Octavian covered up family immorality, self-indulgence and crime. Roman religion, whose gods betrayed and cheated one another, could not serve as an example for the people.

But John did not turn with his criticism to the Romans. He focused on Antypas who considered himself, as did his father, the builder of the temple of Jerusalem, an exemplary faithful follower of Moses.

Whoever wanted to be considered a loyal Jew was bound by the law of Moses. Whoever wants to be known as a Christian must be bound by something greater than a little cross around his neck.

79. A person in need of us

When I wrote about voices that answered, after thinking seriously in the name of pity and humanitarianism, regarding the problem of whether it is necessary to deprive handicapped children of life, I received letters accusing me of concern only for the children and not saying anything about the elderly, the sick and the disabled, who suffer greatly from the selfishness of their environment.

I have written about this problem more than once but I do think it deserves to be returned to once more.

The terrible condition of the elderly and the disabled is a frightening matter! Just a few days ago a certain woman told me of this incident. In the house in which she lives the water system broke down. Because the administration did not want the rooms of the more influential residents of the building to be disturbed in any way during the repair work, all the work was done in the rooms of a few old, single, and sickly residents. For many weeks these persons had to endure the presence of the repairmen in their rooms, the drilling in the walls and the streams of water covering the floor. These few helpless women who should have had the maximum consideration were burdened with all the troubles that befell the whole house.

We have only too few institutions that care for the disabled elderly. When it becomes evident that it is necessary to find such a place for somebody, the whole family is feverishly aroused in locating one. The persons thus provided for in an institution easily fall into despair since they have to be separated from their family and friends, for the place is usually far away.

As for the care received there, institutions differ. Not always can we immediately say "terrible" or "cruel." Not everyone who undertakes the care of others, even from the noblest of motives, can fulfill it properly. If the lot of the disabled is heavy, it must be said that the care of them is also an unusually hard task. Not only is it necessary to "serve" the needy, it is also necessary to do so in such a way that they are not humiliated. It is necessary to smile, but smiling in the presence of a person in pain and complaining does not come easy. Just a quick remark, and the poor disabled one is hurt to the core. Patience eludes both the one and the other: the patient cannot bear his inadequacies, and the nurse, her helplessness. Even when caring for our dearly loved ones, we are often thwarted. What can we say about people who have undertaken this very difficult task for the sake of strangers?

The care of the disabled elderly is becoming the burning question of our time. Their number is constantly increasing. Families are getting smaller. The time has passed when in a large family house there was always a place for grandpa or grandma. Today grandma is necessary only until the grandchildren grow up, and that on the condition that she stays well on her feet. Grandpa is not generally necessary.

The problem requires a solution. But nothing can take the place of the most important ingredient: real love of the person who needs our help. Wherever he is found, in our home, in his own, or in a nursing home, our duty is to serve him, to have a heart, to help him, to smile, and to be willing to exchange a few words. There have been tragic instances of severity whence came the conviction that only "genuine people" ought to be given the privilege of caring for disabled persons. Who are these "angels of mercy"? Where do we look for them in a society ever more deeply steeped in egoism? We have to begin with a change in ourselves, by evoking in ourselves a feeling of obligation to help others. When we change, the environment will change. So let us look around to see if there is anyone in our neighborhood whom we can help?

80. Indifference is the worst thing (Mt 11:25–30)

There are times when Jesus relinquishes his usual controlled tone of voice and bursts out in fiery words. In this yielding to his emotions, he is all man—totally human.

Speaking of John the Baptist, Jesus is on fire. The indifference of the people directing the chosen nation stirs up his indignation. They did not even care to notice the warnings of John, or the signs and miracles that he, Jesus himself, was performing. And, unexpectedly, from sharp words of condemnation he passes over to a joyful prayer. He gives honor to God the Father for allowing matters unnoticed by the wise and learned to be perceived by the common people.

John and Jesus were not followed by the priests, the doctors, the sadducees, or the pharisees. They were followed by a crowd of poor people, the hated publicans, and the despised street girls. Those to whom no one extended a helping hand. Those who knew their own misery and were looking for help. Those others, the wise and learned, were well satisfied with themselves and their lot. They did not need anybody. If John and Jesus disturbed them, it was only because they could now become the leading molders of opinions for the angry masses of people. The world of poverty and misery was very large and embittered with its lot, while the world of practical wisdom and abundance constituted but a tiny group of people fearful of losing their goods.

However, Jesus did not bring on a civil war. He brought freedom from sin for everybody, including the sadducees and pharisees, Romans and Greeks. All he demanded was the shedding of their indifference. Indifference is the very worst thing—an abominable condition. For even he who seeks good in an evil way, is always closer to Jesus than he who seeks nothing. When Jesus permitted the street girls to follow him, did he see nothing bad in their fallen career? Yet he did not cast aside such a woman of loose living when she appeared at the banquet in the house of the pharisee, washed the feet of Jesus, and wiped them with her hair. She was not the most guilty for the sins of her life. And perhaps those who forced her to prostitution were those very wise and learned men, indifferent to good, despising the woman today, and yesterday taking advantage of her service?

This woman wanted to love and to be loved. She was cheated. Her desires were converted into a shameful career. She was told that love is exactly that, and then treated with contempt. But Jesus told her that is she is still able to love she can start her life anew, in a different way.

And this gave Jesus much joy that so many yearnings for love remained in the hearts of the simple and the poor.

Today when we complain about indifference all around us, we ought to rejoice that there is much more yearning for love. But first that desire must be awakened. Love is awakened only by love. Taking up the battle with indifference in ourselves—we are fighting the indifference of the world.

81. Weeds (Mt 13:1–23)

A few years ago, I was coaxed into seeing a documentary film representing the life of today's maturing girls. I looked at the film and left with a bad taste in my mouth. The producers of the film, under the pretext of creating a document, simply showed a long series of extraordinarily bold erotic scenes. Crowds were hastening to see the film, and they were not the parents concerned about their daughters.

However when I voiced my criticism, I was told that I do not appreciate the revolution that has occurred in the approach to sexual matters. The opinion of the people who spoke was that films of this nature break down the "squelched impulse," "sexual timidity," etc., and so are fulfilling a positive role.

I was not convinced. I agree that there has been a revolution in the approach to sexual matters. And it is not wholly a bad thing that today problems of sexual life are discussed openly, that their meaning in married life is well understood, that thanks to this knowledge people can now be helped who at times are in serious trouble and who formerly had no one to confide in or consult.

However it is one thing to understand and discuss problems of sexual life and quite another to present them in such a way that not the problem, but the picture is the main thing.

One may say: That's a work of art, and this is pornography. But when the discussion reaches the themes of sexualism it is evident that even otherwise serious-minded people do not see any harm in pornography. One such person asked me recently in an ironical tone, "Well then, sir, do you consider that we are not mature in the matters that the West is engrossed in?"

I replied that I do not think that all the matters of concern in the West are an expression of greater maturity. When the discussion begins to deal with matters of pornography it becomes clear that nobody is able to draw a line of demarcation between certain themes in "art" and pornography. The West no longer recognizes any boundary between them. Does this mean that we should not see it?

The concern here is not that there exist themes dealing with important matters of life about which we should not speak. The real concern is how we should speak of them.

An open discussion about sexual matters should promote human love. And it can truly do so. But when the discussion turns into a casual exchange of "bold erotic scenes" its result is simply the igniting of sexualism, with the inevitable killing of true love. For sexualism must be subjected to love, directed and determined by the human will. The deeper we want to treat love, the stronger we must be masters of our instincts.

Jesus speaks about the seed which fell among weeds. In the world created by God there are no unnecessary things, and weeds have their value. The pulled-up or torn-out weed makes excellent compost. However the weeds may not be allowed to stunt the growth of the seed which is the most important.

82. The chain letter

The mail brought me an envelope in which the anonymous sender enclosed a short prayer: "St. Anthony, pray for us, for success in our families, for those dear to us, and for peace in the world."

If this was all—everything would be in order. St. Anthony is a great saint somewhat forgotten by us lately. Not too long ago there were still found in practically every church in front of the statue of the saint little sacrifice boxes indicating bread for the poor, or so-called "Bread of St. Anthony."

Last year being in Padua, I saw the fervor with which people surrounded the tomb of the saint. In the beautiful *Fioretti* of St. Francis we read that Anthony ws named his "successor" by Francis, and that when in Rimini, the people did not want to listen to his teaching, St. Anthony went to the seashore and preached to the fish which came swimming in from all sides to hear him.

He was a learned theologian when he entered the Order of the Brothers Minor. He undertook the work of a missionary among the Albigenses and became the protector of the poor. Although a professor and scholar, he abandoned his studies in order to serve those in the greatest need. He earned for himself the reputation of a man loving people so much, and being so desirious of freeing them from the least worry, that in their opinion he came the patron of lost articles.

As I stood at the tomb of St. Anthony I thought that it was right and proper to recall this Saint in our times. We who stand in the face of misery and starvation for millions ought to learn from this saint that nothing, including knowledge and wisdom, can overshadow the needs of suffering humanity.

But... the proffered prayer was completed with the injunction to transcribe it in so many copies and send it to so many persons. Moreover, the author of that leaflet warned the recipient that the one who would not fulfill the request would be met with many terrible misfortunes, while the one who did fulfill the directions would find great good fortune. An example of this "good fortune" was cited. A certain priest after having distributed the prayer in thirteen days won $300,000 in a lottery. Someone else, "in punishment for breaking the chain," lost a son.

What blindness on the part of those who type out such nonsense on a machine and send it out to people! But the authors of the little chain letter who play such foolish games in the name of the great saint and blackmail gullible people premising them "monetary luck" or threatening their loved ones with death, those people deserve a much more severe appraisement. They are the sowers of the weeds that grow between the grain of the Word of God.

83. Examen on manliness

A few weeks ago on television we viewed the Soviet film entitled "Such High Mountains" with Bondarczyk playing the main role.

Perhaps we should feel sad that this wise thought-provoking film did not reach the movie screen. It portrays the story of a village teacher, single, experienced in the hard ways of life, who takes upon himself the task of bringing up some war orphans. An onerous job, and how ungrateful!

Often teachers imagine that their task is to pass on to the children a certain amount of knowledge. Our hero however is convinced that his first and most important task is the training of the personality. Before the acquisition of concrete knowledge comes the all-important development of honor, honesty, goodness, appreciation of nature and proper relationships with other people.

War is not necessary to make this work arduous. Changes in civilian life, especially as great as they are today, and above all the improper behavior of adults who by their own unfortunate living experiences burden their children and who do not train their children, but rather demoralize them—all of this militates against the devoted teacher. The real tragedy of our times is that the generation of the parents has ceased to feel responsible for the generation of their children.

In the film there is a scene in which the teacher has an interview with a young physicist who asks him ironically, "Are you a humanist, sir? Do you teach the children verses? Today the important thing is the mathematical formula, not—poetic verse." The teacher gently answers, "I think the time will come when everyone will have to pass an examination not on verses, and not on mathematical formulas, but on manliness." It is very high time indeed for us to come to the conclusion that we will not bring forth a healthy generation if we ourselves do not pass the examination on manliness.

We Christians believe that the truth of our religion is the best school for training a person. But it is not enough to believe. This learning of truth must be incorporated in life—daily, at every moment. Every minute of the day we are in the eyes of our children. They hear every word we say and they see every gesture we make. We ourselves have to give an account of our manliness daily if we want our children to be able to pass this exam some day.

We all have to become genuine educators—all the parents, grandparents, uncles, aunts, teachers. Erroneously does one think that as soon as a child gains some knowledge he becomes a man. On the contrary, a child must become a man in order to know how to use the given knowledge!

The strength of the generation that was lost thirty-one years ago on the barricades of Warsaw was not merely courage in battle but the understanding of self-sacrifice for the sake of a cause. They passed their exam on manliness. Will we who were saved in those days also know how to pass that exam? The conduct of our children will testify to that. What is it like?

84. Playing with fire

I was an eyewitness when three thirteen-year old boys, in a certain garden, poured some chemical on the trunk of a beautiful maple tree and ignited it.

It was a real shock to me. A double shock, for what seemed to me to be more terrifying than the play of the boys was the gross indifference of their parents who were not in the least concerned about the destruction of the tree. "Boys must surely have their fun," they simply stated.

In a collection of stories by Flannery O'Connor *In a Ring of Fire*, there is a striking novelette about a few thirteen-year-old boys also who, having come from the city to the farm, set fire to the woods. What was their motive? The authoress suggests: they liked their life in the village so much that they burned the woods in order that when they returned to the city no one else should enjoy the delightful woods. It seems to me that the writer endowed the little barbarians with extravagant feelings and thoughts. They destroyed the woods not because they liked them so much. They destroyed because they really do not appreciate nature, greenness, and trees. Instead they wanted to change and disturb it, imagining themselves as creating something better in its place. In truth, however, they are not up to creating anything.

This matter is not at all significant and I think we ought to give it serious consideration. The instinct to create something new is in itself a very valuable thing, indeed. But new creations cannot be erected on ruins. Into every new thing there must enter something left over from the old. It is easy to cut off or burn a tree. To plant and bring a new tree to maturity—that will take longer than the lifetime of a whole generation.

Who is to blame when children destroy trees, trample on the green grass, and abuse nature with garbage dumps? Evidently we, the parents, grandparents, and grownup people. "Parents cannot be militarists," said the mother of a barbarian child to me. Of course not. But a militarist is not an educator. He steps in and has to step in when the educators fail. Parents who are unable to train their children will have to at certain times take over the function of the military if they do not want their problem to be taken over by the true representatives of the law.

Where are the parents when the child throws garbage all around? A little child throws a small piece of paper; an older child breaks off branches of trees; the thirteen-year old sets fire to a tree; the twenty-year old.... A lack of respect and love for the world around us leads to terrible things.

Let us again consider the children destroying their surroundings. What good will it do to call for protection of the environment if there will be a growing generation of barbarians? But first of all let us take a good look at ourselves. Training is not done by negative commands. Effective training is done only by example.

85. Sound the trumpet (Mt 14:22–33)

".... You shall sound the trumpet throughout the land. You will declare this fiftieth year sacred and proclaim the liberation of all the inhabitants of the land. This is to be a jubilee for you.... Let none of you wrong his neighbor.... I am Yahweh your God."

Thus the ancient Jewish Holy Year is spoken of in the Book of Leviticus 25:8-12.

The Old Testament Jubilee Year was a year of joy because it brought liberation and restoration of property. But in this joy was embodied also the prediction of something greater: the Jubilee Year was a symbol of what was to come: setting men free from the slavery of sin and winning back the grace of the lost sonship of God. For this reason the messianic age begins with bursts of overwhelming joy. Coming to visit Elizabeth, Mary intones the rapturous hymn: "My soul magnifies the Lord and my spirit rejoices in God my Savior...." "Mary is the Mother of the Greatest Human Joy because she understood better than anyone else," says Pope Paul VI in his exhortation on Christian joy, "that God performs miracles, that his name is holy, that he shows mercy, that he lifts up the humble and that he is true to his promises. This does not mean that life was to change its regular course. She perceived even the tiniest of God's signs and pondered upon them in her heart. This does not mean that she was to be spared sufferings, for she was to stand at the feet of the Cross, immersed in the Sacrifice of the Innocent Servant, the Mother of Sorrows.... But to her will be opened the joy of the Resurrection. She will be swept up with body and soul into the glory of heaven.... Therefore turning to her, the Mother of Hope and Mother of Grace, we see the cause of our Joy...."

And yet there is so much evil, pain and suffering! We fall asleep with the desire of forgetting about disasters and we wake up with the bitter feeling that these disasters did not disappear during the night. People continue to die of starvation. Animosity continues to reign, maybe even hatred in the family circle. Other people that we love continue to abandon what we consider the Truth and Goodness. That horrible sickness lingers on....

Where are we to seek happiness? Yet the Holy Father reminds

us that the Holy Year is to be a year of joy. If the Jewish Jubilee was the joy of the promise, this Christian Holy Year is to be the joy of a new awareness of the mercy of God.

The frustrated Apostles were returning by boat across the lake. Jesus having performed an unusual miracle instead of standing at the head of the loud enthusiastic crowds hid himself somewhere. The sea was turbulent, and the gusty winds against them. All their hopes seemed to fall apart. The windy night oppressed the hearts of the people who threw everything aside to run after the Teacher from Nazareth, and now they had the feeling that all their haste and sacrifice had been in vain.

Suddenly on the rough sea they beheld something that seemed to be a frightening apparition. Somebody was walking on the waves. The threatening figure was coming closer and closer and they began to cry out in distress.

And then at once they recognized him—it was Jesus. The fear became an outburst of joy. In this gladness, all the feelings of bitterness and sorrow disappeared. The night became as luminouse as day.

Perhaps the essense of the Holy Year consists that we might perceive on the turbulent sea of our fears the Savior Jesus coming to us, and experience the joy of knowing that he is always with us!

86. Speaking in silence (Mt 15:21–28)

The teaching of Jesus is not a collection of prescriptions regulating every life situation. The words of Jesus spoken in the Gospel are few indeed, but each one of them has so much content that it will cover millions of situations. It is only necessary that each little phrase of the Gospel be filled with the silence of thought and then we shall find an answer for every question, especially our own.

Speaking in Silence (Mt 15:21-28)

Jesus does not impose himself upon us. He wants us to draw sense out of his words ourselves. The Gospel is not a book for rapid reading. It is a book to have always at hand and always in mind.

Alas—we like the noisy sound of words too much, without worrying about what the words say. That is why we have become surrounded by the ubiquitous transistor radio. Wherever we move, on the field, in the woods, on the mountains, wherever the deepest silence should reign, there the radio apparatus is sounding off. Children are working out their lessons with transitors on; infants are tuned out with their loudness. What's even worse—nobody listens to what the radio is saying. We listen only to what we ourselves are saying. That's all that interests us. But we want to have a partner that also speaks but whom we do not have to answer.

In this hubbub of two voices: ours and the radio, the words spoken to us by Jesus are lost. He does not speak to us as does the transistor, in a stream of loud shouts, nor the way we speak ourselves, a mass of positive statements and assumptions with which we immediately refute all doubts (even those that sprout within our very selves). Jesus speaks softly and little, and after each word hides himself again in silence. He waits until his words reach us, are received and understood. He waits like the father of the prodigal son who came to the door of his house, and stands at the threshold in the figure of the waiting beggar until he is recognized. . . .

We have to become silent. We have to find time for a moment of silence, shut off the radios . . . begin to listen to the roar of the waves, the rustling of leaves, the echoes in the hills. Those natural sounds will not deafen the words of Jesus for us. They will not dissipate the silence with which he speaks the loudest.

God? So many times I asked him! But he is silent! He does not want to answer me, is the bitter complaint we often hear.

Maybe the Pagan-Chanaanite woman whose daughter was possessed by Satan had the same desire to say just that. Or maybe she should have left, shocked and disappointed when she heard the words of Jesus that he came only for the Jews.

But the woman felt that behind those seemingly unkind words, unkind yet truthfully spoken, because Jesus while living on earth was the Jewish Messiah and only his death and denial caused the spilling of his mercy on all mankind, is hidden a silence which is the love of the everlastingly loving God. The woman then addresses herself to history but turns to love which does not identify with history.

Before history announces its decree, man today may also address himself to the One awaiting him in the stillness of mercy.

87. Grandparents, children, and grandchildren

In the days when families were large, grandparents found their place in them as figures surrounded by general respect and love. They were well taken care of and appreciated.

Today's grandparents are people in the best years of their lives. They work, and create. The son, or grandson wears a beard, but not the grandfather. The grandmothers do not sit in easy chairs and are not knitting away. Full of life and energy they hurry from meeting to meeting, are interested in everything, and have time for everything.

How often the grandparents are "better off in life" than their children! Toward their grandchildren they can be more generous than the parents. This is interpreted by the children as, if anyone is to give, it is grandpa or grandma.

"Grandma will not give me any old thing," says the eight-year-old little girl. "I cannot impress my little Pete with just any old thing," says the young mother. He looks at Grandpa and expects at least an automobile."

These last words sound like a complaint. And who knows but

that it is a legitimate complaint. The possibilities of grandparents can be ever-magnified in the eyes of the grandchildren, but often they are big enough for the parents to feel hurt or embarrassed. They can give and give, the parents say, we cannot give such things. They are spoiling the children.

But grandparents are not only giving, they are also demanding. Parents are overworked, overrun, and concerned about themselves. The children are left unsupervised. Those who are disturbed by this are the grandparents. They set standards. They give and they demand. Parents do not give, nor do they demand.

The child will always love his parents. Not always so with the grandparents. The fact that grandparents give is not yet enough reason to love them, especially if they demand so many things at the same time.

Thus slowly a real conflict is created between the adult generations but the victim is the children's generation. The children learn that expensive gifts come from the grandparents, but when the grandparents want something then it is best to resort to the parents.

How can this problem be solved? Should grandparents disappear from the lives of their children and grandchildren? Are the children to be dependent on their wealthier grandparents all their life?

Only the right kind of training can solve this problem. Both grandparents and parents must understand that the most important are the youngest. There must be a common understanding and attitude. Not a "common forefront of the elders," but a positive fundamental training. A certain number, and possibly the least, of "forbidding rules" equally demanded by the adults in a consistent way and simultaneously the greatest amount of goodness, love, kindness, close relationship and understanding. If the adults are not able to live in this spirit themselves they will not train their children to do so. Grandparents should not seek selfsatisfaction in giving presents to their grandchildren. Parents ought not absolve their children from disobeying their grandparents' wishes or demands.

88. To forget oneself

What was the meaning of the words that Jesus addressed to Peter: "Get out of my way, Satan!" Stop tempting me! I am also a human being who must overcome temptations of fear, weakness, desire of human triumph. But my way is the way of self-conquest... and you are like a stumbling block under my feet."

Therefore, if you want to follow me further, let everyone "deny himself, take up his cross and imitate me."

Maybe it would sound better: let everyone forget himself.... "Deny himself" can be misunderstood. There were people who in the fervor of religious zeal abandoned their home, wife, children, work, obligations. That's what they understood by "deny yourself." But that was seeking self, one's unusual self. Fr. Bernard Kryszkiewicz, the heroic Passionist, wrote in his memoirs: "not to seek self, not to seek self... Self-seeking is often very subtle, dressed in various deceptive appearances...."

To forget self does not mean to forget about our obligations. Self-forgetfulness means to remain a father or mother, the provider and caretaker of the family, to serve the country, to give the required strength to our daily work. To forget self, is meant to forget others, to serve them by sacrificing oneself for their good, often one's own opinion, one's authority. "Indefatigably to soften life for others," again I cite Fr. Bernard, "to give all of self, not to desire anything for self, no gratitude, no understanding, no appreciation.... To take the mistakes of others upon oneself, to sympathize, to console, not to separate oneself from others by feelings of superiority."

To forget self is to understand that we will not draw people by force, but only when they themselves in their own way receive the Truth which we want to pass on to them. To forget self is to respect the law of freedom and self-dependence of man. If you have to exaggerate, then let it be with kindness, deep understanding, and patience. Pope John XXIII did more by his kindness than others by their thundering. Genuine goodness is also self-forgetfulness. Such goodness is not easy for it demands resignation from giving orders. It compels one to accept a person just as he is, to transform him by first transforming our relationship to him. True goodness is to love a person before he becomes what we would like him to be.

And our cross, is not the one we have chosen for ourselves. In looking for the proper cross for ourselves, we are seeking self. To forget self is to accept the cross which life has brought us; the cross which often we cannot get rid of, a troublesome cross in its effectiveness, not gloriously heroic but a cross of humiliation. That is the best cross for us. Self-denial is to acknowledge that the cross which we must bear is our cross—and get to love it.

89. Communion of Saints

Everyday we pronounce the words, "I believe ... in the communion of saints." But not all Catholics know what these words mean. When questioned they reply that the words refer to the influence the saints have upon the life of the people on earth. That is only part of the truth.

The words "communion of saints" do not speak of canonized saints nor of the saved saints. They apply the ancient meaning of saints to all those who are in the state of grace.

There is an intimate union of all mankind, of all the people who are in heaven, suffer in purgatory, and live on earth. It is a living union, that is, embracing numberless personal relationships. Those who are in heaven help those who are on earth—

that is the intercession of the saints. The people on earth pray for the souls in purgatory and those in purgatory very possibly pray for us, the living (as Fr. J. Zieja writes, "We are free to trust that those fulfilling their penance—the souls in purgatory—can pray for those living on earth and care for them").

Those living on earth are divided into those who are in the state of grace and by their prayer as well as voluntary suffering can help other living people, especially those who have fallen into sin or are suffering, and into those who are not in the state of grace. The communion of saints is an uninterrupted exchange of good deeds. Jesus "wants us," wrote St. Therese of the Child Jesus, "to participate with him in the salvation of souls; he does not want to do anything without us. The Creator of the world waits for the prayer of a little soul in order to save other souls." While praying, the soul gives not only her own merits but above all, she draws from the vast treasure chest of the Church in which are found the priceless merits of Jesus, the merits of the Mother of God, and of the saints—the common prayers of all.

The Communion of Saints is a human brotherhood in time and the hereafter. Nothing is done on earth that cannot touch the human heart even though it be at the other end of the world. We are responsible for the hungry, for the suffering, the disappearing, and even those who have already died but whom we are helping today by praying for them, for the laws of time do not bind in a unity like that of the Communion of Saints. By prayer we can make up for and correct the sins and mistakes made by us.

The already redeemed souls and those in purgatory are not somewhere far away from us. They are right next to us. We do not see them, but we believe that they are with us in this unity.

Sunday is a parochial feast. A parish is not merely an administrative unit of the Church. It is also a Communion of Saints in miniature—a brotherly meeting point of saints from heaven, the people on earth, and the souls from purgatory. Maybe it would be well today, when the ties of parochial life are weakening, to look into the parish activities from the viewpoint of the spiritual relationships of its members, and from the angle of the importance of serving one another.

90. When the pain is greatest

It may be that someone of us has lost a child. That is one of the most painful losses that man can endure. The loss of even the most beloved parents is almost a normal occurrence. The loss of a spouse is such a deep tragedy at times that one cannot be reconciled to it even to the end of life. But the loss of a child is, besides the pain, also the bitter frustration of hopes that were nourished.

Children leave their parents nowadays. The conflict between generations is greater than ever before. Still parents place all their hopes in their children even when they leave. Love makes them feel that someday the children will return to the ways of their parents, even if it be only after their death.

Therefore, when a child dies, we live through the most excruciating pain. And it's hard to tell when this pain is greater: when a child dies suddenly in some catastrophe, or when the child dies slowly after years of sickness for which there is no help.

There are people who have lost their faith because of a child's death; they can not reconcile themselves with God's will, which seems to them to be too cruel. Yet that is the very "cruelty" God showed toward his own Son. "God so loved the world that he gave his only-begotten Son. . . ."—that means offered up without taking back, for loneliness, for suffering, for the most painful death that can be imagined.

Somebody will say: Jesus is God. He suffered only as man. Pain is not so bad when one knows its limits, when one is sure of the victory that it brings. But we know that Jesus lived fully as a man. He took upon himself the ordinary nature of man, fearful of pain and susceptible to pain. There are people who can bear great sufferings without a moan. Jesus could not have been our exemplar if he had been such a man. There are people whose lofty ideal in suffering diminishes pain.

Although Jesus knew better than anyone else why he was suffering, he desired that the "chalice of suffering" would pass from him and asked God the Father why he had abandoned him. He chose for himself the greatest pain and the greatest sensitiveness to it. He agreed in his human nature to leave the matter of victory to faith.

His Passion brought us redemption. But our pain too is the coin for which much can be bought. We can give this pain to God and then it takes on an unusual value. Maybe our child had need of something? Today when contacts between children and parents are broken so easily, our children need more help than ever before. Ordinarily we can give them nothing. They turned away from us. This conduct often rouses our anger. And yet we love them; we want to protect them from harm. For their good, we can give them our suffering.

In doing so, we help them the most. There, or here on earth. And in reality always here, because with God there is no time measure and our later offering can have an earlier effect. Accepting the will of God is pain, but also in humility, it may be that gave our dying child the chance to say to Jesus, Do not forget me in your Kingdom!

91. Our Christianity must be strong (Mt 20:1–16a)

Valentine Majdanski, the great apostle of the sanctification of the family, was accused by his opponents that he expected women to give birth to children without limiting their number.
Evidently Majdanski was not a promoter of childless mar-

riages, nor of families with one child. But that is exactly the stand of the Church which teaches that one of the two fundamental objectives of marriage, besides love, is the birth and upbringing of children. There should be as many children as can be brought up. The Church knows that in modern times, the number of children must be smaller than it was some fifty years ago. Modern life demands regulation. But the Church acknowledges only one trustworthy method of limiting descendants, the method of temporary infertility (so-called Knauss-Ogin).

Let's be sincere, this method of temporary infertility is neither easy nor pleasant. Its use is possible only in marriages truly united in love and in understanding for each other. It is a method requiring heroism and sacrifice, especially today when there is a real cult of sex, when films and novels are full of erotic scenes, when it is proclaimed that sex life is something without which man cannot get along.

It is true that the sexual instinct is an immensely important factor in human life. It should not be squelched, but neither may it be allowed to get out of bounds of acceptable discipline. It is only one of the phases of love and the more it is controlled, the stronger marital love will be.

Control of the urge, as it was said, requires love, but control of the urge also increases love and gives it a lasting character. In spite of the objective truth of these views, living according to them requires dedication and courage; it requires a strong Christianity.

In his address to the general audience on June 18, 1975, Pope Paul VI said, "We would want a triumphant Christianity, a comfortable Christianity, profitable and applauded. We would want it to be absolved from its true element which is sacrifice. We would want a Christianity without obligations.... Christianity without unsafe conflicts, without the duty of witnessing unpopular truths—Christianity without heroism.... But no. Just the opposite. Our Christianity must be strong...." In this difficult matter, it must be especially strong. It must overcome all the traps and temptations provided by modern life.

92. Angels

Modern people belittle the devil and do not remember the existence of the angels. Satan and angels seem to them to be simply the personification of evil and good. But Christ says plainly, and the Church teaches, that pure spirits exist, always at the service of God, and with his consent serving man; also that there are angels that rebelled against the command to serve, maybe because of the unusual raising up of man above the dignity of the angels, they became devils and strive to harm man.

God permits the activity of Satan, but turns the temptations to man's greater benefit, only if man does not voluntarily yield to them. We speak of nine choirs (hierarchical steps) of angels. Holy Scripture mentions four great archangels: Michael, the conqueror of the rebellious Lucifer; Raphael; Gabriel, who announced to Mary that she would be the Mother of the Savior; and Phanuel. The prophet Daniel said that every nation has its own angel. Jesus assured us that every person has his own angel-guardian.

"Angels," says John Henry Newman in one of his sermons, "help to spread our activity among us, in the Church.... There is no Christian so miserable that he does not have an angel to serve him.... People are wont to speak of the next world (the world of invisible beings) as if it didn't exist just yet, but that it will only begin to exist after our death. But it is not so: it exists now although we do not see it.... We live equally in the world of spirits as in the world of sense and we are in union with it—albeit unconsciously...."

When we were children we said our daily prayer to our guardian angel. Afterwards we forgot about the one who constantly stands beside us and removes the evil that could overpower us. We will not get to know this "someone" in this life, but still we must believe—we who so often complain about loneliness and abandonment, that we have a faithful friend devoted to us, leading us on to the gate of salvation. Having reached it maybe we will be able to see him and in a human way thank him heartily for his care.

93. God's share (Mt 21:33-43)

Everyone of us is in one of those tenants of whom the Gospel speaks. Each one has received a "vineyard" to cultivate—i.e., a certain field of life's chances: some talent, some intelligence, health, education, good family relationships.... Realizing what we have, we ought to make the best of our endowments.

We were not gifted equally. God gave one more, another less, precisely in order to create ties of mutual dependence amongst us. God does not want us to live only for ourselves. We are to live together with others and help them when they need help. But the aid we give another does not come only from our desire. We not only *should* give, we also *must* give. A certain amount of our "income" constitutes "God's share," and this "share" belongs wholly to the needy ones. The Church formerly called this share "tithing" which was to be given to the poor without any special call for it.

So we must remember that our help to another person begins only after paying God his "share." Today the Church does not set a norm for giving. We must decide ourselves how much we are obliged to give (and it may be that with a clear conscience we can say that we can give nothing, that everything we earn with our labor hardly suffices for sustence God in that situation will demand nothing). And then we can decide how much more we will want to give "from ourselves."

Hunger has again made itself known. The press spreads the alarm about starvation in Honduras and Ethiopia. The deadly drought appeared again in certain parts of the world. Again people are dying daily. Again children are dying of hunger!

We have come to the point of counting on contributions. They will, no doubt, be short of the number needed as the world magazine of feed stuffs announced.

Thus hunger will continue to exist and may even become worse. We cannot remain deaf to the cry of the hungry; especially in this Holy Year, we cannot forget about the sufferings of people. Everyone of us who considers himself a Christian ought to determine how much he can offer to help the hungry. It is not a matter of exorbitant sums. God is not a financial bureau which does not take into consideration a person's situation. A little goldpiece multiplied by a million givers will produce quite a handsome amount. Moreover God does not await the absolute effectiveness of our gift. It is he himself who will make it bring results. He wants only one thing: He wants us to remember that everything we have, we have received from Him, and that we are obliged to share it with the needy. Whoever does not share, he appropriates what belongs to another.

94. To pray for the Pope

The Holy Year comes to an end. Millions of people passed through Rome. There are some who started out as tourists and became pilgrims, but there are more who went as pilgrims and sought the tourist attractions. Especially the travelers from the United States and from Western Europe, as the western press relates, simply looked upon the trip to Rome as a pleasant tour.

This should have been taken into consideration. The world has become entirely indifferent to religious affairs. This does not mean that the reverse process has not already begun. But it is very slow, because it had to begin so deep. It will take years to notice the change.

Pope Paul VI announcing the Jubilee Year did not stress a pilgrimage. He laid the emphasis on renewal of spirit and on reconciliation. What good would it do for millions to go to Rome if they did not care about changing their lives? This aspect of the Holy Year is the most important, and it alone can leave a permanent mark on the life of the Church for the two heraldic slogans are not for one year only.

Remembering this, do we think of the man who gave this particular substantial meaning to the Jubilee of 1975?

Paul VI was an extraordinary pope. The impact of the whirl wind bringing such gigantic changes was broken in the pontificate of John XXIII but its effects, blessed, no doubt, but also painful, appeared in the pontificate of Paul VI.

In one of the last stories of B. Marshall "The Bishop," the English bishop Finbar is talking with Paul VI. Looking at the pope, who "although he had so many dioceses from Gdansk to Punta Arenas in mind, knew about everything exceedingly well." Bishop Finbar became aware that he had before him a man who is bearing an unusual burden. All the contests, criticisms, outbursts, blunders, departures, were striking at him. The Church seemed to be torn apart, and falling in, but the man who was upholding it, bending at times under the superhuman weight, attacked by some, criticized by others, was the pope.

Just a few years ago such a wave rolled past the Church. And when it receded, indifference took over. It had to come. It too was foreseen by our Savior. It is also neccessary for the Church to elicit new strength from within itself.

But all this the man has to suffer who is the earthly representative of Christ. Today the papal crown is a veritable crown of thorns. The Vatican has become the Garden.

Do we pray for the pope? Do we aid him with our remembrance? Do we sustain him with our prayers in his heroically difficult task? Do we pray that hope will not abandon him, or that he will know how to see what has already begun but will go on growing slowly, almost imperceptibly?

In the Garden the Apostles fell asleep. We too often fall asleep over our trials and troubles, yet how small they are at times, leaving the Man alone dragging the saddle of the changes. We have to pray for him ... often ... as often as possible. We have to offer our sufferings for him. He is only a man, hence he needs our help.

95. Missionaries

On October 19, 1975, the Holy Father announced the beatification of Mary Teresa Ledochowska.

Mary Teresa was born April 19, 1863. She was the sister of Julia Ursula, the foundress of the "gray" Ursulines and of Vladimir, general of the Jesuits. As a young lady in the court of the Grand Duchess of Tuscany she suddenly left the gay dancing crowd to take up the battle, by word and pen, with the greatest crime committed against man, the slavery of the black people.

Only the shores of the African continent were known at the beginning of the nineteenth century. Soon caravans of hunters looking for slaves were forcing their way into its depths. Those dealers were snatching Negroes and selling them to America. We know these frightening stories at least from the book of Jules Verne, *Fifteen-year-old Captain,* which no doubt everyone of us read in his childhood. The slaves were forced to work in the cotton fields of the southern United States, in British Guiana, in Spanish Cuba, and in French Santo Domingo. Unheeded were the protests of the Church and the people that could not in conscience look upon the work of the black slaves. The countries officially condemned slavery, but the plantation owners and dealers did not intend to resign their profits.

In the nineteenth century the colonization of Africa began on a large scale. The soldiers of European dynasties who followed the discoverers took possession of even larger tracts of Black Land. Instead of shipping the Negroes out to enrich America, they engaged the black people to work for the good of the colonists. Thus colonization provided a new form of slavery.

But the process of colonization also opened the way for the missionaries. The governments of the countries colonizing Africa could not object to this. Furthermore they expected the missionaries to be helpful to them in their action. Therefore, France, although fighting with religion in the nineteenth century, promoted the activity of the French missionaries in the colonies.

However the missionary movement from its very foundation had to be in opposition to the doings of the colonists. It was bringing the Faith to the African people, and simultaneously proclaiming freedom even when individual missionaries, as sometimes happened, by their conduct were supporting the colonists, convinced as they were that they were performing a great mission of civilization.

In Rome, especially after Vatican Council I, the work of organizing missions was begun with great ferver. Mary Teresa Ledochowska became the main representative of this activity. In 1894 she organized the Sodality of St. Peter Claver. She issued her own and contributed articles to publications in various languages, Polish included, such as: *Echo from Africa* and *The Little Negro*. These periodicals informed the Christians with the situation in Africa and collected contributions to aid the missionaries. Mary Teresa herself was able to collect $1.5 million, which for standards of those times was a staggering sum, not counting all the material articles brought in for her cause. All her life she was a model of zealous industry and sacrifice. She used to repeat:

"Let us work! We will have time enough to rest for all eternity." She died in 1922.

As the African countries were liberated from colonial slavery they did not perceive at once that missionary work had nothing in common with the policy of exploitation by the colonists. With time however they discovered the truth. Today's missionaries cooperate closely with the local clergy and enjoy the protection of the black African bishops, something that seemed impossible, or improbable in the days when Mary Teresa Ledochowska began her work.

96. Death and life (Jn 14:1–6)

Daily when I open the newspaper I look for the list of death notices. Whoever has lived sixty-five years in one city as I have will find some dear one among the deceased practically every day.

Each day the number of "my" dead grows. I have many more "there" than living "here." Such is the law of life. The new generations grow taking our place. Besides those who are dying in "their" good time there are many dying too soon, it seems to me.

Such a death seems tragic and evokes rebellion. Then we have to repeat and convince ourselves that God sends death at the very best moment for each one. Only such a conviction is consonant with our faith in the most merciful God, who foretold that he would take us to himself. God does not break the free will of man but he gives us the maximum chance. It depends upon man whether he is able to profit by it. Death is not a "punishment." From the eternal viewpoint it is a reward: the end of the period of painful tests. A person dies in order to meet Him who loves Him much more than any other mere man could love Him. Those of us remaining on earth, suffer because someone dear to us has disappeared from our sight. But the departed one continues to see us and can help us.

Such a view of death has nothing in common with disregard for life. It is a test. It brings pain but also joy. Life ought to be the fulfillment of duties, but obligations fulfilled are both a hardship and a joy.

The first obligation of a living person is to preserve his sanity, and openmindedness. Only then can we do what we owe the Church, our country, our community.

More than about the thought of death, we should be disturbed by the news in the press that the amount of liquor consumed in the first half of 1975 is greater than the amount taken in the first half of 1974. Alas, we do not drink only a little. We drink very much. Indeed much too much, and that amount is growing! With it is growing what is less easy to control, the number of marriages broken by liquor, with abandoned, neglected, often retarded children, accidents involving excessive drinking, instances of poor workmanship, drunken brawls, fights, malicious destructions, and killings at times....

When we come to think about our near and dear ones who have died, let us entrust them to God. Let us believe that their fate is resting in good hands. But when we think of those who are living, let us do all we can so that they will live conscious of their present tasks and obligations. Let us fight narcotics, that is what liquor has come to be. Let us stop minimizing the harm it does and not make a joke of it. In memory of those who preceded us in death, let us demand of the living, ourselves included, a real understanding of why we are living.

97. Guidelines for a missionary

Missionaries are not only priests and religious people who travel to do mission work in Africa or Asia. They are often also lay people.

In the Brazilian jungle Walter Dowbor, a Pole, lives and

works. An engineer and educator, having reached the age when other people retire as "emeritus," he liquidated his home in the city, went into the heart of the jungle, settled in a little village and there began to work as a missioner. In my novel *Burned Bridges*, I tried to portray certain experiences of this exceptional man which he graciously shared with me.

Walter Dowbor set down ten precepts by which a lay missioner ought to guide himself. They are:

1. Take the initiative in action but be sure to be able to take the responsibility for every initiative made
2. Forget yourself and your past
3. Melt like sugar in the bitter coffee of daily life
4. Learn to pray, think seriously and love
5. Love those whom we like and those whom we don't like
6. Love those who like us and those who don't like us
7. Share your time, your intelligence, your property
8. Get to know Jesus, believe in him, and love him
9. Have Jesus within you and remain in him
10. Choose the way of holiness and saintliness.

To choose the way of holiness? Isn't this precept going a bit too far? And yet Pope Paul VI said that there is placed before man demands of perfection, and this perfection is not "just a faculty but a duty." "Does this paradoxical perfection have a name?" asked the pontiff. Yes indeed it has, and you know it: it is called holiness. Saintliness ... attracts far less than it frightens away. So many people excuse themselves to easily by saying: I am not a saint ... But ... it is not true that holiness is impossible.... There is a saintliness which we might call ordinary; although it is equally woven of extraordinary material, it demands only two factors cooperating mutually ... the first is grace ... the second, our own will....

Hence the slogan, "Choose the way of holiness," is a most realistic watchword because everyone can receive grace and everyone has a will.

Walter Dowbor completes his guidelines with two assertions: "The more you give the happier you are," and "Everybody can be a missionary in his own community."

That's a great truth. Missionaries go on mission, but missions also come to us. It is not necessary to sink in the Brazilian jungle in order to work for man. Human needs are knocking on our doors every day. Children, the elderly, and the sick are waiting for our help. It is only necessary to take our eyes off ourselves and we will see those who need us.

98. There must be time for children

Nasfeter's film about children, *Butterflies,* is both beautiful and wise. The time of children's coming to maturity, and a very early maturity it is these days, is immensely trying and often dramatic. Never more than today did the duty of being with one's children at the decisive moment weigh so heavily on the adults, to be able to perceive and understand their troubles, to help them discreetly but without minimizing the seriousness of their problems. Alas, how often adults are too busy at that time with their own affairs, and perhaps very important ones too, but can there be anything more important than the need of a child?

The more a child is neglected, the faster he matures and the more impetuously. Such maturing is sometimes accompanied by freakish flings that can ruin a child's whole life. Deprived of the affection of his parents he seeks help from companions, equally immature, or he will closely observe adults and learn the worst from what he sees.

Modern parents feel young a long time. Even when they have maturing children they often think about their own "heart conflicts." Others again live through great ambitions in their careers. One dedicates all his time to social work; another is passionately devoted to matters of his profession; still another assumes work beyond his strength for the purchase of a car in view of a long trip beyond the border. However, he is a poor civic leader who sees social problems in his community but does not see them in his own home. Nor is he a good doctor who perfects himself in healing strangers but does not notice the illness of his own children. Bad is the politician who wants to fight for peace in the world but does not see that the problem of peace begins with little things, to all appearances, in family affairs.

A feverish passion for travel abroad has gripped the generation of parents today. Allowing for the benefit of such travel, it must be said, that these trips are greatly conducive to breaking contact between parents and children, if the parents leave the children more or less unsupervised at home. How often it happens that parents returning from a pleasant trip fall into a whirl of dramatic conflicts which the adolescents had raised during their long absence, because of their absence.

Children do not ask to be born. Since they have come upon earth they are entitled to proper care and upbringing. Parents must have time for their children. No "ravishing" matters must overshadow their first duty—the upbringing of their children. A certain infantilism seems to weigh down upon the parents of today. They seek their own satisfaction too passionately. Too zealously and too long do they seek themselves. What Nasfeter said so beautifully and discreetly is a cry of alarm.

99. What then? (Mt 25:14–30)

The Holy Year is coming to an end. Any day now the bronze doors of the Basilica of St. Peter will close, only to reopen in the year 2000. How many of us will live to see that day? What will our world look like then?

In the meantime, what will go on here? What will happen with the benefits of the Holy Year 1974–1975? Will the religious zeal cool-off and disappear? Will the slogans of renewal and reconciliation, slogans in their essence as old as Christianity itself, continue to ferment?

The Holy Father anticipated this. In one of his addresses he mentioned that today's world is living in expectation of a better future. The Church, too, is sharing this expectation, although for the Church this better future is not just a growth in material goods. The dynamic awaiting which the Christian world is experiencing, awaiting being always a "working" not a "getting," is the waiting for unity. The Holy Year has passed but the problem of unity is still before us. We must continue to work for it.

And the Pope repeated what he had said the year before: "We ought, in accordance with our first Christian obligation, create anew and bring to life real love within God's Church. Dear brothers and sons, try hard to call to mind and consider the apostolic exhortation, on December 8, 1974, about reconciliation within the Church. We must be one, we must walk together. We must put an end to the divisions within the Church. Let the devastating interpretations of pluralism cease, the attacks of Catholics upon Catholics. Enough of disobedience! Today more than at any other time, it is necessary to build one Church, a Catholic one, and not destroy it! The spreading of love, renewed and strengthened, in God's holy Church—that is the first concern in the postjubilee era!"

In the beginning and at the end of the Jubilee Year, Pope Paul VI stresses the same theme, unity among Christians.

Doesn't that unity exist?

One would like to think it does. In truth there are no big public accusations. But let us look not so much at the accusations as at the deep silences and omissions. People are not noticed, their works, their labor, their efforts, although objectively they seem to be important enough. There are, sad to say, many Catholics among us who notice only their own "clan," their "group," in general "their own." They look over the heads of others. But let it happen that a Catholic-foreigner arrives in Poland. Then the talk with him is only about those who were usually unnoticed. And what a talk that is! What is not dragged out!

Would it not be worthwhile to consider this after the celebration of the Holy Year which was to bring us reconciliation?

Each one of us received from God a certain number of "talents" to spend. The one who received more, must also attain more.

Christianity, the Church, the Holy Year, the Pope—all ask us to work for unity. Everyone can do something according to his abilities. Every gesture of kindness and benevolence shown to another, not because he belongs to "his own," but because that is the way to unity, is already an input into this universal problem. The Holy Year is over, but the question remains.

100. Whatever you have not done for the least of these... (Mt 25:31–46)

There was a time when many Christians were of the opinion that a missionary's work is to speak to the pagans about God. When they want to hear him, then he tries to provide for their necessities: clothing, food, medicine, helps them in every possible way. If they do not want to listen, so much the worse for them. They are looked upon as "black sheep" from whom he has to turn away. There is no help for them!

Today practically everybody understands the matter in an entirely different way. The commitment of the missionary is, above all, to help the needy, the poor, and the sick. The work of the modern missionary does not begin with talking about God. It starts with feeding the hungry, strengthening the sick, interceding for the life of the prisoner. It is helping every needy person because he needs it, not because in the future he might become a Christian. Naturally, at an opportune moment the missionary will try to speak of God. But even if he feels that some people will never listen to his words, he has to help them.

We discovered this approach from the fact that when the Black people began their war with the oppression of colonization very often they treated the missionaries as cooperators in this oppression. And yet the approach of which we speak is as old as the Gospel! Speaking of the Last Judgment, Jesus does not accuse the condemned for not preaching his word. He accuses them of not helping man and identifies himself with every suffering person.

We should all be missionaries. The missions have come to us. And yet how often we say: What? We are to help him? Never! He's a drunkard and a rascal! We should help this woman? She's a trouble-maker, a shameless crone who envies all and hates everybody! We are to take care of this child? Why he's a brat! We are to care for this family? But they do not pray, they do not go to church, they live immorally. Let those who are like them, help them!

Are these the words of the Last Judgment?

The Militia of the Immaculata organized by Fr. Maximilian Kolbe, in 1917, was to be the vanguard of the Church against the masonic foe. But the essence of this organization was based on the conviction that since the Masons are enemies of the Church they are specially "entrusted" to the Blessed Mother of God for she takes the most tender care of those who do evil without knowing what they are doing. Mary loves all people, she wants the salvation of all; therefore, she must be most concerned about those who are threatened the most with the anger of God. The Immaculate Virgin is the first act of God's mercy toward man since he, God, created her to save people from his anger. To want to fulfill the desire of Mary is to pray for those "entrusted" to her. The members of the M.I. ought to recite this prayer at least once a day: "O Mary, conceived without sin, pray for us who have recourse to you, and for those who do not have recourse to you, for the masons and those entrusted to you."

To be a missionary, that is to help all the needy, pray for everybody, especially for those who need prayers the most.

101. Man, the unknown

A person who survived a very serious illness said to me, "I have come to the conclusion that the only medicine we can count on is prayer." Both of us laughed at this as if it were a joke. Yet, I thought, what I just heard is a great truth.

This does not at all mean that modern medicine is to be despised and ought to be thrown out in favor of quacks and witch doctors. Medicine on a level with other sciences has in the last decades made enormous progress. Surgery especially has performed miracles. Internal medicine has remained far behind.

The insides of man's body are continuously a great mystery in scientific research. In the 1930s the learned American, of French descent, Alexis Carrel, wrote an astounding book *Man the Unknown Being.* Even to this day the book has not lost its actuality. In man there are powers of life and powers of death which react upon the organism and often cancel the "mathematically" calculated diagnoses of medical men. The prescribed medicines always have a double effect: they heal the disease but after a certain period they themselves begin to react in a poisonous way. Hence the frequent return to the use of medicinal plants which had already been relegated to the realm of quakery but whose effectiveness although less striking is incomparably better for the organism. Young doctors are not always sufficiently humble in acknowledging their inability to identify the strange growth in the human organism. The ever deepening research in specialization is leading to the conviction that the countless operations performed upon man provide full knowledge about his insides. In the meantime how often it still happens that in spite of these scientifically calculated data, the man himself is able to elicit unknown powers opposing the disease, or the reverse some gnawing unknown "sorrow" or "injury" is worsening his condition in face of the apparent improvement.

Once more let me repeat: I am far from the conviction that we ought to relinquish medical help. It is only reasonable that we consult a doctor and take the prescribed medicine. At the same time, however, we ought to seek within ourselves the power that can perhaps cure the illness.

For the believer, prayer is the force that releases this power to conquer the inner "sorrow" within man.

Fortunately we have the right to pray for health. Health is man's great treasure, the indispensable condition for his performance in the face of the obligations weighing upon him. When we pray for health we do not pray only for relief from pain; above all we pray for the right to return to activity which is our reason for living. Maybe the illness was only a warning, or a reminder that we are careless about our health, without which we cannot perform our duties, exposing ourselves to harm especially by drinking and smoking.

Whatever the circumstances, we must constantly remember to pray for reverent submission to the holy will of God Who knows better than we do what is necessary for us. And if He, in spite of our prayer, allows the illness to continue, it may be that this sickness is the means which in an "unusual" way will be conducive to our good.

102. Before the earth arose....

During the last two centuries all the most important functions in the Church traditionally either begin or end on the feast of the Immaculate Conception of the Blessed Virgin Mary.

The feast of the Immaculate Conception was known in Christendom already in the eighth century. In Poland it was introduced in the fourteenth century thanks to the Franciscans and Benedictines. In the fifteenth century Pope Sixtus IV advised the erection of a chapel in the Vatican in honor of the Immaculate Conception, the so-called Sistine Chapel, well-known because the election of a new pope takes place there. Finally, in 1854 Pius IX, urged on by the whole Christian world, proclaimed the dogma of the Immaculate Conception. Four years later Mary appeared to Bernadette Soubirous in Lourdes. When asked by Bernadette who she is, Mary answered in words unintelligible to the illiterate little girl, "I am the Immaculate Conception."

What does this dogma signify? Even among Catholics there are misunderstandings. It says that Mary in deference to the great honor that was to be bestowed upon her was conceived without original sin and came upon earth in the same stainless nature as her first ancestor, Mother Eve.

But it is worth turning our attention to a particular aspect of this matter. Before original sin, people were different from us. They knew no suffering. They were not to experience death. They were indeed capable of committing sin, but their senses were so controlled by reason that it required full understanding and consent of the free will to commit a sin. Therefore, Adam and Eve sinned so grievously because they were fully aware of what they were doing. It was a conscious revolt against the will of God, just as well-understood as was Lucifer's rebellion.

We do not really know why God did not pardon Lucifer, yet deigned to have mercy on man. Perhaps it was because Satan was somewhat responsible for the sin committed by man. From the very beginning, people were the possessors of a promise of redemption. They were to receive something, even more than they had received at first. But they had to bear the burden of the effects of their nature wounded by sin.

Before the earth was created, the plan of redemption was

ready. This plan envisioned the appearance of a Woman who would be willing and would be able to become the Mother of the Savior. And it took place already then: "I am conceived before the hills . . . before he made the earth and the fields. . . ." says the Book of Proverbs. We see everything too much within the frame of time. For God, time does not exist. The first sin was barely committed when redemption already took place. But this act of tremendous mercy had to become incarnated for the people in human time. Centuries had to elapse before finally she was born, the one chosen before time.

Mary was born free from original sin, but she was not freed from the effects of that sin. We know that she suffered, she died, although she was taken up to heaven immediately. Although she never committed a sin, we are convinced of that, she was not exempt from human weaknesses, temptations and doubts.

God wanted that everything would take place as though the miracle of the Immaculate Conception had never happened. The holiness of Mary was hidden in the simplicity of her human life. Mary remained a human being, but certainly a most beautiful person. She had the possibility to refuse God. Since she said: "Be it done," she did it in a transport of love and of her own perfectly free will. But because she agreed, things happened as they were supposed to happen, the Son of God became her Son, while the Holy Spirit gifted her with all his graces. Without ceasing to be human Mary stood above all other men, for having all graces she could dispense them as gifts. It is as though she is the trusted treasurer to whom the Ruler-King entrusts his treasure and says, distribute as you see fit among the needy.

One dogma gives birth to the next. The dogma of the Immaculate Conception completed the dogma of the Assumption.

We trust that just as all the graces of the Holy Spirit finding themselves in the hands of Mary are poured out upon the people through her hands, so likewise all our petitions addressed to God go through her immaculate hands. There is no doubt about that, as St. Therese of the Child Jesus said, "We can ask

Mary for everything because she knows whether our petitions should be presented to Jesus. And if she judges them worthy of presentation she will graciously present them most efficaciously."

We hope that all our petitions of the Holy Year have landed safely in her hands. Let us trust her, for she being "born before the ocean came to be," knows what to do with them.

103. Death of Father Tom Roztworowski

They are passing away, one after another, people of my generation. Fr. Tom Roztworowski, a man who was a true symbol of this generation, has left us.

I became acquainted with Fr. Tom just before the war. In the blustering, happy crowd of the youth of that day he was the loudest and the merriest. He was bubbling with life, humor and joy. Later on when I asked him how he does it, how he can always manage to present a smiling face, he answered that he made it the aim of his life: always to wear a smile. Fr. Tom's smile did not only betray his interior joyousness. It was, plainly speaking, a form of mission: with his smile Fr. Tom wanted to remain young among youth, share their enthusiasm, gain them with his smile for the Highest Cause. Fr. Ricci once became a Chinaman for the Chinese; Fr. Nobile became a Hindu for the Hindus; Fr. Tom became a smiling friend for the smiling!

When the occupation came, Fr. Tom was still working, even more intensively. I met him at ever so many conspiratorial meetings. His confessional was always swamped. In front of his door there was always a waiting line. He found time for everything. He arranged his hours so that he could prepare my daughter for her First Holy Communion, and in between classes he played the piano and taught her joyful songs. He helped in secretly hiding

Jews. Best known for his nonsense and gags, he generously served the most persecuted.

We met in Starowka at the very beginning of the uprising. He was chaplain of the Main Command, and I a staff member of the Midnight Group. When Colonel Wachnowski asked me to find a chaplain for his staff I went to Fr. Tom for advice. Thanks to his directions, I found Fr. German-Paczek.

After the tragic explosion of the tank I discovered Fr. Tom in the midst of the massacred people. The Main Command left Starowka and Fr. Tom was now devoting his strength and care above all to the wounded. I sensed that this work was the hardest for him, that's why he took it upon himself. Nature was pushing him elsewhere: on the line, under the barricades. He was born to the horse and the charge. It must have been very hard for him to kneel beside the cots of the mangled and butchered people to console them and inspire them with hope. Time after time I noticed the beautiful profile of Fr. Tom between the cots in the hospital on Long Street, or in the corridors of the cloister near the church of St. Hyacinth.

I also found him among the smoldering ashes of houses after a raid whose bombs had buried tens if not hundreds of wounded people in rubble. Together we searched for the living among these unfortunates, for my niece Basia to whom as well as to others, Fr. Tom had brought Holy Communion every day.

He was the one who remained with the battalion "Gustaw" during the attempt made by Group Midnight to get to Midtown, with the soldiers who were ordered to "coverup" during that attempt without the hope of being able to leave Starowka. The next day when the evacuation of the Group began by means of canals, Fr. Tom decided to remain with the wounded. And this time he was choosing between his cavalier nature which was demanding action in battle and the obvious work of necessity, the duty of serving the suffering and the helpless.

Coming to understand that the Germans would no longer permit him to care for the wounded Fr. Tom ran away and hid himself among the ruins of Starowka. He lived alone in the midst of ruins and corpses up to the time of the capitulation. Then luckily he got a chance to leave the town and make his way to the convent of the Magdalen Sisters in Walendow.

After the war, Fr. Tom resided in Lublin and in Lodz. As usual he worked with the young. As usual too, he was always smiling, hiding behind this smile his determined will to serve the needy. At one point he was torn away from his work. I recall that at some literary gathering, Isabelle Czajka-Stachowicz walked up to me and said, "You really know Fr. Tom Roztworowski well, sir. We ought to help him. We must really help him. I spoke to him already. He is such a person... so..." In vain she tried to grasp the right word. When he returned to his chosen work she said, "You were certainly happy about this, sir, weren't you? For I am very happy. You are too close to each other, so maybe you do not really know what he is like...."

"It's a great thing," Bishop Klepacz said to me one time during our most intimate talks about the "twilight," "that I have with me a man like Fr. Tom."

In 1963 Fr. Tom went to Rome to become director of the Polish section of the Vatican Radio.

I remember him in this role from my last sojourn in Rome. I was wandering a long time through the spacious corridors of the building on Via della Conciliazione before I found the Polish section. The large hall was sectioned off with wooden partitions into small rooms. Fr. Thomas was late for the appointment but his secretary, a sympathetic Miss Hanka, talked to me about him with rapture and enthusiasm. So here too he aroused enthusiasm in the young. Then the door opened and I saw a bald head, pink cheeks, a classic Roman nose and the always smiling lips of Fr. Tom.

A few months ago he returned to Poland. I hastened to St. John's, but was told that he was sick and was resting outside of Warsaw. It was said that this condition was "nothing serious." But the appointment of a new director for the Polish section of the Vatican Radio made me uneasy; maybe this illness is something more serious than it seemed to be at first. I never saw him again. He died on March 9, just two days after the feast of his great patron.

I said that he was the living symbol of our generation. He began his activity with the same overwhelming drive of faith, hope and zeal which attracted all of us. But where we, in the course of years grew lukewarm, he remained fervent. Our resolutions diminished, he fulfilled his unremittingly. He chose to smile and kept on smiling! He chose serving the most needy. This cavalier decided to serve in the infantry.

How sad we felt that he left us so soon! But perhaps we ought to envy him that he has already reached the place where awards are given and received ... not for words ... not for the charge or rank, but for life! For the humdrum daily toil!

104. A Polish saint

Mother Ursula Ledochowska, foundress of the congregation popularly called the Gray Ursulines, but officially the Ursulines of the Most Sacred Heart of the Dying Jesus, came of a well-known family in our history. She was born in 1865 in Loosdorf near Vienna.

Her grandfather, Ignace Ledochowski, general of the Polish armies, was the defender of Modlin in 1831. After the downfall of the November insurrection, he had to move to Malopolska. His son, Anthony, studied beyond the border and married foreigners. In spite of this, he did not become denationalized.

The second wife of Anthony Ledochowski was a Swiss lady, the countess Salis-Zizers. Three of the children of this second marriage are worthy of note: Vladimir, the Jesuit, Provincial in Krakow and finally General of the Jesuit Order; Blessed Teresa, foundress of the Sodality of St. Peter Claver for African Missions;

and then the one about whom I want to speak: Julia, later on in the Order known as Ursula.

Julia spent all her childhood and youth in Austria. She studied in a school conducted by the English Ladies. She was brought up in a deeply Catholic spirit but obviously with little Polish. And yet when in 1883 the Ledochowski family transferred to Poland to Lipnica near Bochniew, the meeting with her father's native and was not merely a joyous thrill. In this girl, speaking Polish rather poorly at the time, there would be born a deep patriotism and a remarkable feeling for the needs of the Polish nature.

In two years after his return to his own country, Anthony Ledochowski died. Smallpox, which was the cause of his death, also attacked his oldest daughter Teresa. Teresa got well, but the disease ruined her beauty. An interesting fact is that the girl, who had no idea in her head about a religious life, who was given to entertainments, suddenly became of necessity, directed in another direction. After a period of searching, she became a great organizer of African missions. Thanks to her work on the international level, she attained recognition sooner than her sister.

Julia was different. From the beginning she united piety with love for maternal and domestic affairs. An extraordinary organizer of time, she helped her mother bring up the numerous younger family members, took charge of the house, and helped her father in managing the property. Seh did not think of entertainments or even of marriage. The cloister was drawing her, but an active order dedicated to the education of children and youth. Still she was unable to choose a congregation for herself; hence only because of circumstances she decided on the convent of the "black Ursulines" in Krakow. She entered it in 1886.

For twenty years Sister Ursula worked in the cloister as educator and teacher. Well versed in linguistics, she taught language courses. But above all she trained the young people. In this field she attained exceptional results.

In 1904 she was appointed superior of the convent.

This did not tear her away from her work of training. Mother Ursula, just like Julia Ledochowska, had time for everything. Her special attention was given to the academic world. More and more women were pursuing higher studies. The structure of domestic life was changing. Now mothers will no longer be engaged in caring for children only, they must know how to combine child care with a career. Mother Ursula introduced a boarding school for girls in Krakow. She had hardly laid the foundation for the project when she had to hurry to another.

After the revolution in 1905, the changed situation in Russia made it possible for the gymnasium of St. Catherine in St. Petersburg to be opened to Polish Catholic girls. Mother Ursula was permitted to establish a boarding school. She herself became the directress.

The work in St. Petersburg was not easy. The czarist government, forced to make concessions, did not look kindly upon the activity of the Polish religious. Mother Ursula had to throw all her talents, her tact and industriousness into the task. In her work she adhered to the principle that "Catholicism and the spirit of Poland are necessary and complementary elements in the upbringing of children. Both call for effort to battle with any halfheartedness and place before the soul the postulate of holiness achieved in the honest fulfillment of daily duties."

These words clearly portray the stand of Mother Ursula Ledochowska. Her aim was the education of youth who are to undertake in the spirit of sacrifice the daily ordinary duties of life. Not the culture of "superhumans," not the production of seekers after "great adventures," not the creation of "stars," as we would say today. Hers was a school of family life, home, career, and citizenship. Also a school of holiness, but holiness born of daily effort, a holiness accessible to all and a possible aim for all. For the life of the nation it is better to have an army of unrecognized saints, saintly mothers, saintly wives, and saintly teachers than one single saint, even a canonized one, but clinging alone and tragically in an environment detached from the common good.

The work of Mother Ursula was causing greater and greater dissatisfaction on the part of the czarist government. Her educational work was too obviously a preparation for a new kind of Polish society. In 1911, she was told to leave St. Petersburg. She went to Sertaval in Finland where some time previously on the seacoast at Merentaht (meaning Star of the Sea) an affiliate of the Petersburg gymnasium was established, which destined for physically weak girls.

In Merentaht, Mother Ursula carried on mission work in addition to her educational enterprise. Finland was a country long lost to the Church. In that territory only two Catholic churches were found. Mother Ursula learned the Finnish language with lightning speed and was translating the church hymns and Christmas carols into Finnish. The house in Merentaht with its singing and pleasant atmosphere was soon attracting the local people.

In 1914 the war broke out and Mother Ursula, as an Austrian subject, was ordered to leave the country. She left for Stockholm.

Her sojourn in Finland directed Mother Ursula's attention to the Scandinavian countries, so beautiful, so heartily devoted to human affairs, yet so far removed from Catholicism. The desire to organize help for Poland in the first place, but also with the mission ideal in sight, moved Mother Ursula to make contacts with the few Swedish Catholics. Naturally, in that place she began to speak Swedish. The Poles who were settling in Stockholm in ever greater numbers began to crowd around her. This caused Mother Ursula to call other sisters from Russia to come to Stockholm. Together with them, she opened a Language Institute. Now she could begin to work with the Swedish youth.

In 1915, Sienkiewicz organizing in all of Europe not engaged in war committees of aid to Poland entrusted this project in Scandinavia to Mother Ursula Ledochowska. Mother Ursula took to this task with all her usual vim and generosity. She traveled through Scandinavia, made innumerable addresses about Poland, and always in the local language. She drew into cooperation with her, Selma Lagerlof, Alfred Jensen (secretary of the Library of the Nobel Foundation a Slavist, translator of *Pan Tadeusz* and *Irydion*) and also Professor Benediotsen (translator of *Ojca zadzumionych*).

In one of her addresses these words were found eminently descriptive of her position: "We have not lost hope," she said, "God has made us a nation and a nation we will remain. Send us to American cities or to the Sahara desert and you will be convinced that we will always love Poland courageously, sure that we are going to meet freedom...."

In Mother Ursula's stand there was no lack of soldierly assurance. A soldier is not only some one who bears arms. Mother Ursula was a soldier of propaganda in Scandinavia. And the measure of her effectiveness in this field may be the fact that among the people she was able to win over for the cause of Poland, was the one-time mortal foe of Poland, the writer George Brandes.

In 1918 Mother Ursula could return to an already free Poland to whose liberation she had contributed so loyally.

However, the year of separation from the motherhouse of the order in Krakow and the introduction by Mother Ursula of new styles of work created a certain dissonance between the established community and the group of sisters who came from Scandinavia. Mother Ursula felt this lack of harmony very keenly, but in her sorrow she realized that it was a ferment which always appears when there arises a need for a new congregation. The contemporary papal delegate in Poland, Msgr. Ratti, upheld her in this conviction. The group of sisters that returned from Scandinavia settled in Pniewy near Peznan where a school of domestic science for girls was established. In the same year, 1920, Mother Ursula went to Rome to settle the affairs of the order. She wrote from there: "I have suffered a lot here in Rome for which I am deeply grateful to God. Our work is leaning on the cross, that is always the safest, and so we can hope that something will come of it...."

A new congregation did arise—Polish, evoked by the needs of our country, the "gray Ursulines." The constitution for the new congregation was approved by Pope Pius XI, the same former papal delegate Ratti who from the very beginning promoted Mother Ursula's idea and who often repeated: "Be what Divine Providence made you."

Providence required a congregation that would rightly mold the souls of the Polish girls working for the first generation of children born now in the liberated country. It would be worth noting how many women who later on, in the bloody years of occupation, knew how to fight and how to care for themselves and others, came from Ursuline discipline.

Gradually from the motherhouse in Pniewy whose patron and protector was the Apostle of Scandinavia, St. Olaf, the work of the "gray" Ursulines was spreading first to Wielkopolska, later to Lodz and vicinity, and finally to Warsaw and all of Poland. A convent was also established in Rome on Vis del Casalette.

In the year 1931, an Ursuline boarding school for student girls was established on the corner of Dobra and Gesta. How many times in my student days did I go there for assemblies, conferences, meetings and prayers in common!

And in Rome on May 29, 1939, Mother Ursula Ledochowska died.

Mother Ursula Ledochowska did not perish at Auschwitz. She is not the author of illuminating works of theology. But she was the mother of motherless children, an educator in the best sense, a soldier. And she is a saint.

The second half of the nineteenth century up to the 1930s—that's the time of the great rebirth of religion and morality in our country. At the beginning of the nineteenth century, Poland was a country subject to partitioning, not only politically but also morally. A breakdown of national character was taking place. We were still strong enough for heroic outbursts, but no longer able to work unsparingly and wholeheartedly for the common cause. However, the process of breaking up was halted and reversed. Today if Polish Catholicism belongs to the best lived in the world, we owe it to the work of holy people like Mother Ursula Ledochowska.

Some years ago for the centenary of the birthday of Mother Ursula, a little booklet was issued, such a beautiful one, comparing the directives of the last Council with the teachings of Mother Ursula. The Rev. Primate Wyszynski was right when he wrote that the chief concern of the Council was: "Don't fence yourself away from the life and needs of the man of our times." From the very beginning this precept lay on the heart of Mother Ursula. Already in 1930 she said: "The difference between TODAY and YESTERDAY lies in this: YESTERDAY the sheep grazed only in pastures and did not need much help; TODAY instead they fall into precipices, and climb up on the highest cliffs, therefore we have to leave the peaceful lanes of work to go after them and try to catch up with them, here and there, like a true shepherd. . . ." And two years later: "I have to share something with you which should be a great joy to all of us. The Cardinal Vicar wants to entrust us with a mission, not in Africa, but where it is equally necessary, on the outskirts of Rome. There are only barracks and they will give us one like that. I asked that they build us nothing better. We will live there together with the poor, we will teach them Catechism, we will nurse them and love them. . . ."

105. Nicodemus—one of us (An article published in the Spanish weekly *Jesus Christ*)

On a certain night, as St. John's gospel tells us, there came to Jesus a well-known and highly esteemed pharisee, Nicodemus.

I made this Nicodemus the hero of my novel *Letters of Nicodemus*. It gained many readers in my native country, Poland, and also in Spain, Germany, Italy, England, the United States,

Portugal, Czechoslovakia, France, Sweden, South African Republic, Austria....

Why should there be such an interest taken in this story everywhere? I think that it drew so many readers, because of the contemporaneousness of its hero, Nicodemus. In spite of his historical setting, Nicodemus is a man of our day.

The story was written in the years 1949–1951, but the beginnings of its conception reach back to the early 1930s. At that time I wanted to write a story, just as Nikos Kazantzakis did later, about Christ who comes to this world the second time in our modern age. In my book, Jesus was to be born again in Poland in those prewar years. The war spoiled my first plan. Five years of conspiracy and battle in arms threw me off the track of my first aspirations. Biblical studies led me on to history. I decided to portray Jesus in the light of his epoch. But I did not resign from the dialogue with contemporaneousness. This contemporary in the story, whose action took place 2,000 years ago, was Nicodemus.

I did not have to "make" Nicodemus a contemporary character. It seems to me that hardly any other of the evangelical personages fits the picture of contemporary life so well as does the person of Nicodemus. The Gospel is an astonishing book. It was written by four men of varying intelligence and coming from different localities, and yet not one of the four imposes himself upon his work. We writers know how heavily we weigh upon the personalities of our heroes. The authors of the Gospel do not weigh upon their work at all. They barely indicate their authorship with some insignificant details. They disappear in the history written by themselves.

Four stories having as their hero the same historical personality would create four distinct people. Each author would see in his hero, something different, something specially dear to him. The four gospels always show us the same Man. Such a Man, no one could "fabricate." He really existed. The evangelists did not create Jesus, as did the authors of the literary works such as the apocrypha. In the apocrypha, Christ is subjected to the conditions, or ideas of the authors. In the gospel he is a wholly independent personality. The authors disappeared, and he remained such as he was. In a certain era of history, the Church cut off the gospels from the apocrypha inserting the gospels into the canon. That was a blessed decision inspired by the Holy Spirit. But it was also a fully human decision based on the dissimilarity of the works.

This objectivism of the picture as seen in the Gospels relates equally to personalities of other protagonists of evangelical history. People are shown with the exactness of a photograph, and not even the best portrait. Peter or Judas, Antypas or Pilate, are so real and distinct that their characters, not losing anything of their historic position, have also become human symbols and types.

Such a typical man is Nicodemus. And Peter and Judas and Pilate could have lived in our times. But Nicodemus is specially fitted for our era.

Nicodemus is a pharisee. In the field of religion, the pharisees preached against a spiritless ritualism; in the realm of national life, they called for the independence of Israel; in the community they led a movement adverting to the large crowds of people. It could be said that they were renovators of religion, patriots and civic leaders. They expressed the direction so highly approved in our day.

But we know that man betrays his own ideals, not by abandoning them, but by allowing them to lose their internal values.

Phariseeism, in a hundred years after its zenith, when it was the soul of the nation fighting for its mission, fell into disunion. Abandonment of ritualism became a spiritless formalism; patriotism degenerated into a sickly nationalism; the movement toward the masses was converted into a tendency of ruling the masses without any regard for the people ruled.

Chesterton said this about the old virtues which in our times "went wild": "The pharisees in the time of Christ truly believed that they were the representatives of the best aspirations of their nation. Even today, in Jewish literature, books appear which are proof of the apologia of pharisaism. That is what R. Aron treats in *The Obscure Years of Jesus* and R. Travers Herford in *The Pharisees*.

The man who visited Jesus at night was a man believing himself to be the possessor of the highest ideas. And yet that assurance was linked to a certain mistrust which impelled him to go secretly to the house where lived the Man so bitterly opposed by the whole pharisaic sect. Nicodemus voices opinions the trustworthiness of which he is not at all sure of in the depths of his heart. The set mind of Nicodemus excluded defeat. But defeat was already hanging over his head.

Nicodemus felt bad. He came to Jesus and we understand that he was seeking salvation with this Teacher upon whom they, the teachers of the nation, had declared war. He was like the man of today who runs to the fortune teller with the crystal ball. He was ready to fulfill every foolish thing she might ask him to do.

Jesus recognized at once with whom he had to deal. He spoke to Nicodemus about the necessity of being born anew. Nicodemus looked for a formula to escape the impasse. Jesus pointed out that the truth he was seeking was within himself; it consisted in discovering the real meaning of the formulas that Nicodemus was professing.

Modern man often lives by the magic of words and formulas. Naively he declares: Progress is a good thing; hence everything it brings must be good. Progress is the formula for success.

But if success changes to suffering, what then?

Jesus did not underrate the formulas of Nicodemus. He simply told him to look at the world in a different way than he had been looking, with the eye of a child. Children are the ones who see the things of the Kingdom. For a child, too, the importance of the matter must be measured by a feeling of its worth. Of what value is renewed interest in religion, what is patriotism worth, or social work for the people if they do not proceed from the motive of love?

Was Nicodemus ready to dedicate himself to some cause all his life? Does modern man know how to love? Never was so much said and so much sung about love as today. Love, it is claimed, is something irresistible, but also something that is very quickly forgotten. But Jesus said, "God so loved the world that he gave his only-begotten Son, so that every one who believes in him will not perish...."

In my book Nicodemus lost a beloved child. That's the only being that he loved. Modern man does not know how to love on a broad scale. He knows how to talk a lot about the sufferings of the hungry, the sick, the homeless. About the sufferings of people whom he does not see. Their suffering is a problem for him. The thing looks entirely different when he stands in the presence of a living, suffering man. Then he would rather try to close his eyes. He is even ready to assert that death is the most humanitarian solution for the suffering person.

But the narrow-minded love of Nicodemus gripped the dying body. This pharisee had lost the child-like spirit. Now he was losing his own child. That was the only cause for which he was ready to fight.

For Nicodemus, suffering is the opposite of love. But Jesus showed how closely related these two are. The brazen serpent was the medicine in the desert for the people bitten by serpents. Christ came to be "raised" on the cross for suffering mankind. Suffering is both simultaneously: a disease and a medicine.

Modern man is afraid of suffering. He tries to escape from any form of it. But the realities of this day bring him more suffering than ever before.

Nicodemus was one of us, a contemporary. We are so sure of the truths we possess, and at the same time so helpless when they fail us. We want to love so much, but we do not know how. We dream of a generous offer for the cause, and yet we are afraid of the pain.

If my Nicodemus who, as I intended, is the evangelical Nicodemus, gained so many people, it was perhaps because he laid bare all the fears, weaknesses, and doubts of each one of us, the need of greatness within us, and the subtle seeking of self which deprives us of the greatness of our dreams.

106. To pay with life for the welfare of man

When we speak of Polish candidates for sanctity, and there are about thirty of them at present, mention must be made of the Passionist, Fr. Bernard of the Mother of Beautiful Love.

Sigismund Kryszkiewicz, later Fr. Bernard, belongs to those "saints" whose secret we can discover thanks to the constantly growing familiarity with the thoughts of St. Therese of the Child Jesus. A typically human boy of the lower middle-class, lively, strong, athletic, member of a large loving relationship. He was born May 2, 1915, in Mlawa. Not for religious reasons, for the family was not too keen on religion except for the mother, but because the boy was a slow learner and had to be "pushed," he was sent to a school conducted by the Passionists in Przasznycz.

Sigismund found his way to the Passionists, and stayed with them. No objections from his father and relatives could move him. Suddenly a vocation was born in the boy. In 1934 Kryszkiewicz became a Passionist.

The Passionists, a congregation founded by Paul Daneo, later called Paul of the Cross, a saint little known by us, a hermit and mystic of the eighteenth century. The Passionists came to Poland rather late, only in the 1920s. The work of the Passionists covers every form of mission activity, but their specialty is the direction of the hearts and minds of people to the "life-giving Passion and Death of our Lord Jesus Christ." The Passionists have, as their aim, to teach the people to meditate frequently on this Passion and to "suffer something daily for Christ."

One would judge the specialty is but slightly characteristic. The Passion suffered by Christ is and must be found in the very center of Christian thought. But the beginning of the

Eighteenth Century, that was the victory of the counter reformation and the return, albeit only apparent and external, of the temporary influences of the Church. A sense of power steers the mind away from suffering. The slogan hurled by Paul of the Cross was the call for the future. So often that happens with the great appeals of the saints. The idea of the Passionists was to become the dominating force at the end of the eighteenth century through the nineteenth and into the twentieth century. Italy, where the order originated, was to be drenched in a sea of suffering. Afterwards, all of Europe and then the whole world.

Human sufferings are a mystery which cannot be explained except in the light of Christ's suffering. Christianity in the nineteenth and twentieth centuries had to give the answer to the sufferers. This demand gave the order the power to spread so that in the course of two centuries it grew to unheard-of proportions, took on great significance, and produced two canonized saints: the young cleric Gabriel of the Sorrowful Mother, and the famous Gemma Galgani.

To these Passionists came Kyszkiewicz. He began his studies, first in his own country and then in Rome. But during his sojourn in the Holy City, Bernard developed a troublesome, unidentifiable disease, severe headaches which made it impossible for him to finish his studies. This must have been very painful for a boy full of enthusiasm who doubtless thought that having overcome the opposition of his family, he had already attained everything. God loves to send such surprises to his most fervent adorers. Kryszkiewicz was ordained a priest (without the exam permitting him to hear confessions and preaching sermons) and was sent back to Poland. It was the end of the year 1938. War was hanging in the air.

A bitter return. Unfinished studies, incomplete pastoral rights, unknown illness, which to some seemed to be the beginning of a mental disease.... Really surprising that such trials did not break the 23 year-old man. He was like a bird caught in flight. God, it could be supposed, had refused his sacrifice. For what is a missioner worth if he cannot absolve sinners, or preach the Agony of Christ?

When the war broke out, Bernard found himself in the monastery at Przasnysz. There followed days of dangers, flight, and homeless roaming about. A number of religious from Przasnysz met death. Bernard recovered however with the feeling that "I never even imagined that I was such a coward." But at once a strong determination was beginning to form within him, "to await with peace and patience the moment when help will come from the Father on High."

He took up residence, for the whole time of the occupation, in the monastery at Rama Mazowiecka. The dearest years for Bernard, as well as for the whole generation to which he belonged, would be years of real maturing. The "defeated" religious regained his efficiency; the priest was awarded his rights. After passing his examination in Siedlice, he received his coveted rights to hear confessions and preach sermons. The somewhat naive and overly sentimental, sometimes too sugary type of devotion with which he entered religion, took on vigor. And his head? "Hurts when it isn't needed," he wrote in a letter, "and stops when it is needed."

Crowds of people moved through Rawa, people torn away from their own homes during the war, separated from their nearest and dearest ones, thrown out to wander alone, forever threatened by roundups and dumped to the bottom of misery, hunger, cold, and despair. Suffering people who did not understand suffering! The abyss of all the pain he sees around him tears Bernard away from thinking of his own suffering. Maybe that is the well-known way of the saints: through their own suffering they reach out to the sufferings of Jesus and from the sufferings of Jesus they stoop down to the suffering of another person. Somewhere along the road they lose themselves. To lose self, that is also important. Bernard quickly catches up with this mystery.

Kryszkiewicz gleaned a lot from the thoughts of St. Therese.

The little one, but great saint offered herself to Jesus as a sacrifice of love. Bernard repeats her words, but adds to them these of his own, "With what kind of loving sacrifice of self am I to honor your merciful love? Dear Lord, I do not know how to choose.... Therefore, Lord, I give myself to you entirely so that your most holy will may be fulfilled in me. Everything, whatever you wish...."

From Therese, Bernard learned the truth: God himself ought to decide our way. We should put ourselves in his hands and he will direct us. If on the road, there will be unconquered obstacles, let us not be disturbed, let us leave it to God to remove them. He would not give us our desires if he did not want to satisfy them.

With this understanding, the young religious throws himself into the whirl of action. He becomes the protector of the suffering, the afflicted, the desperate, the rebellious. He utters beautiful words and hurries on to action. In this "coward" appears an unsuspected courage, in this nervous wreck, unusual composure and peace. In this sick individual, incomprehensible powers and strength. He would drag one person out from under the rubble; another by endangering himself he would warn against danger; still another he would take to the hospital between bombings. He would feed one, overcome another's doubts, and snuff out despair in another soul. The war continued, the number of sufferers kept on increasing, but also the popularity of this young, slim, unprepossessing monk who spoke in a soft voice from the pulpit but in the parlor or in the confessional became an unequalled polemist. More and more people began coming to Rawa and to the monastery to seek advice from Fr. Bernard.

He knew how to deal with people. From the time of war there remained a small notebook containing directives written by Fr. Bernard about dealing with a person. Performing the functions of a so-called "spiritual father," he was educating three Passionist-clerics. But the written directives go beyond this narrow sphere, they speak not only of relationship toward religious brothers. They speak of relationship to man, and they speak of the man who wrote the notes.

The pedagogical guides of Bernard state: "Never impose your own view forcibly.... To show the maximum of possible consideration for the convictions of X (one of the three brothers with whom Bernard had the most trouble).... Not to want to be perfect too soon... Not to point out mistakes just for the sake of proving their presence.... Frequently the pointing out of errors is the result not of a sincere concern for the improvement of one's neighbor, but rather of a desire of relieving oneself of a subtle kind of revenge.... To come out of a dilemma, I may be mistaken, and he may be right.... To try to identify with the desires, preferences, fears, and to make allowances for everything in the greatest possible degree (and in the margin the note: how hard this is for me).... Not to seek self, not to seek self.... To be passionately desirous of the good for X; therefore not to count anything too hard, to consider no sacrifice too great, not even one that hurts very much from the viewpoint of one's own greatness, like a mother wearing herself out to the last, never saying: too bad, I'll stop, it's not worth it... At any cost unwearyingly to make life easier for others. To give everything of oneself, and not to demand anything for oneself, neither gratitude nor understanding.... To overdo with kindness.... Not to wait until someone comes to me for help with his trouble, but to go to him myself.... To always have a sincerely pleasant countenance...."

When one reads the Pedagogicum of Fr. Bernard, one is suddenly reminded of John XXIII. The same understanding, goodness, love for man, need of responding with gentleness and self-sacrifice, self-effacement. How much modernity in this "holy" Passionist!

On November 11, 1944, the last anniversary of his religious vows, Fr. Bernard entrusted himself into the hands of her who stood nearest the cross at the moment of the Death on the Cross, and whom this monk had chosen as his teacher of the most beautiful love. In the act of consecration he said: "O Mary, my Mother, Mother of Beautiful Love and Mother of immeasurable sorrow, allow me to love God, to love him without limits or measure, to love him with my own heart and the hearts of millions, to love him as He himself told us to love him. Therefore, allow me to wear myself out, wear out constantly, uninterruptedly, but slowly and imperceptibly, as you yourself did for me, O my incomparable Mother..." We can learn much from this prayer about the man who composed it.

Fr. Bernard must have been aware of the fact that the work he was doing was "wearing him out." No one noticed this on him, but he was conscious of it. He knew. Jesus died for him, and Mary was taking care of him as a most tender mother. He had to answer them in style, caring for other people and dying for them. To die for another, that is to bring up, and to educate a man. There is no other way, if it is to be the way of sanctity.

In March 1945, after the battle for Rawa Mazowiecka, in which the city was destroyed, came the liberation. Kryszkiewicz went to Przasnysz where he was advised to take in hand the restoration of the ruined monastery. But first of all, Fr. Bernard began to take care of the people in the devastated town. Again he went about helping the sick and lifting them up in spirit. In the contaminated air he was stricken with typhoid fever.

He died July 7, 1945, honored by all who knew him.

Fr. Jan Twardowski wrote a verse which begins with these words:

> Father Bernard, Passionist true
> With my clumsy pen I beg of you
> Tell the story of Poland's suffering love
> To all our saints in the realm above.
> Tell them how many people were deathly sick
> While battles raged on, heavy and thick.
> O Holy One of the occupation time,
> Who ate bread with us in dust and grime!

107. God's miser, the story of Blessed Maximilian Kolbe

Introduction

Niepokalanów—the City of the Immaculate Virgin—is spoken of in various ways: respectfully, affectionately, sneeringly, maliciously, ironically. But when we stand within the confines of these low gray huts—unpretentious little wooden barracks—we are convinced that as far as Niepokalanów is concerned it is a matter of utter indifference what people think of it. This does not mean that it is a world wholly separated from ours by a surrounding wall. Niepokalanów is deeply involved in this world, for nothing human is alien to it; at the same time, however, it is so preoccupied with its own business, its own mission, that neither vain praises nor sarcastic words can touch it. For us, people accustomed to loud noises in boisterous streets, it is not easy to understand Niepokalanów. We, as well as non-Catholics and nominal Catholics only, are wont to tie-up our endeavors with foreseeable results; hence only a tangible power do we consider real. Niepokalanów's something that belies this axiom. It does not pursue perceptible effects; nor does it seek power. That is precisely why we are witnesses of the most incredible results, and of a force that can move mountains.

Here at Niepokalanów began to appear publications of the greatest output imaginable; here was a confluence of the thought of many people that would not have been reached by other means. And this is an extraordinary fact: Niepokalanów was never a triumph of an "electoral college"—that is, people of a strong head on a strong neck. No, Niepokalanów passed through various phases in the course of its fifty years of existence. Many friars broke down and left. Others perished, died. Niepokalanów lived through diverse experiences and endured many trials. Yet it lives today and exerts its influence.

What then is Niepokalanów: people or an idea? Above all, it is the concept of an ever-living Franciscanism. Today's civilization with all its grandeur is a constant mortal peril for mankind. We are like sorcerer's pupils who unwittingly have set free the imprisoned powers in his laboratory. We did this with the best intention, but as the old proverb says: the road to hell is paved with good intentions. What was originally created to help man has become a threat to his welfare.

Contemporary civilization wants to create for man, but it has ceased to care for man himself. It promises him an ever easier life, but an ever easier life is too low an ideal for man. Man must know that he is living for *something*—and not merely for ever greater comforts, ever more numerous pleasures, ever faster movement. In portraying man's future, contemporary civilization has forgotten that the man who sees only ever greater comforts and pleasures for himself in the future becomes a monster of egoism. To release the atom and expose the universe—and place all this in the hands of a thoroughly egoistic man—that would be creating a perspective of a cataclysm that could tear a whole world apart.

Niepokalanów is not a denial of progress and civilization. It is an idea which says that technical progress is necessary and very important, but it must be in the service of something greater. Progress must not be hindered but man must be educated to fit this progress. The higher the human mind reaches, so much more humble must man become. The more good civilization produces the more important is the equal distribution of it in brotherly love. Niepokalanów is the concept of bringing progress into the role of serving human needs—not whims or fancies.

However, even so profound a concept would be worthless it if were not for the people. People had to be found who would conceive and incarnate such an idea. In the history of the Church there are such people; they are the saints....

A saint is not merely a hero, a discoverer, a creator. We can easily deal with those titles. The title of saint has a mystic meaning. Only God designates his saints—the known and the unknown.

Let us not say that there are no saints today! Perhaps no other generation has seen so many in their midst. The time will come when others will speak of us as of those who saw and heard and touched with their own hands. Then we will witness and we shall have to bear witness.

God Himself designates saints, but it is given to man in his human dealings to bring to fruition the making of a saint. Hence wherever there arises an all important idea so definitely predestined for a certain period, there, underneath all the trappings, will be found the pulsating heart of a saint.

That saint had to be laying the groundwork of the little barracks in the city of the Immaculata, as I had already written in 1946. Today we know that it is really so. And there may be the blood of more than one saint.

Is it surprising that we were seeking a saint in the man who was the founder of Niepokalanów, who himself lived by its sublime idea and grafted it like buds onto others, and who at last voluntarily gave up his life for this idea?

Whoever visited Niepokalanów had to see the face of its founder, Fr. Maximilian Kolbe.

The man

Let us take a look at his photograph. A man with a long beard in the prime of life, a high and wide forehead, determined, bespectacled, with deeply penetrating eyes, furrowed brows giving the face a somewhat severe appearance, well-nigh forbidding. Upon further scrutiny, the look begins to lose its grim aspect, the eyes appear more and more tranquil, almost tender, and at the same time betray hidden pain. Looking a little longer, the large lips surmounted by a bushy mustache seem to quiver slightly as though about to smile....

At first sight we meet a man full of willpower, startling energy, determination and decision. Courageous—not afraid of hunger, cold, inconvenience, antagonism—fears neither slander nor prejudice. There is no hesitation about him, nor weakness. He is a calculator: he counts and measures, figures endlessly, appraises and makes estimates, draws up budgets and issues financial estimates. He is well acquainted with everything; with motors, presses, linotypes, and radios. He knows what is cheap and what is expensive; what, where and when to buy things. His letters are replete with original sketches drawn with one stroke of his pen and with plans which transcend the present moment. His handwriting is determined, masculine, resolute. He writes anywhere and everywhere, on the edge of a table, on his knee in a moving train. Thus the individual letters overlap somewhat, but the context retains its full concrete strength. Never does he have enough time for correspondence; his letters consist of fragments added to at times even on the sealed envelope. He sprints to the letter, writes without thought of style, and returns again to his interrupted work. He is everlastingly in a hurry... never has any time. "Life is short," he writes, "therefore we must use time well... be MISERS OF TIME." Sick as he was with tuberculosis, he would outrun the youngest of the brothers as they dashed from building to building. Riding a bicycle, his companions would inevitably be left behind. No vehicle was fast enough for him; had he lived to the era of jets he would have used nothing else... or maybe missiles. It was not a matter of importance to him where a man dwelled, what food he ate or clothing he wore; the all-important thing was the speed of action. He lived feverishly to accomplish as much as possible. In a letter he writes,... "to overwork, to tire oneself out, to be counted as nothing... looked down upon as not much less than a maniac even by one's own... thus annihilated, to die for the Immaculate Virgin. And since we live only once in this world, and not a second time, it behoves us to deepen the meaning of the above phrases in a truly miserly way so that our love for the Immaculata can prove itself by conquering the whole world, the hearts of all and of each one individually beginning with oneself. He signs the letter: "One beside himself for the Immaculata" (A fool for the Immaculate Virgin).

Here then is the first impression, the unadorned external appearance of Father Kolbe: impetuosity personified, a firebrand, a fool for Christ who destroys himself and drives others to action.

But underneath the skin of this man of God we see another individual well-nigh crushed by the onslaught of a fatal disease. A consumptive since the year 1921, he lived with only one lung in an unabated feverish condition. Time after time doctors consigned him to the next world. In the pocket of his habit he carried several death notices. He suffered severe gastric pains that lasted several days at a time. In the summer his frozen hands caused him much trouble. He very nearly lost the putrefying finger of his right hand, which would have been tragic because without it he could not have been ordained. One of his confreres wrote of him: . . . "He was extremely nervous. Due to complete exhaustion, he often suffered a severe shock during which, if at a meal, he could not even hold on to a spoon. At times he could not sit still, then he would get up and walk. In this nervous state he would sometimes hear confessions, and there in the confessional in utter misery, he would move his body from one side to the other. . . ."

For a man with his infirmities it was not an easy thing to volunteer for the missions. After he had gone, he would write "Just imagine what it means to go on mission. Someone goes on a mission full of enthusiasm and satisfaction. But in this zeal there is a good bit of self-love, seeing new countries, oceans, etc. That is all right if it is not the real objective. Then he arrives at his destination—everything is new and fresh. Children love variety, as St. Teresa used to say. But when the ordinary day-to-day work begins—hot in summer—a person perspires and weakens; in winter it is wet and cold. In another place the mosquitoes bite and there is no rest even at night, bedbugs too are plentiful. The climate is bad and hardly bearable. The food is so different. I ate only bread and some fruit because I could not consume their dainty dishes. However, I had to overcome myself in order not to offend anyone. Suspicion is rampant; the secret police can be found everywhere; no one is trusted. Contemptuous shouts are heard and at times even a stone is hurled at an unsuspecting missioner. When the children are given anything, they take it with one hand and grab it with the other... Then too, disagreeable differences can arise among the friars... Add to all this homesickness for your fatherland... frustration, disillusionment, temptations. Mission is no guarantee against temptation; hence only the soul that perseveres in prayer will overcome everything...."

The furious energy of his activity was balanced by many sufferings. We understand why he was in such a hurry. He knew that he did not have too much time for his work, and that work was growing from an idea that was no trifling matter. Father Maximilian was concerned not merely about the friary, not about the City of the Immaculata, not even about Poland. He was concerned about the whole world! His watchword was, "To conquer the world for the Immaculata!"

We return to this matter again. There was in Father Maximilian a third personality so deeply hidden that it was not always recognized even by the best of his friends. Father Maximilian was a man with the gift of knowledge. Not just human knowledge, which very often is simply a lack of knowledge. Father Maximilian *knew*. What he knew he did not always want to divulge, nor did he always know how to say it. Human thought is often lost in words. And what about knowledge that cannot be weighed on a human scale? Once he said with a touch of melancholy in his voice, "I am not able to explain everything about the Immaculata to you!" On another occasion, "I would tell you something, but maybe this is not yet the time for it...." And concerning himself (In the year 1938), "I will not live much longer and I will not remain with you much longer...."

At times in conversation with others there came upon him such a bright flash of knowledge. One day during the war, Father Maximilian was playing chess with some of the brothers. He liked to play and during the game he would chat. He said, "One of the brothers was telling me that in his sleep he heard a voice saying to him that in thirteen days we will not be here. I said to him, "Let us wait and see. Well, thirteen days have gone by and we are still here. You know, my children, that was the devil talking to our brother just as he cried out to Bernadette of Lourdes, 'Run, run away!' But the Mother of God with a frown on her face looked in that direction and immediately all was quiet. At that time Mary also wrinkled her brows...." He stopped short... and said to his partner: "Hurry up, brother; move, for I am waiting." This secret knowledge of his, he fearfully tried to hide from his brothers which created the appearance of something abnormal, a thing so inconsistent with his open nature. Until he gave evidence of being a talented organizer he was not really appreciated in the Order. It was said, "Yes, saintly, but a tiresome bore." They made fun of him, jocosely calling him "holy marmalade." Years of strenuous work were necessary to prove the obvious, that this secrecy and deep concentration was Father Maximilian's conscious way of hiding his flourishing life of the soul. Father Kolbe feared that he would be misunderstood, that he might be more highly appreciated than he deserved. Hence he tried to conceal his knowledge as did St. Francis, his stigmata.

But one of his mysteries we know. To understand it, however, we shall have to leave Father Maximilian for a while and revive the once lively lad of Pabianice, Raymond Kolbe.

The choice

The Kolbe Family was a family of fabric weavers for the growing industry in the city of Lódz. The mother, nee Dabrowska, reared her boys in the Catholic tradition. She had three sons: Francis, Raymond, and Joseph.

Raymond was born in the year 1894. When he was eleven years-old the city of Lódz was sizzling with unrest. Revolutionary feelings took possession of the workers. They were all for the revolution because their exploitation was enormous and the industry was in foreign hands.

The Kolbes moved from Zduńska Wola (where Raymond had been born) to Pabianice. Here the father "kept" a small grocery store which barely provided for the family a sustenance. This store was a trade-in for his former weaver's shop. The mother added a little income by serving as a midwife. Thus, both were involved in the very undercurrent of the labor trouble. In the store where the wives of the workmen came to buy provisions, and in the homes of the new-born babes, they heard constant complaints about the unconcern of the capitalists and the "jungle" of furious battles going on for profits, such as W. Reymont described in his novel *The Promised Land.*

Both parents were practicing Catholics and they understood that wrongdoing could not be eradicated by hatred of the individuals. Raymond's father and mother belonged to the Franciscan Third Order. Before her marriage, the mother had thought about a religious vocation. When she consented to the marital union she resolutely declared that it must be a truly Christian marriage. Mr. Kolbe agreed, and that was not an easy promise, because it required real heroism of poor people in a world of gangrenous egoism. Of their five sons, only three survived; the other two succumbed to the weavers' disease, consumption. But it was difficult to provide for the education of even these three. Therefore the little store was assigned to Raymond who was the best of them in mathematics.

In their home, behind some cupboards was a tiny chapel ... a crucifix on the wall, a picture of the Blessed Mother of God ... some flowers before them, fresh ones in spring and summer, and paper ones in winter. No doubt there was some holy water in a bottle and a glass paperweight with a picture of the Bright Hill. The boys' certificates of their First Holy Communion were most probably hanging on the wall too. In this private little chapel the young Raymond often knelt to pray and weep. That attracted the attention of his mother who took her son to task. But he only said, "It's a secret."

She convinced him that a small boy should keep no secret from his own mother. Then he told her that when he prayed in church and asked our Blessed Lady to tell him what will become of him in the future, the Mother of God became alive for him in the picture and showing him two crowns—a white one and a red one—said: "This white crown is the crown of chastity; the red one, that is the crown of martyrdom. They are both destined for you. Do you want them?"

He answered: "I do,"—words that were not an empty promise for him. Just as his father, when he expressed his consent to the marital condition of his betrothed, so now Raymond accepted the decision for life. It would be useless to try to determine whether the episode related by his mother only after the death of Father Maximilian was a real miracle, or only a miraculous response of his interior life. Teresa of Avila experienced a physical shock upon looking at a sculpture of the crucified Jesus; Teresa of Lisieux saw a smile on the face of a statue of the Mother of God. Neither one of them ever claimed that she witnessed a miracle; and yet what each one saw determined her way of life.

Now something ethereal broke through in little Raymond. Slowly—for only very slow transformations are really lasting—in his mind an idea began to crystallize that would in time become the call of his knighthood: "To conquer the world for the Immaculata!" In the meantime, however, little Raymond Kolbe was preparing himself to be a storekeeper while his older brother Francis attended school.

But lo and behold! A fortuitous meeting! There would be many such eventful occurrences in the life of Father Maximilian. The pharmacist in Pabianice took an interest in the bright boy and decided to tutor the boy in his own home. Thanks to the earnest teaching of the druggist, Raymond caught up to Francis and the two of them together finished their third class in the commercial school, the highest educational institution in Pabianice, and both desired to become priests.

In the same dramatic year of 1905, Franciscan missionaries from Lwów came to Pabianice. The main speaker was Father Peregrine Haczela who announced from the pulpit that the Franciscan minor seminary was accepting candidates for the Order. At once Francis and Raymond applied for admission. There was no doubt about the suitability of the first one, the parents decided to let him go. But as for Raymond, they shook their heads. Who will help them when Raymond goes? Who will run the store when this son who is so brilliant in calculation will not be there anymore? Raymond pleaded but was not insistent. He had a natural ability to make his own decisions but at the same time he feared succumbing to his own self-will. He knew what he wanted, yet he waited. In the monastery he would saddle decisions on his superior. When he himself became the guardian he would cast the burden of decision upon the Immaculate Virgin.

And so it was in truth that she made decisions for him in everything in his life. He did not insist, but his parents yielded. Both brothers went to the minor seminary in Lwów.

Life in the monastic atmosphere was quiet and peaceful. The boys studied, and Raymond excelled in mathematics. His head was full of exotic ideas, e.g., of building a sky-rocket-like missile, calling it ethereoplane that would go the moon. At another time he would dream about an apparatus that would let him hear sounds from ages past. His imagination was fantastic, but controlling it was his good sober business sense so that more than one of his foolhardy ideas came to reality in his lifetime. He did not fly to the moon, but surely only because the Immaculata did not want to see him there. The voices from ages past, however, he did hear later on, in the subterranean cells of block 11 in Auschwitz.

Together the two brothers reached the seventh class, a time of decision. Both wanted to be priests but both had doubts about becoming Franciscans. It is not easy to observe the rule of the Friars Minor approved by Pope Honorius III at the request of St. Francis and his companions. It takes up the matter briefly and succinctly: "The life of the Friars Minor is this: to observe the holy gospel of Our Lord Jesus Christ living in obedience, without possessions and in chastity."

The hardest thing for Raymond was probably obedience. For a man determined as he was to shake the whole world, that was not an easy decision to make. Raymond was born with the fever of greatness in his heart. In the world he could certainly become someone outstanding. But he felt that on his path to eternity, submission to obedience is essential. He wanted to be obedient to the Immaculate Virgin, but she asked him to be obedient to man.

Poverty? Raymond's parents were poor people. Ordinarily, the poor thirst for riches. However, both his parents and Raymond himself understood the value of moderation in all things. But from moderation to total deprivation is a long way. The feeling for ownership was imbedded in Ray's blood. He knew from experience what it meant to have your own shop, your own store, your own piece of land. If he followed St. Francis he would not have the right to call anything his own. "Real communism," he would say later, "is right here with us." And chastity? It would be naive to think that the future founder of Niepokalanów had no temptations to overcome in this regard. One does not get the white crown for nothing. Man does not take the necessary precautions if he feels no dread of danger. Setting out for Rome he wrote to his mother: "Please say a special prayer for me, that's all I need... for there will be many temptations. I have heard, for instance, that women in Rome accost even the religious...." All his life, Father Kolbe continued to edify his religious brothers with his apparent fear of the danger of losing this virtue... not only losing, but even of diminishing his power of resistance,.. of suffering the slightest imperfection. Raymond must have known well the heavy burden of these three vows. He had vowed chastity early in life and meant to keep his promise. But obedience and poverty seemed to be a bit too hard for him. He decided to leave the monastery and was on his way to the provincial to report his decision when the bell called him to the parlor. His mother had come to see him.

What was Mrs. Kolbe doing in Lwów? She had come there with a big decision. Religious at heart, although she had yielded to the will of God in becoming a wife and mother, she still yearned for the peace and quiet of a convent cell. Her life as mother had come to an end. The last one, her youngest son Joseph, had also gone to the Franciscans in Lwów. Without responsibilities must she remain in a world full of gossip and noise? After an understanding communication with her husband, Mr. Kolbe joined the Franciscan tertiaries in Krakow; and the mother, having made an unsuccessful attempt to join the Franciscans in Assisi, decided to enter the Benedictines in Lwów.

That was what she came to tell her son. This talk with his mother caused Raymond to change his plan and he decided to become a friar. He would enter upon his novitiate September 4, 1910.

From now on there was no Raymond, only Brother Maximilian: he who aspires to maximum: the greatest.

Twenty-two years later this same man who hesitated to take upon himself the obligation of obedience would ask his superiors and would try to persuade his confreres to voluntarily take a fourth vow of absolute obedience to go on mission to whatever place the will of the superior will direct them. He wrote in a letter from Japan in March 1932, "The brothers here (and I with them) have taken into consideration these four points: 1. that neither our rule nor our constitutions oblige us to be ready to go on mission; 2. that no one can truly be a client of the Immaculate Virgin without surrendering himself to her without reservations; 3. that "de facto" at present our Father Provincial cannot command anyone of us to go to a place beyond the boundaries of Poland; 4. that no war carried on under such a system wherein the general would have to ask a soldier whether he likes his assignment... would have much of a chance of victory. Hence we have sent a petition to our Father Provincial to permit us to add to our present monastic vows this one also... that we will be ready to undergo anything and everything for our Immaculate Virgin, even the loss of our life, if need be."

Danger discovered

Two years later we see Brother Maximilian in Rome. The European horizon became gravely darkened; underground thundering resounded throughout the Balkan State. Poland found herself at the crossroads. On the one hand she sought self-preservation from Russia, undergoing so many internal conflicts; on the other hand, fighting brigades and future legions were preparing for a confrontation with the Central Powers, Germany and Austria-Hungary.

Brother Maximilian hurriedly finished philosophy, then theology at the International Franciscan College. He studied much but even more he deepened his spiritual life. He flung himself on the road of understanding the mysteries of sanctity. Two saints drew him with special attraction: the recently beatified Joseph Cottolengo, founder of the House of Providence in Turin, and "little" Thérèse of Lisieux, not yet even beatified. The writings of Thérèse, then known by the title given by the sister of the saint: *The Story of a Soul,* were highly recommended as unusually "valuable" reading. Maximilian practically devoured the book. He was spellbound by the theory of "footpaths"—childlike trust in Divine Love. Maximilian who seemed to be the incarnation of energy and creative art, entrusted himself to Thérèse and lets himself be guided by her experience, in spite of the fact that for many, she seemed to be "passive" and "sugar-coated." There was something striking in this paradox: to unite the desire of the greatest effort with blind trust!

Maximilian saw the way to Jesus leads through the Immaculata. "Let us try... to be a perfect instrument," he says, "to allow the Immaculate Virgin to direct us, for that is the essence of sanctity." Another time, he writes that, God gave us Mary, "in order not to punish us, to restrain his justice as much as possible. Thus by dedicating ourselves to her we are instruments of God's mercy in her hands, just as she is the instrument of mercy in God's hand."

He wrote to his mother, underlining the words... "in everything I acknowledge the special protection of the Immaculata."

On April 6, 1914, he experienced the miraculous cure of his gangrenous finger threatened with amputation. Where medicine failed, Lourdes water helped.

With his eyes fixed on the picture of the Immaculata, Maximilian was constantly coming closer to the view which he finally expressed thus: "Mary, as the Mother of Jesus, our Redeemer, became the co-redemptrix of the human race; and as the Spouse of the Holy Spirit she participates in the distribution of all graces." In 1921 Cardinal Mercier obtained for Belgium the permission from the Apostolic See to celebrate the feast of Our Lady, Mediatrix of all Graces. From 1934 the Franciscans also had the privilege of placing this feast on their religious calendar. Father Maximilian would be one of these who contributed to the finalization of the principle on which will rest the future dogma of the all-powerful mediatorship of Mary.

In 1914 Brother Maximilian pronounced his final religious vows and received Minor Orders. To his mother he wrote, "As I took my vows I added the name Mary." In the meantime World War I broke out. Brother Maximilian as a "Russian subject" had to lead a hidden life for some time in the monastery at San Marino. Later on, he returned to Rome to resume his interrupted studies.

After many years he reminisced: "War broke out in Poland.

Large numbers of Polish patriots joined the army. Not a few clerics exchanged their monastic habits for soldiers' uniforms. Some returned; other did not.... Had I remained in Krakow, no doubt I would have done the same for I was strongly attracted to military service." One of those who went and did not return was Brother Maximilian's older brother, Francis. His father Julius also enlisted in the legions. Taken as a captive in Olkusz in 1914, as a Russian subject he was treated as a deserter and executed.

While war raged in Europe, Italy was being overwhelmed by a powerful wave of Masonic demonstrations. By focusing on Austria's pro-Catholic beliefs, Italian Freemasonry, always anti-Catholic, posed a serious threat of anti-Church violence. Brother Kolbe observed this phenomenon and immediately sought a remedy in his own energetic way. Freemasonry wanted war. Very well, then let there be a war. But war for a Christian always means a war for the sake of a person. "Napoleon said, to win a war three things are necessary: money, money, money. To attain heaven, sanctity, three things are also necessary: prayer, prayer, prayer. Everything depends on the quality of the prayer."

Only through prayer, by means of holiness does the road lead to victory. Brother Kolbe communicated with a few like-minded enthusiasts and in great secrecy but with the approval of their immediate superiors, on October 17, exactly four days after the great miracle at Fatima, seven zealots organized the Militia of the Immaculata (M.I.). They were, besides Kolbe, Peter Pall, Kwirikus, Pignalberti, Anthony Glowinski, Henry Granata, and Anthony Mansi.

What was the Militia to be? The army of the Immaculate Virgin! Its objective: To work for the conversion of sinners, heretics, schismatics, etc., but especially of freemasons, and for the sanctification of all men under the protection and through the intercession of the most holy Immaculate Virgin Mary. The conditions of membership in the Militia were: "To surrender oneself completely to the most holy Immaculate Virgin Mary as a tool in her spotless hands and to wear the miraculous medal." This is the medal that was coined on the testimony of St. Catherine Laboure in her visions of 1830.

"The members of the M.I." wrote Father Kolbe, "surrender themselves to the Immaculata unconditionally to be used as an instrument for whatever she herself is doing, i.e., to conquer the devil and aid souls in self-sanctification." Two texts served as a motto, "She shall crush thy head," and "You have destroyed all heresies yourself. It is not written that she destroys all heretics for she loves all souls."

What were the particular means of the activity of the M.I.? "Every legitimate means allowed by one's state of life, conditions, and circumstances." Later, Father Kolbe completed the directives: the acts are personal good example, prayer, suffering and work.... Concerning prayer, the members tried to turn to the Immaculata daily with the prayer engraved on the miraculous medal: O Mary conceived without sin pray for us who have recourse to thee, adding, and for all who have recourse to thee, especially for the freemasons and those recommended to thee.

"For the consolation of fervent souls," Kolbe continued, "it must be noted that the essence of the consecration to the Immaculate Virgin does not depend on the actual constant remembrance of her, but on the will to do so. Thus a soul wholly engaged in the perfect performance of her duty does not cease to belong to the Immaculate Virgin; and so even without thinking of it, all her thoughts, words and deeds do not cease to be those of the Immaculate Virgin."

The little medals and this prayer were successful. Maximilian bestowed medals upon everybody, and when war came with its murderous occupants—to them too, his future murderers—Father Maximilian would offer his soul saving little medals.

Misunderstood

From the very beginning, the formation of the Militia placed Brother Maximilian (who in a short time, April 28, 1918, became

Father Maximilian) in a difficult position in his own monastery. Not many friars understood him. Only a few saw in him the consistent accomplisher of the will of the Immaculate Virgin. The majority looked upon him as a harum-scarum tossing about unrealistic idiotic ideas. They spoke of the Militia with forbearance: "Oh, just another pious devotional organization."

Not even statistics could convince them, and they were interesting numbers. The Militia, with 25 Polish members in 1917, grew to 450 in 1920, to 84,000 in 1926, and reached 700,000 in 1933. Daily, three quarters of a million people recited the prayer for sinners and freemasons. Whoever knows the influence of prayer understands why so many people were converted during the war.

But all of this happened gradually.

Father Maximilian returned to a free Poland in 1919. His mother was now with the Felician Sisters in Krakow. He returned homesick. Consumption, which had killed two of his brothers, now attacked him, too.

In January 1920, just half a year after his arrival, he notified his friends in Rome that in Krakow there appeared the *Knight of the Immaculata,* the official organ of the Militia, with a circulation of 5,000 copies. It was a premature announcement.

In August 1920, the superiors sent Father Maximilian to Zakopane at the foot of the Tatra Mountains. Here he spent eleven months while tuberculosis consumed his lungs and hemorrhages exhausted his system. Although confined to a chair or couch, he was not idle. He planned projects, organized the Militia for distant centers, prepared his *Knight,* and at the same time was concerned with the people around him. He gave them all his little medals.

Somewhat improved in health, although far from cured, he returned to Krakow. Since he could not teach in the seminary, to which he had been assigned, he spent his time on the *Knight.*

The initial publication of the *Knight* was a bombshell that shook the very foundations of the whole monastery. Years later he would tell his brothers, "You will hear many comments and jest on the subject of the consecration of oneself to the Immaculata. The bishop expelled Blessed Grignon de Montfort from the diocese, albeit the Holy Father personally approved of his spreading devotion. His own brother, a Dominican, would not speak to him, not the pagans, but his own people were his greatest adversaries."

"Have your head examined Maxie," they said to him time and time again. "Are you out of your mind?" Sickly, a hemorrhaging invalid wants to edit a publication! Where will you get the means? You will only plunge the Order in debt, compromise it, and expose it to ridicule."

But what could be done with the obstinate fellow? His projects found favor with the Franciscan Master of Novices, Father Venance Katarzyniak who died shortly in the "odor of sanctity." The early difficulties were verily overpowering. Later on, Father Kolbe would reminisce, "I sent the question to Fr. Venance as well as to others: what about it?" (that is, the publication of the *Knight*). He answered humbly, "If my advice can do any good, I am of the opinion that the organ of the Militia should be published as soon as possible." In a short time he was forced to take to his bed by the ravaging powers of consumption, and died. A whole year elapsed before I made an attempt to put the advice of the deceased Father in action. On November 25, 1921, the Militia treasury owed 40 Polish marks. There was no source of income or dependable support. One of the Fathers expressed himself thus: If the monthly were to come out in January, that would be a miracle; but since there will be no miracle, there will be no January issue. Turning to the clerics he said, "Pray to the Mother of God through the intercession of Father Venance." And, I do not know myself how it happened, but the first number actually appeared in January. The entire capital collected paid for that issue, and again there was no money for February. In addition I became seriously ill. Burning with high fever, I turned to Father Venance, and unexpectedly came the necessary money. I cannot refrain from making known such evident response from Father Venance . . . and his last words cry out to be heard: "I am sick and can no longer do anything, but after my death I will do much for the Order."

Not doubting the preternatural intervention of Father Venance, I am reminded that it is very much like the interventions of St. Philomena whose aid St. John Vianney called upon. "I am nothing," he would repeat, "St. Philomena does everything."

Father Kolbe issued the first of the *Knight* practically alone. He collected the necessary funds by going begging from store to store. That was not easy for him, he acknowledged that he did not know how to do it. What he collected he had to spend immediately. The prices were rocketing sky-high and inflation was running wild. In the monastery the cry could be heard: Into what troubles will the idiot hurl us? How will we pay our debts? We are a religious order, with the vow of poverty. Does father understand this?

He understood. Poverty obligates only people, for the Immaculata, nothing should be spared. The *Knight* is for her; it will teach the people who the Immaculate Virgin is, and that the whole world is to be consecrated to her.

One day when there was no money to pay the printer the 500 marks for the publication, an unknown woman placed an envelope containing the exact amount of money on the altar in the Franciscan church. She had also written a verse on the envelope. The verse was very poor but the money served to pay for the monthly.

In 1922 there was a printers' strike in Krakow. The *Knight* could not be published. But that was no great problem with Father Maximilian. He decided that since the monthly could not be published in Krakow he would find another place and suddenly the whole publishing outfit was transferred to Grodno.

But here too, it was no easy job. They worked first in one print shop, then in a second, finally in a third one without satisfaction. All at once it dawned on Father Maximilian—open his own print shop.

Again there was the outcry in the friary by those who knew little of the world. Buy a printing press? That "chief of the Knights" has completely lost his head! The monastery cannot make sacrifices so that he can "play" at editing a magazine!

Yet it came to pass that Father Maximilian found a willing "listener," and obtained the necessary permission from his superiors. The unexpected money fell, as it were, from the heavens—the entire sum of $100—and an old printing press was found.

Then the work began. The machine had to be turned by hand which required the utmost effort since for a 16-page *Knight* with a circulation of 5,000, the wheels had to be turned 80,000 times, and the whole staff consisted of three persons. They took a respite when momentarily something broke in the machine, and there were many such breaks. Then they cranked again. It took ten days to print an issue. It had to be folded, packed, and addressed, then, the type rearranged, the copy written and prepared for the next number. In March 1925 the circulation was up to 25,000 copies. They began to look around for a little motor.

Maybe the steadily growing job would have been too much for Father Maximilian if he had not found among his helpers another candidate for sainthood: Brother Albert Olszakowski. However, Olszakowski worked so hard he exhausted his strength and died in 1926 . . . but what he did, he did. After many years, Father Maximilian wrote, "Some people claim that Niepokalanów is already existing in heaven where the Guardian is the Immaculate Virgin, and the workers are Fr. Gorden, Fr. Venance, Fr. Alphonse (the youngest brother of Fr. Maximilian who later on in the Order had become a very zealous co-worker of Maximilian), and Brother Albert." Father Kolbe spoke up about receiving new applicants for the brotherhood and again there was a violent outburst of opposition What? So many brothers? And what will we do with them when the whole print shop breaks down? Who will feed them all? Everyone that comes to work on the *Knight* immediately becomes a brother, and even holds an important office in the establishment. Surely, the world is turning upside down!

After some years, Father Kolbe confessed to his brothers, "I wanted to remind you of certain graces that the Immaculate Virgin granted you. In the first years of the *Knight,* how much unpleasantness I had to bear! In December, when the doors were open to the brothers in Grodno, they said to me: Sure, it's a manorial farm; the friary supports them all. But when he will have to go on his own resources, the brothers will have to go. Just recently (in 1938—the year of the greatest flowering of Niepokalanów—my observation) I heard the same kind of prophecy: As long as they are all young, they can help themselves; but when they get old, who will keep this up? Moreover, when they start to die off, we will have to offer Masses for the dead all year long! There's no end of difficulties, as there never has been. If the Immaculata had not given me the necessary strength and light, there would not have been a place here for you..."

The publishing staff now numbered twenty-two members for whom it paid the cost of maintenance to the friary. It should not be assumed however that the sudden and numerous recruiting of friars was due solely to the urgent need of many hands in the huge workshop required at that time by the *Knight.*

Fr. Maximilian considered the question of vocation and total consecration to the service of the Immaculate Virgin a matter of principle. "Only he who has dedicated himself entirely to the Immaculate Virgin," he used to repeat, has the right to live off the offerings people give to the Mother of God." So there must be a place here for everyone that has a true vocation. But those who do not have a genuine vocation, let them leave as soon as possible. At one time the Rev. Provincial limited the enrollment to a certain number, and those that came beyond that number did not persevere. I consider it a great grace of the Immaculate Virgin that I did not yield then; there is a place here for you and there will be for many others and Divine Providence will sustain us. I had to listen to much talk from various sources. Indeed the Immaculate Virgin had to uphold and reassure me a lot not to change my mind..."

During the war he would keep saying, "Even if you would have to die, for the many graces you have already received in religion it would be worth dying."

This man actually democratized the monastery. He raised the brother from the position of subordinate assistant to the role of knight. He opened the door to the brotherhood and created at Niepokalanów a characteristically genuine community. He put spirit into the technical work of publication.

Niepokalanów

However new difficulties arose. Grodno on the eastern border, far from the center of the country, was not the ideal spot for the publishing business of a magazine growing so fast in popularity. Moreover, a living contact of the editors with the readers demanded a change of location. Father Kolbe had been thinking about this for a long time.

Five years had elapsed since the first publication of the *Knight*. The magazine had received the blessing of Pope Pius XI and the Polish episcopate. Father Kolbe had a relapse and was obliged to rest at Zakopane from September 1926 to April 1927, during which time he was forbidden by his superiors to have anything to do with the publication. That did not come easily to a man whose whole life was the Militia and the *Knight*, but he was an obedient friar. "Obedience," he wrote, "that's conformity of our will with the will of God; that's the essence of holiness."

Again a stroke of luck! In June 1927, Fr. Maximilian, in speaking with the pastor of Adamowicze, Father Ciborowski, learned that there was a possibility of obtaining a piece of land in Teresina near Sochaczew from Prince Drucki-Lubiecki. Immediately he started negotiations. "For the price" of offering perpetual Masses, as though Masses could be paid for, Fr.

Maximilian obtained a five acre piece of land. The provincial chapter, however, refused to accept the terms laid down by the prince of twenty-six Masses annually in perpetuity—two of which were to be offered in the palace of the prince. In spite of this, the prince, persuaded by Father Maximilian, offered the land to the Order unconditionally. On August 6, 1927, the statue of the Immaculate Virgin was blessed on the newly acquired land, and construction began in October. On November 21, the printing establishment with two Fathers and eighteen Brothers transferred from Grodno to Niepokalanów. On December 8, the canonical blessing took place. Thus Niepokalanów came into being. Wooden barracks went up one after another and the printing presses were assembled in them. Niepokalanów was not to be a traditional brick monastery. It was envisioned as a cluster of primitive little huts to serve simply as a shelter, comprising the bare necessities for human occupation with no luxuries and no conveniences. A few years later Father Kolbe wrote from Japan in a distressful tone, "The announcement about building a permanent monastery aroused a feeling of fear that Niepokalanów may be slowly moving toward mediocrity...." Before the founding of Niepokalanów Father Kolbe wrote to his brother Fr. Alphonse, "I was telling you that one of our Fathers proposed, not to expand any more—there are enough machines; now we will have an income... Let souls perish, we will have an income—what a bailiwick! Then indeed the curse of St. Francis would have to fall upon such a thing ensuring a peaceful existence, as it did at one time on a thriving bailiwick of the "lordly Franciscans" (as we were called in Italy). The breakdown of such a factory, or its confiscation would then be a blessing from heaven so that the lordly Brothers might again become the poor Brothers Minor and take to the work of saving souls, even if it be under the threat of not having a piece of bread to eat...."

Miser? Yes, a miser who regrets spending extra on a more convenient house, or a brighter, cooler cell? It is still heard in

Niepokalanów: "... if it weren't for the will of Father Maximilian we would have much more spacious buildings here." If anyone ever poured the old Franciscan wine of poverty into new leather bottles of the 20th century, it was Father Kolbe.

It was said, "He's in a hurry; that's why he builds any old which way." Indeed he was in a hurry. But when it concerned the building of Niepokalanów it was the principle that determined his action: everything of the best for the *cause*—the newest, most modern machines and the swiftest means of transportation. Then the miser ceased to be miserly. But no luxuries for the people; Franciscans must remain a wandering fraternity. Only those wholly detached from the comforts and things of this world can go to preach to the fishes, the birds, the people....

In 1930, Fr. Maximilian, leaving Niepokalanów in the hands of his brother Fr. Alphonse and his plans in the hearts of his brothers, resolved upon traveling to the eastern coast of Asia to establish the second Marytown there. One man plows, another sows the seed, yet a third will reap..., that's the principle of missionary effort. Father Kolbe dreamt of new Marytowns: in Japan, in India, in China, in America, England....

But when he spoke of these plans the outcry burst forth: What? What? To Asia? What a dreamer! Has he lost his mind? This man will never learn to think in a realistic way!

Mu genzai no Seibo no Kishi

There came a day when Fr. Maximilian said to the brothers, "Whenever there are irritations among you, I feel them most painfully. That's the only affliction I have in general. If with the aid of the Immaculate Virgin I could help such a brother to sanctify himself, I would gladly give up my life for him...."

To give one's life for another—for others... strangely this conviction grew to intensity in the thoughts of Fr. Maximilian. He had already met with human weakness, and animosity, including those with whom he shared his faith but who did not share his confidence. He did not run away from them; he did not seek an easier or "greater" life beyong the oceans.

There is in the life of a saint, (how good it is that now we can write of Fr. Maximilian in these terms!) periods of time which I would call "periods of ripening" or maturing. Before his departure, he was activity itself. He worked, he wrote, he took part in polemics. He could be very firm in argumentation. He knew that prayer was the most efficacious weapon against the Freemasons, yet he also knew how to put them on the spot. He could be a fighter. Later, upon his return, there would be no more fight in him. There remained only a great love for his fellowman and an insatiable need of making him someone above human weakness. He understood that to be a saint does not mean to want to fight for holy causes, or even to seek one's own sanctity. To be holy, is to desire holiness for others.

It was necessary for Fr. Maximilian to go to Japan to pass through this last phase on his way to sanctity.

But why to Japan?

Once when Father Kolbe was returning from Zakopane he met some Japanese students. He had discussions with them and as usual when they were leaving he pressed his miraculous medals into their palms. Maybe at that precise moment some words were said which he did not remember exactly later on, but the thought of Japan, the land of the Cherry Blossoms, did not leave him. When the mission call came, at once his plan was formed: we are going to Japan.

In the winter of 1930 five friars prepared fervently for the journey. They did not know much about Japan. For them it was simply the country of martyrs. They had read the bloody history of the followers of St. Francis Xavier and the 250 years of unparalleled persecutions beginning with the crucifixion of 26 Japanese Catholics on Mt. Tatayama. No doubt Fr. Kolbe also knew the history of Fr. Adalbert Mencinski of the Society of Jesus, a contemporary of Andrew Bobola, who set out for the Far East with a deep-seated desire to offer his life for the faith; who wandered over to Japan, to the green port of Nagasaki in the depths of the ocean gulf, and there after seven months of indescribable tortures, found what he so fervently sought—

death for the faith. Surely our own sacrificial seeker of the souls of others was well aware of these facts when he placed his finger on the southern end of the island of Japan and said with full determination: here we will publish the Japanese *Knight of the Immaculata!*

However before they left for Japan, Fr. Maximilian made a reconnoitering trip through Europe: Vienna, Paris, Rome, and Assisi.

In Rome, "I offered Holy Mass at the altar where the Immaculate Virgin appeared to Ratisbon because it was the anniversary of this apparition." From Italy he went to France, to Marseilles. "I am writing on the ship, *Champollion,* which belongs to the company most convenient for us perhaps . . . The cost of the trip for five is 6,600 and then some . . . not quite 7,000 zlotys. I am growing a beard already . . ." From Lourdes: "I offered Holy Mass in the basilica at Lourdes but the dearest place here is the grotto. . . ." He turns to Lisieux and spends the first of February there. To his brother he writes a short note: "I am writing in the room of St. Thérèse of the Child Jesus in Bouissonets . . . I will spend only three hours in Lisieux. Let St. Thérèse, patroness of the missions, look out for that." In a postscript on the margin of a little photograph of the great Saint he added: "Among the things of St. Thérèse, while she was still at home—there is a chessboard and a set of chessmen to delight our chessplayers. A very pleasant atmosphere. It is after twelve now. At one o'clock I may perchance have an opportunity to speak with one of her three sisters living in the convent at Lisieux. . . ."

Three Martin sisters were still living in 1930: the oldest, quiet Mary; the next in line Agnes-Pauline, the "little mother" of St. Therese, elected to a life-long position as superior of the convent, still bemoaning the fact that they seized a part of her jealously guarded words of St. Therese and obliged her to have the *Novissima Verba* published; finally, the youngest sister Genevieve-Celine, the one who would bring about the disclosure of the real unaltered writings of St. Thérèse. But Fr. Maximilian was told that he must not disturb the sisters in their recollection. So this visitor from Poland did not appear important enough it seems, and he left Lisieux without seeing any one of the sisters.

He returned to Poland through Berlin. Three weeks later, on February 26, all five friars (among them Bro. Zenon Zebrowski, known today in Japan as Bro. Zeno) traveled through Vienna, Rome, Marseilles and then on the ocean liner *Angers* through Port Said, Djibouti, and Colombo to Singapore and Saigon). Thirty days on the ocean! In Saigon, "we had the opportunity of meeting the local clergy of the native people. They were favorably disposed toward us and wanted us to settle there. I promised them that in a short time, about six months, two brothers would arrive and start publishing the *Knight*. . . . Leaving Saigon was like leaving home . . . the streets were lined with people bowing to us and we had to be careful to bow back."

In Hong Kong the stay was brief, Fr. Maximilian offered Holy Mass in the cathedral and visited the Salesian print shop.

In Shanghai, "lots of trouble, but our trust is in the Immaculata." "Difficulties upon difficulties, but today . . . the auxiliary bishop gave us permission to open negotiations and to spread the *Knight,* but was not in favor of publishing it in Shanghai. A well-known Chinese benefactor, Lo-Pa-Hong, promised to give us a house to use." He added: "It seems that I will not be able to leave the Orient for some time because the brothers unacquainted with the language would not be able to help themselves."

Before the ship reached Shanghai, Fr. Maximilian had sent a message to the Bernardines in the city. To his astonishment when on the quay, he was met by a crowd of people with axes, hammers and long poles; they were led by bearded missionaries. They were expecting the Franciscan missioners to have a sizeable baggage. And here they saw five friars, each one of whom could in all sincerity say, "All my belongings I carry with me."

The above mentioned Lo-Pa-Hong had promised to provide a building, printing presses and paper for the *Knight.* It seemed that the Chinese *Knight* could be edited and published right there. But unexpectedly something went awry. Fr. Maximilian did not write about it explicitly. He just mentioned that the Bishop was averse to the publication of the *Knight* from the very beginning. The mission field of China was allotted to certain respective religious congregations. The Franciscans, and especially the Polish Franciscans, had nothing to do in the field where the French Bernardines were working.

"The only place left for us is in the depths of the province of Shensi where we have a mission, but that is an impossible place without communication," wrote Fr. Maximilian, and added, "What I sensed in Niepokalanów has come to pass, our greatest difficulties will be caused by European missionaries."

On April 24, 1930, the ship bearing Fr. Maximilian arrived at the port of Nagasaki. The wide harbor was filled with vessels, big and small, whose white walls were gleaming in the sun. Colorful Japanese letters proclaimed the name of each. Unnumbered junks with their uplifted crests and cabins covered with cane mats, were floating in the water along the entire length of the quay. A chain of islands along the seashore is inhabited by a swarm of fishermen. The Japanese are a mysterious people. When in the middle of the last century the first missionaries to be admitted to Japan came to Nagasaki, the people greeted them with the touching declaration, "You and we are of one heart." They are the descendants of the first Christians whose numbers reached half a million after the very fruitful missionary era at the end of the Sixteenth Century. But alas, at the beginning of the Seventeenth Century, a persecution broke out, due mainly to the Protestant English and Dutch merchants who accused the missionaries, especially the Spaniards, of wanting to hand over Japan to the king of Spain. The Franciscans and the Jesuits, although set at variance, suffered death together in the bloody hecatomb of February 5, 1597. However, Catholicism survived in spite of the persecutions. Cut off from the Church, the Catholics of Nagasaki gradually knew less and less of the fundamentals of their faith. And yet in 1867, several hundred Christian families were condemned to hard labor for professing their Christian faith. For hundreds of years in the poor huts of the fishermen were preserved statuettes of the Mother of God, Seibo, similar perhaps a good bit to the goddess Kwanon, and even called Seibo Kwannon or Maryka-Kwannon.

By 1930, about 60,000 Catholics lived in Nagasaki and its environs; the city had its own bishop.

Towering above the town, situated in the valley, were the surrounding hills overgrown with a dense mass of greenness: reeds, grass, and dwarfish Japanese pine trees. One of these hills, occupied today by a pagan temple, was the place of the massacre of the Japanese martyrs. Fr. Maximilian looked longingly for the sight of this hill. Frequently he repeated what a joy it would be for him to seal his dedication to the Immaculata with his blood. A few years later he said, "If one is not ready for anything and everything, it means that he is not devoted to the Immaculata unconditionally.... To die in battle is simply the normal thing.... A father or brother who goes on a mission is a seed thrown into the soil and he must produce many native, indigenous seeds.... He might even get a bullet in his head for that; for working too hard. That would indeed be an honor...."

The bishop of Nagasaki, Hayasaka, greeted the newcomers from Porando very heartily. Actually, the idea of publishing the *Knight* struck him a little humorously, but he was pleased with the fact that in Fr. Maximilian he found a professor of philosophy for the seminary in Nagasaki. That decided it. Fr. Maximilian would teach in the seminary, and the *Knight* could be published.

The three Franciscans (two remained in Shanghai) rented a house near the cathedral church and immediately set to work. The missionaries arrived in Nagasaki on April 24 and on May 1, Fr. Maximilian wrote to the General of the Order: "Thanks to the Immaculate Virgin, the Japanese *Knight* has already been printed in one of the print shops here. At this time we are issuing 10,000 copies. Yesterday, I returned from Osaki where on Saturday, Our Lady's day, I bought a printing press of moderate size and 145,000 Japanese stamps. Long live the Immaculata!"

On this press Fr. Maximilian imagined that he would be able to print the Chinese *Knight* and send it to the brothers who remained in Shanghai. Already he was weaving his plans; "After regulating all these affairs, I would like to open a larger place in India (for all the languages of India) and in Beirut for the Arabian language (Arabia, Syria, Egypt, Tunis, Morocco: 100,000,000 souls then the Turkish, Persian and Hebrew languages. In this way the *Knight* and the M.I. would reach over 1,000,000,000 souls, that is, over half the population. But after all, let the Immaculata direct this work herself as she wishes. I only fear that I may omit something I should do."

The Japanese *Knight* was coming into existence amid substantial difficulties. The missionaries did not know the Japanese language, but by overstraining themselves they learned. They pondered how to translate Immaculata. Happily they translated it as: without sin the Mother of God, Mugenzai Seibo. The *Knight* of the Immaculata became *Mugenzai no Seibo no Kishi*. So they had a title, now they also needed the contents. Fr. Maximilian wrote articles in Latin, or in Italian, and different people of good will translated them into Japanese. The first, ardent, coworkers of Fr. Maximilian were Protestants and pagans. But the editing of the periodical was not the only problem. The post office refused a flat rate. There was no Japanese typesetter; no cutters, no folding machine, and no money. When Father Maximilian bought the printing press the police demanded that he buy a very expensive industrial license. The machine he bought did not have a motor, so again it was necessary to use the old method of Grodno, turn by hand to the death, in sultriness and scorching heat.

How did they live? Fr. Maximilian writes, "During the night and today there is a snowstorm. The snow was falling on my face so that I had to cover my head in order to sleep. The whiteness surrounds the brothers on the garret, and the washbasins are filled with snow."

In the meantime Fr. Maximilian, who had barely started the presses going, was called to Poland for a chapter meeting. Preparing for the journey he sent this joyful letter ahead of him: "The Japanese *Knight* is being received here very eagerly even by the pagans. Yesterday, from Tokyo came an order for 150 copies of the May issue with the payment enclosed. One of the non-Catholics is thanking us for his copy and asking to be placed on the mailing list. Offerings are beginning to pour in."

At the chapter meeting on July 24, 1930, Fr. Maximilian was confirmed as superior of the brothers in Japan. He returned to Nagasaki by the end of August and was stupefied. All the work was at a standstill!

He wrote to the provincial: "In Nagasaki I was informed that after my departure the priests were withdrawing more and more from cooperation, counting on closing the enterprise. Only when the telegram I sent to the bishop after the chapter announcing my return, did the work come to life again and the July issue was brought out. The copy for August had not even been touched... !"

Fr. Maximilian immediately sized up the situation. He wrote: "I set in order the most important affairs... To tell the truth, the buzzing mosquito is giving me trouble again even though I still feel pain in my left hand where he or his comrade bit me, but this too is for the Immaculate Virgin. At night I must cover my face to be able to sleep without waking because of the mosquitoes, but then one cannot sleep because of the heat and perspiration. However, this too is for the Immaculata, to gain as many souls as possible for her..." How could this feverish consumptive suffer all this? Only the Immaculata would know.

Requisitions for the periodical grew steadily. The missionaries traveled through the country and pressed it into the hands of the people they met. Pretty soon the 10,000 copy circulation was not enough. The pagans came to the Franciscans, even the Grand Panjandrum, and started discussions. They left with a gift of the miraculous medal.

Fr. Maximilian sacrificed long hours in conversation with the seekers of truth. Daily, several people waited for him in front of the publishing house. He had a tremendous amount of work to do. Lectures he had to prepare along with conferences, editorials, work in the press room. He wrote about himself: "I am somewhat slow in learning; I pound it in, but the words do not want to stay in my head, especially since I have so little time for pounding. When I actually do apply myself, my head begins to ache, my nerves jump, I feel feverish—that's incompetent of me."

From the chapter Fr. Maximilian brought the permission to build another Marytown in Nagasaki. The title was quickly decided upon: The Garden of the Immaculata–Muganzai no Sono. Land and a house were needed. It wasn't easy to buy them with the funds allotted. Fr. Maximilian searched and searched. . . .

In the meantime, "we are printing 20,000 copies of the monthly and expect to print 25,000 in December because the Japanese are reading the *Knight* very earnestly. . . ." Still, there was a shortage of workers. Some dropped out hysterically demanding a return to Poland. New Japanese applicants were coming in.

All this time no house had been found. On the other hand there were successes. He wrote: "So far, over twenty of the pagan Grand Panjandrum have become readers of the *Knight*, glory be to the Immaculate Virgin!—and many other pagans as well. Today the little figurines of the Immaculata came from Niepokalanów. The leaders among the pagans opening the boxes said "kinejdes" (pretty) and asked: 'Whom does it represent?' "

Finally, a place was found for the "City of the Immaculata"; Hongoti, a suburb of Nagasaki, a steep mountain declivity densely overgrown with reeds. In the midst of the shrubs were plum and orange trees. On the hill was a cemetery for cows and on one of the cliffs, a statuette of a crooked little god. It was quite a distance to the center of the city. "Therefore, the price is moderate, 7000 yen."

The land was brought in March 1931; the transfer was completed on May 16, the day of the feast of the Blessed Virgin Mary, Queen of the Apostles. In two months stood the building of "Mugenzai no Sono" which literally means Garden of the Immaculata though it is difficult to express the exact meaning of the title in Japanese.

He wrote on June 6, 1931: "I am enclosing three photographs from the period of construction. Toward the end of May everything was paid off for the grounds. A debt of some 700 yen remained for the construction of the building which in itself is very simple. The walls are of the thinnest boards with cracks and openings in them. The kitchen is a little iron stove (with one burner) in the open air without any enclosure around it. At the same time our joy is great because it is really Marytown already, and we have our Lord Jesus in the chapel."

At the end of October there were new investments: "According to our means we will try to complete the fencing, even if it is only with barbed wire; to think about a dwelling for the brothers in winter for now they are sleeping in the garret directly under a cement roof, and here at times snow appears; to build a kitchen, for at present the cooking is done in the open (without walls under a tin roof) and near it a pantry or larder; then something like a bathroom or shower, for the summer heat is almost unbearable, and some kind of laundry facility. As for the chapel— even the bishop does not consider it adequate to be called semi-public, although it is much more polished than our first one in Niepokalanów in Poland; so we must think about that, too, especially since the present one is barely big enough for us ourselves."

"What else? Oh, yes, they are digging our first well. Up to this time the brothers had to go to the public well for water down the street together with the women and girls who in summer go half-naked here.... This digging is not like that at Niepokalanów in Poland; here you have to bore into the rock...."

All this steady boring, these troubles brought forth the old cry: the erection of Mugenzai-no-Sono here was just another "crazy idea" of Fr. Maximilian's.

Yet when the cataclysmic day of the atom bomb came, Nagasaki disappeared along with 100,000 people in a moment but Mugenzai no Sono remained! Why? The slope screened the building from the rest of the town. No walls fell in; no one perished within the precincts of the monastery. An accident?

Construction was not everything. The hard labor that Fr. Maximilian exacted from his handful of brothers did not always bring good results. He wrote to the guardian of Niepokalanówo: "We have troubles galore in both cities of the Immaculata, and we shall have many more. Is not this perhaps the hour when the Central M.I. should think about circles of prayer and suffering for the intentions of the M.I.? How much of it would be to our profit if the religious women, especially the contemplatives, would offer something, some of their suffering, their adoration of the Most Blessed Sacrament! Likewise the sick people with their pain could win many souls. Maybe this is the time for such circles!"

It was not easy to deal with people. Not all his helpers were as fervent as Fr. Maximilian. Some gave way, weakened, complained, got sick, moaned and groaned. They would want to, but it all ended in their wanting-to. They perspired profusely and threw themselves exhausted on their couches. They considered the work at Mugenzai no Sono a stint beyond their strength. They were not shamed by the sight of Fr. Maximilian whose health was beginning to falter. Diffidently he wrote about it, and only because and as much as holy obedience demanded of him: "For a long time now I have been getting ulcers, sores that break open, one after another, so that today one of the brothers had to support me at Holy Mass. My fever goes up and that makes my work harder.... "My lungs hurt me so badly that I really feared a hemorrhage.... I'm afraid that I will be pampering myself. I do not feel a bit well and lately because of the heat and the sultriness, I almost fainted on the train.... In the evening at times I even moan, and my nerves are violently jarred." In spite of this, daily he rode a distance of several kilometers to reach the city (sighing vainly to his bike), traveled time after time to Tokyo and other cities, taught, gave lectures, wrote, planned, lived through every concern of the two cities of the Immaculata.

It was these men who wanted to. There were others, however, who had ceased wanting-to. Fear of the foreign land had overcome them and they hysterically demanded an "immediate" return to their fatherland. Still others were willing to work with all the earnestness in them, in any place on the face of the earth, but not in Mugenzai no Sono....

Fr. Maximilian wrote about one of his co-workers: "He told me himself that he feels alien here and is not happy; therefore his work is not going well. Truly, it is not. He has time to spare, but no zeal for learning the language, and hope for help in the future is very small... Although, as I intimated, he is a good man and tries not to cause me any annoyance, I cannot demand anything beyond what he vowed; furthermore he has not had adequate training and maybe even not enough ability to be able to get the education necessary for future work here. Hence it is doubtful whether he will be able, or even want to remain here permanently. Here real dedication and intense work are required.... What disturbs me most is that some of the brothers are beginning to follow this direction and imbibe in that spirit...."

But there *were* others. With joy Fr. Maximilian wrote that in Mugenzai no Sono a veritable "gang of madmen" for the Immaculate Virgin had been found. Ready for everything, they were not intimidated by the hardships of building on the slope, nor by the danger of arson, of which envious pagans, who had broken the statue of the Mother of God several times, were capable. Nor did they fear the strain of carrying water, the turning of the printing press or the learning of the language. Besides the brothers from Poland there were now also brothers from Japan. "Our professor Yamaki, a Japanese Protestant, who is industriously translating the *Knight* (from Italian)... said recently that he believes it is time for him to become a Catholic. The professor of Medicine of the local university looks in on me for a conversation in German... and he offered to translate for the *Knight*.... The pagans who were helping in the print shop are also learning the catechism." "One of these pagans was coming to work without pay for the Immaculate Virgin. His dying father disinherited him completely. He is working and preparing himself for baptism and the habit."

Crosses, the heaviest being those inflicted by our estranged loved ones are intertwined with moments of joy. In moments of grief Fr. Maximilian succumbed, "I too feel at times that I am unnecessary for the Immaculate Virgin, rather a hindrance...." But immediately he rouses himself, "In truth, she picks the blunderers!" He loved his good and bad coworkers very tenderly and often signed his letters, "Maximilian Kolbe and children."

Only now did this intrepid warrior for the cause of the Immaculate Virgin touch the bottom of his knowledge of man and his need of loving him in spite of everything, of always offering himself for another irrespective of what he really is.

Between May and July 1932, Fr. Maximilian set out on a journey to the Asiatic continent with the intention of establishing a third City of the Immaculata, this time in India. "Today I told the brothers," he writes to Niepokalanów, "to commend this intention to the Immaculate Virgin that I may know her will and it became clear. China, with the city of Heiman, grew faint, Annam with Saigon could wait and other ideas became silent, as there appeared before my eyes, India with Ernaculam."

Seemingly all went well. The local church authorities agreed, the place was chosen, and even the name of the Indian

Niepokalanów was designated: Amalam. It was, one could assume, a definite sign on the part of St. Thérèse. In spite of all this, the Indian City of the Immaculata did not come to be.

"I think," wrote Father Maximilian to his brothers, "about so many things, or maybe just rave about them for it's more than warm here, about the future Niepokalanów, and the Polish one, the Japanese one and others . . . and back again about the Polish one and the Japanese one . . . and again my thoughts would like to tear apart the curtain of the future and see where I would land. . . . And the hopes, the concrete visions, words of the joyful telegram, and doubts again . . . and the flash of hope. "And what if, Niepokalanów should fail?" and immediately the joyful answer, "If the Immaculate Virgin should want it to fail, then all of us would help in the destruction of it most assiduously." After all, She is the Proprietress, and has a perfect right to say at any moment, if she so desires, "That's enough now." It suffices that we give ourselves over to her together with all that we have spoiled. She will know how to turn it all into greater good. . . ."

On April 7, 1933, Fr. Maximilian again set out on his way to Poland for the meeting of the provincial chapter. The chapter convened in Krakow and appointed Fr. Czupryk guardian of Mugenzai no Sono, leaving Fr. Maximilian in full charge of the *Knight* and the M.I. During his sojourn in Poland Fr. Maximilian prepared the Japanese ambassador to Poland, Minister Kawai, for baptism. He returned to Japan only in October.

Troubles in Mugenzai no Sono had somewhat abated during the last few years. There were printing presses already and a folding machine had come from Poland. On his trip to Europe in 1933, Fr. Maximilian was in Rome where there was some talk of making him a bishop, but the Franciscan superiors opposed it. In 1934 a church was built in Mugenzai no Sono. The *Knight* reached a circulation of 65,000 copies.

In 1936 the new chapter appointed Fr. Maximilian guardian of Niepokalanów in Poland. The events that were going on there demanded his presence.

When he was leaving Japan, on his way to the chapter, Fr. Maximilian had the feeling that he would never return. In a letter to the brothers in Mugenzai no Sono he wrote from Shanghai, "When this ship was already bearing me farther and farther away from the shore, I thought to myself: Perhaps this is really the very last time I am seeing you on earth and tears welled up in my eyes. But it is all for the Immaculate Virgin."

Likewise on the way, he wrote to one of the brothers, "Avoid sadness whatever may be its cause, even if it be most justifiable. Always peace and serenity of spirit. Let us leave all our troubles to the Immaculate Virgin."

In Poland Again

Not for a moment during the sojourn of Fr. Maximilian in Japan did the thread break that connected the founder of Niepokalanów with the people he left near Warsaw. This was not due to the fact that the two cities of the Immaculata, situated on two extreme ends of the globe, belonged to the same Franciscan Province, but because the Niepokalanów in Poland, the Mother of other cities of the Immaculata, was to be, in the opinion of Fr. Maximilian, the main watchfire of the idea that issued from the mind and heart of the son of the little shopkeepers of Pabianice.

When Father Alphonse, his own brother Joe, would no longer be at Niepokalanów, Father Maximilian wrote to his successor, the new guardian, and beseeched him, "protect the cause of Niepokalanów and its characteristic poverty, because there are some people in the province who, not of ill-will, but for the greater good of the province, want to obliterate the distinction between Niepokalanów and other monasteries.... Niepokalanów with its broad goal of conquering the whole world for the Immaculate Virgin falls under Chapter XII of the Rule and under penalty of losing its reason for existence and of betraying its ideal, cannot change its objective which is to accomplish the aim of the M.I." At the same time he wrote to the provincial, "It seems to me, maybe it's utopia, that it would be the normal state of affairs at Niepokalanów, if the future workers for the conquest of the world for the Immaculate Virgin would be trained at Niepokalanów in the spirit of Niepokalanów, i.e., of surrendering themselves unconditionally to the Immaculate Virgin ... because others, not being obliged to this unconditional surrender, would have a derogatory influence." And again, "It seems to me that Niepokalanów was built for the saving of souls for the Immaculate Virgin, and if it should change its objective it will cease to have a reason for its existence; it will lose its impetus, its breadth of expansion, and there will follow stagnation, a comfortable life and finally dissolution...."

"The Immaculate Virgin, the objective... and poverty, the capital... are the two things which Niepokalanów cannot give up under any circumstances. Without this objective it would not be Niepokalanów for it would be false to its principles. And without poverty and trust in Divine Providence there is no thought of breadth, offensive...."

Concern for the preservation of this character of Niepokalanów in Poland was Fr. Maximilian's constant companion. He wanted to know everything that happened at Niepokalanów. He was uneasy when it seemed to him that buildings were going up to last permanently. Even at a distance of thousands of ocean miles, he was grieved when he heard about the fire at Niepokalanów. He gave advice as to what to buy, where to put things, how to secure safety. He wrote to individual brothers, counseled them, and clarified their ideas.

Above all the press absorbed his interest. Fr. Maximilian came out with a new project—the thought of a daily paper.

In December of the year 1934, Fr. Maximilian received the first trial copy of the *Little Journal* (27th of November) published at Niepokalanów. He wrote immediately, "It may be that 2 cents will not be enough, especially since there are not many of these coins in circulation. Therefore, let it be 5 cents. A felicitous title. Some verses and even columns forgot their proper places. Too much haste in arranging columns. Very beautiful is the expression in publication of the Immaculate Virgin—it is her work." In July 1935, when the *Little Journal* could boast of more than a year's income from its work, Fr. Maximilian wrote, "It seems to me that it would be good to get closer to other dailies . . . but only in so far as it can be done without detriment to our ideal, so that friction and antipathy does not spread beyond the borders of the country. It must be demanded that the editorial co-workers really write in the spirit of the M.I. and avoid unnecessary stigmatizing of people or parties or other nations. Our foremost aim is always the conversion and sanctification of souls. . . ."

"As to the *Little Journal,* it will slowly become perfect and reach the height of perfection when its text is such that it will be fit to be signed: Editor-in-chief—The Immaculata."

Fr. Maximilian realized that the publication was not perfect. The atmosphere of the bitter, idealistic, political and personal battles that were being waged in the Polish press in the second half of the 1930s must have caused him great anxiety. In the whirl of the heated discussion about nationalizing trade, there appeared tones of anti-semitism, albeit far removed from the tones of the German, Russian and even French press, yet not entirely free from passion and hatred. Fr. Maximilian wanted to warn "his" paper to avoid such tones. Before his departure on mission, Father wrote angrily; today, after his Japanese experience, he became a man in whom love for his fellowman surpassed all injuries and insults. In fact he had never been a publisher condemning all Jews indiscriminately. He knew how to dis tinguish the enemies of Poland from those honest and decent people who were not really Christians, but for that very reason belonged, on a level with the first, to those "committed" to the care of the Immaculate Virgin. At that time he had to remind himself repeatedly of this commitment. Today he felt this "commitment."

Besides the *Little Journal,* the initiative of Fr. Maximilian gave birth to other publications issued at Niepokalanów, among them: *Knight of the Immaculata* for the youth; *Little Knight of the*

Immaculata for the children, and *Miles Immaculatae,* a Latin *Knight* for the international clergy.

This last idea was in Fr. Maximilian's mind for a long time. Way back in 1932 he wrote from Japan that it was time, and necessary to issue a *Knight* in Latin for the priests and seminarians of the whole world, especially for the native clergy of the mission countries. "In this way the clergy of the whole world would rally round the *Knight*.... The *Knight* would be so edited that it could take the place of the press agency."

Keeping the pulse of all the activity at Niepokalanów Fr. Maximilian concentrated on the training of the monastic personnel in the spirit of dedicating oneself unconditionally to the Immaculate Virgin. He knew that he would not live long. His health was declining perceptibly. In Nagasaki in May 1935 he wrote, "I feel completely exhausted and I do not know just when I will end this earthly pilgrimage." On various occasions he interjected unexpectedly, "Let us try to prepare ourselves for death earlier." I will not live much longer and I will remain with you only a short time. The life of a person consists of three phases: preparation for work, the work itself, and suffering. Some here at Niepokalanów are only preparing, others are already working, and for the old ones, such as the one who sits here (pointing to himself, and he was only 45) it would be about time to pass on to the last phase—suffering." But "from Niepokalanow one does not go to purgatory.... Whoever has its spirit, even a lay person, it is hard to suppose that he would go to purgatory."

It was said that Fr. Maximilian did not have perfect rapport with the Fathers. Yet his influence on the brothers was most unusual. At the very beginning of his activities, Father made the religious brother a knight of the Immaculate Virgin. Now he wanted to strengthen all of them, more than 600 at Niepokalanów, and make them firm in their knighthood.

He conducted daily meditations with them. He supplemented these with talks as they went on hikes or met at recreation. When necessary he knew how to be stern. On the whole, however, he reacted to their needs with the greatest love and tenderness. He did not begrudge time for interviews with individual brothers who had problems or were going through critical periods of weakening. Each brother he addressed as "my child." Although still a young man, he treated the brothers as his sons, as his own family.

Lessons continued to flow endlessly, "It is necessary that the Immaculate Virgin educate us. The whole philosophy of the men at Niepokalanów is this: It is essential that we let Her train and form us exactly as She pleases. To be sure, this is not and cannot be our objective, that we should be well-known, written and talked about. No, not even the whole of Niepokalanów should be our aim. What really matters is our interior life, our internal activity which means our continuing commitment to belong to the Immaculate Virgin, to being her knight. Let us remind ourselves that the external activity is simply the overflow of what we possess. What can we do to show our concern about her affairs? Plainly, be a saint! A saint is not an old codger, a sluggard to be pushed around. A saint must be sprightly, enterprising, full of initiative. If the Immaculate Virgin tells you to work here, then put your whole energy, zeal and activity into it; if she tells you to rest, then rest; and when she calls to recreation, then recreate. Such a soul that does all this perfectly accomplishes very much for the cause of the Immaculate Virgin. Hence we must strive that our sacrifice will simmer in this slow fire for fifty, sixty, or even a 100 years. Everyone seems to know how to burn up fast. We have to learn how to work and how to direct our work. That is a very difficult task, but it must be done."

"Lately everywhere they speak of war. How does one prepare for this war? Above all, one must strive to be very fervent. The resolution to be a saint must be very serious and firm."

"It is coming close to a very serious battle. What its stages will be, it is hard to say. We can expect anything. As I was talking with the brothers we said to ourselves that the loftiest ideal would be to lay down our lives for the Immaculate Virgin. We live only once, and only once do we die. But the best will be whatever the Immaculate Virgin wants for we are her property and it is her business."

On Sunday, August 28, 1939, he said to the brothers, "In a knightly manner to suffer, to work, and to die but not an ordinary death, to be shot with a bullet in the head, to seal one's love for the Immaculate Virgin, thus in a knightly way, to shed your blood to the last drop for the hastening of the conquest of the world for her, that's what I wish for you and for me."

And then he uttered something mysterious, "I recalled all the favors I received from the Immaculate Virgin. Yesterday I realized that I do not serve her like I should. I know one thing that she demands of me albeit it is contrary to my understanding."

The war

The war was approaching. Incidents occurred with unusual speed. The year 1939 was a year of lightning transformations and shocking returns. In April Father Maximilian wrote to Field Marshal Rydz-Smigly: "Understanding the important role our army is playing in upholding universal peace, protecting our country and regaining its stolen territory, and appraising the necessity, of an extraordinary effort and individual offerings of all citizens, the brothers of Niepokalanów, 619 strong, who have dedicated their lives to promote the honor of the Immaculate Mother of God, together with the 120 alumni of the minor mission seminary desire to come to your aid with the modest offering of 1,200 zlotych for the needs of the Polish Army."

Speaking to the brothers on October 28, 1939, he said, "Just a little while, and the bombs may fall upon us. Here indeed is the publishing house of the M.I., this Niepokalanów and its expansion, which does not please everybody. But let us be prepared for this at least—to perform our duty as it becomes a knight of the Immaculate, Virgin. Whatever happens anywhere else, here at Niepokalanów there will be plenty of surprises in the days ahead of us. The Immaculate Virgin may permit this for the greater good of her cause. Whoever does not feel able to persevere in a knightly way here, let him pray much to our Blessed Mother for the necessary graces!!"

September 1 witnessed the "criminal" attack on Poland. On September 5, Fr. Maximilian received orders to evacuate, and dismiss the brothers. He blessed them with the words: "It was good for us to be here together under the tender care of the Immaculate Virgin, but the time has come for us to separate. I beg your pardon for any scandal I may have given you and for all irritations I may have caused you. I had hardly any vexations from you. You are going on mission. Let the light of your good example always shine. Wherever there is a man from Niepokalanów, there should also be Niepokalanów. Many of you will never return here. I too will probably not outlive this war. But remember: Love the Immaculate Virgin and turn to her in all your troubles."

Only 50 friars remained at Niepokalanów. Others applied to the Red Cross or returned to their own homes. Fr. Maximilian took charge of the remaining handful in their fatherly care of the huge crowd of deathly frightened escapees from the neighboring towns and villages. He consoled them, reassured and quieted them down, invited them to prayer. His words inspired them, his conduct lifted up their hearts, and his presence filled them with peace. The wounded were taken care of in the monastery. The hungry were given everything that was found in the larders.

On September 19 early in the morning the roar of the guns reverberating in a circle around Niepokalanów suddenly grew dim. At the gates appeared soldiers in globe-shaped helmets drawn down over their eyes and in grayish-green uniforms. "Alle raus!"—this yell—so much like the whistle of a whip which will resound for years throughout Poland, drove the friars out from the house onto the courtyard. "Alle raus!" They stood opposite each other: on one side the blackrobed friars girded with rope cinctures, on the other the soldiers armed to the teeth with bands of missiles. One of them, in broken Polish, told the friars to form a double line. He allowed two friars to remain in the lazaretto; the rest had to go. Where? The soldier did not inform them. A moment of decision. The brother infirmatarian had to remain in virtue of his duties. And the second? Voices were heard "Father Maximilian! Father Maximilian!" He shook his head—turned to Brother Cryiak, "You stay, my child."

The column of friars left Niepokalanów. They followed the road to the highway. In the first row was Fr. Maximilian supporting himself with a cane. Voices trembling with pent-up fear could be heard all along the column. "What will happen? Where are they leading us?" Nothing was known. Parallel to the column the soldiers were marching, their rifles clattered and their hobnailed shoes loudly struck the stones. The people shed tears as they bid farewell to the departing friars, and they in turn wept as they went into the unknown. Only Fr. Maximilian walked peacefully, almost serenely.

In this manner, thirty-seven persons were taken: two priests, one Japanese cleric brought to Niepokalanów by Fr. Maximilian, and thirty-four brothers.

On the highway the German soldiers pushed the friars into trucks. Then began the fatiguing journey through Rowa Mazowiecka to Czestochowo. There they loaded the prisoners onto railroad cars. Pushing the people together in the freight car, a soldier pulled Fr. Maximilian's cane out of his hand and almost struck him with it. On September 21 they arrived in the camp of Lambinowice (Lamsdorf). Three days later they transferred the friars to the camp in Amtlitz.

They lived in the camp, in tents, slept on the bare ground. It was cold and damp—autumn of 1939 came swiftly with waves of cold rain. The first snow fell on October 8. Under the tents was a medley of people: Poles and Jews, priests, friars, and lay persons imprisoned for unknown reasons. The situation was terrible, conditions that would be the tragedy of camp life—the mixing of the good with the bad, the intelligentsia with the rabble, the saintly with the criminals. When some were praying, others were cursing, fighting, and robbing one another.

A group of the friars from Niepokalanów was convinced that they would not be able to endure it. How much patience Fr. Maximilian must have had to constantly uplift his companions' spirit, to invite them to pray, to place before their eyes the ideal of unlimited trust and hope, to convince them that this is an unusual occasion and opportunity since they got a free ride—to go on mission to Germany. The miraculous medals were again on the go. They made their way in equal degree to the prisoners as well as the overseers. The soldiers, the noncommissioned officers, and even the officers came to look with awe upon a man who not only did not lament over his own pitiful condition, but prayed joyfully and imparted his faith to others. In this country where the "fear of God" had come to be the "fear of every authority," where crime could be commanded, where laughter disappeared, such a figure as Fr. Maximilian presented, must have seemed to be a dream.

Fr. Maximilian was consistently serene and inflexible. Daily he gave the brothers a conference. When on his nameday, October 11, the brothers were congratulating him he responded, "I was wondering what I could give you today on my nameday. I wish you just one thing—that you may belong to the Immaculate Virgin even more and more with every moment! When suffering is far from us we are ready for anything and everything. But now that we have this opportunity to suffer, let us profit by it and suffer with the intention to gain as many souls as possible for the Immaculate Virgin."

On November 24 the friars were transferred to Ostrzeszowo and placed in the basement of the school. They were taken to all kinds of jobs until their release on December 8, the very day of the feast of the Immaculate Conception.

They left by train transported with joy. Only Fr. Maximilian rode silently, deeply lost in thought. His offer of blood had not been accepted. He would have given it so willingly. So gladly would he have given his body worn out by illness for souls that would now be serving the Immaculate Virgin. But she did not want it just yet.

In the plundered but not wholly destroyed Niepokalanów, life was awakened anew. The scattered brothers came together again and took up the hardships of daily monastic life.

Fr. Maximilian thus explained matters to the church authorities, "The aim of Niepokalanów, as we know, is the spread of the honor and love of the Immaculate Virgin and of drawing souls to her. Formerly we did this primarily with the aid of the press; at present our main concern is prayer, then hard work, productiveness and charity." The brothers were refurbishing agricultural machinery for the neighbors, repairing watches, making boots and sewing clothes. But Fr. Maximilian was nursing the illusion that maybe the German authorities would permit him to publish the "*Knight*." And actually on November 20 he recieved the desired assent for the publication of one issue of "*Knight*" for the Warsaw district with a circulation of 120,000 copies.

I remember very well what that one and only issue of the *Knight* was in that hard winter of 1941, the second winter of war. I was hiding then in the vicinity of Sochaczewo. In the deluge of Hitler's propaganda, the flood of articles badly written in Polish and German, the ragged words did not really inform us, but their very tone was enough to rouse our hopes.

Before the first issue appeared in 1940, Fr. Maximilian was called to headquarters. He was quizzed above all about the *Little Daily Journal*. This publication proved to be the salt in the eye of Hitler's propaganda. Being ill, Fr. Maximilian wrote to the official who called him in, "I regret that I cannot oblige you with the required numbers of the *Little Daily Journal* because for a long time now, unnecessary printings are obliging us to be sparing our coal. However, while I was still in Germany as Zivilgefangene I heard that the police came here with numbers of the L.D.; hence I assume that you can find them there, sir. As to the monthly *Knight of the Immaculata* I believe it will promote the general good for the following reasons: 1) After 100 or 200 years you, sir, and I will not be living anymore. Then all affairs will cease, even the important ones except the one most important question: what and where will we be then? A religious publication raises such and similar questions. 2) The most Blessed Virgin Mary is not a fairy tale nor a legend. She is a living person, loving each one of us, but not known well enough, and not loved enough reciprocally; therefore, we must publicize her activity. I would like to mention that I feel no hatred toward anyone on earth. The substance of my ideal is contained in the enclosed prints (most likely the enclosure was a little diploma of the M.I. in German). What flows from them, that's mine; therefore I always hope to work and suffer and even to lay down my life in sacrifice."

Alas the published issue brought attention again on Fr. Maximilian—this time it was the Gestapo. One day there came to Niepokalanów a group of German journalists who were publishing the *Warschauer Zeitung,* in the so-called General Government. Arrogantly and angrily they trotted through the monastery. The report of this visit appeared in the *Warschauer Zeitung* on February 1, 1941.

"A monk," thus began the reporter, "allows us to enter the monastery and leads us to one of the nearest houses. On the door we read: K + M + B 1941, written with chalk, initials of the names of the three holy kings. These signs are written on the doors of Catholic homes especially in the villages around January 7. This superstitious sign is supposed to avert misfortune."

One's cultural standard speaks for itself. The reporter had never heard of the three royal magi whose relics, a symbol of pious honor given without pretense to any historical truth, are actually found in the cathedral of Cologne.

"The *Little Daily,* he continues "that's the bird that led

us on that particular pilgrimage to Niepokalanów. The main task of the black monks, those residents of Niepokalanów, is the publication of the monthly *Knight of the Immaculata*—and the title means *Soldier of the Virgin.*

It is not surprising that the *Knight* was published at Niepokalanów but that they also printed the "*Little Journal*" is almost unbelievable. This very *Little Journal* was a harmful paper attacking the Germans. No occasion was omitted of slandering and casting venom upon the neighbor from the west. Without any provocation it was poisoning the good atmosphere between the two nations, neighbors to each other. The *Little Journal* was especially harmful to the Germans because its cost was dirt-cheap and it could be easily printed.

The article ends with this conclusion: "A fact remains a fact—that one of the most notorious and disruptive dailies was printed in the Catholic monastery, contributing to the dissemination of hatred between Poland and Germany and the fruit of the hatred was to be Bydgoszcz."

Today we know enough about the unspeakable doings at Bydgoszcz: who disseminated the hatred and who stirred up dissension in order to have the opportunity later on to perpetuate the bloody massacre of the civilians.

"The instigating daily in the monastery, hence in a place whose guardians falsely claim that they stand to protect morality and the good customs of society. Well do we know the power and influence with which the Catholic Church helped Poland."

When Hans Franck was appointed by Hitler as "governor" of the partitioned province of Poland, he wrote in similar terms in his memoirs, "The Church was always held in reserve as the final center of Polish nationalism. When all the lights of Poland went out there was still the Saint of Czestochowo and the Church."

After the appearance of this article, Fr. Maximilian was convinced that dark clouds were gathering over the monastery. He said to the brothers, "The Germans will not leave me in peace. I feel it."

He could have "disappeared." Ever so many threatened

people were disappearing. I myself lived for years under a pseudonym. The whole conspiratorial organization of hundreds of people used falsified personal papers and false identification cards. But he of course could not and would not leave his charge, Niepokalanów, and the brothers!

When he was still in the camp he said, "Let us make this contract with the Immaculate Virgin. Let us say to her: O Blessed Mother, for love of you I surrender myself to you with the intention of staying in this disagreeable camp even though others go home. I will remain here to suffer—forgotten and spurned." Thus he used to offer himself personally. What more he asked of the Immaculate Virgin he did not divulge, but it is easy to surmise.

And now he felt that he would not outlive this war. A feeling of his approaching end was constantly with him. He had a certain premonition he would not even survive the current year of 1941. But was he to die in his beloved peaceful Niepokalanów surrounded by the brothers whom he loved so much? That would be very contrary to his nature. Once upon a time he said in Japan, "It seems to me that in our Polish Niepokalanów we will not need much ground for a cemetery for most of the bones will rest in various parts of the world. At that time he was thinking of the missions. Today the missions came to Niepokalanow. It was not necessary to go to seek death. It sufficed to wait, it was approaching.

February 17, 1941 ... A gray, foggy, early morning.... Two black automobiles with the terrible sign POL next to the numbers drove in at Niepokalanów. The porter rang the bell from the entrance: "That's for Fr. Maximilian," Just for a moment, a very short time, his lips trembled uneasily. But peace returned immediately. With his usual step he went to meet the arrivals. As he walked forward he became more and more composed, more self-assured. Now at last....

The men approached. Bulging caps with death's head on a black background of green hats. Characteristic leather overcoats. They came nearer and nearer. Some brothers were pushing a little wagon with wood on the premises. He stopped them. "Just wait, children; let these gentlemen go through." He stopped in front of the men and said, "Praised by Jesus Christ!" They looked him in the eye with a searching gaze. They like to drink in the fear evident in their victims' eyes. But Fr. Maximilian stood smiling and at ease. His hand was seeking a miraculous medal in his pocket. Maybe they would agree to take one.? The angry looks of the arrivals were refracted helplessly from the peaceful countenance of the friar. "Sir, are you Maximilian Kolbe?" asked one of the men in Polish. "Yes, I am," he answered. And in his heart reigned joy.

At the stake

Fr. Maximilian was arrested together with four other priests and driven to the Pawiak. In vain, twenty brothers volunteered to take his place but the Gestapo wanted him, not the others.

On February 24, he sent an official letter from the prison with a request for clothing.

On April 2 he informed them, "For some time because of a fever I am in the infirmary." On the first of May he thanked them for the package of eatables he received. He wrote: "I am glad that you have much work to do. Thanks be to God! The Immaculate Virgin, like a loving mother, will think of her children in the future as she has done in the past. I have already left the infirmary, but I still receive hospital food. At present I am working in the library..." May 12.... Acting on the command of the prison official he asked for civilian clothes.

On June 15 he informed his mother, "Toward the end of the month of May in a transport of people I came here to the camp in Auschwitz."

That was the last direct sign of life from Fr. Maximilian. At Pawiak Fr. Maximilian had been assigned cell no. 193 in the 5th division. The prison was overcrowded and the atmosphere was tense with apprehension. Deportations to Palmir had already begun, where massive executions were taking place. Transports were also being sent to Auschwitz. Prisoners were being taken for questioning to the Gestapo building on Szucha Boulevard. They returned from there horribly flogged. With his peaceful attitude Fr. Maximilian exerted a truly beneficial influence upon the tense atmosphere of the cell. He was greatly loved and admired.

One day the guard, an SS man, Scharfuhrer, came into the cell. He had a mean look. He scanned the cell and the well-nigh petrified inmates. He seemed to be looking for a possible pretext to explode. And suddenly, he noticed it. One of the prisoners was dressed in a habit. A spasm of rage distorted the guard's face. He burst forth with a choking cough. With his paw he snatched the rosary suspended from the priest's cincture. His foaming mouth came close to the face of Fr. Maximilian.

"You cleric"—he muttered, "You fool! Talk! Do you believe in Christ? Speak up!"

"I believe," answered Fr. Maximilian. His voice trembled lightly, not fearfully but zealously.

The blow struck like a thunderbolt. The friar felt the sweet taste of blood on his lips; the cheek painfully grew numb.

"Now what?" asked the guard, "Do you still believe?"

"I believe."

A fiendish bellow issued from the lips of the guard. His face became ashen as if he was the one struck. He hurled himself upon Fr. Maximilian, pounded him with his fists, kicked him, turned him over on the ground, and tugged at the crucifix on the rosary.

"Do you believe in this? Talk! Say it!"

"I believe."

Another terrible blow, and the SS man rushed out of the cell. He slammed the door shut after him as if something was chasing him. They heard him running wildly down the long corridor.

Fr. Maximilian struggled slowly to his feet. He had a hard time quieting his comrades in the cell. They foamed with rage. All fear had left them and they were ready to grab the guard by the throat if he should again appear before them. Fr. Maximilian spoke softly, "Gentlemen, take it easy, I beg you. It is not necessary, nothing is necessary. This is of course for the Immaculate Virgin."

The prison hospital, and after hospitalization, work in the library. Fr. Maximilian now knew that he would go to Auschwitz.

In the library there was a meeting with another prisoner, Stanley Piasecki. They knew each other. Piasecki was the editor of the fighting weekly, *Straight from the Bridge*. They used to see each other at various editors' meetings. On the night of the occupation, December 4, 1939 (feast of St. Barbara who was to become the patroness of the underground press), Piasecki established the underground publication, *Battle* to be the organ of the National War Organization constituting the armed formation of the National Party. There were six of us when we talked over the first issue that day. There was Johnny Mosdorf who was arrested soon after and found himself in Auschwitz. There was Szczesny, the director of the print shop, who died a year later. I was the only one who outlived them and remained to be a coworker on all the issues of *Battle* that were published during the occupation.

A year later, the Gestapo crawled into Piasecki's house at night and found on his desk instructions written by him for the N.O.W.. "He was accused," wrote Grzymala Siedlecki about Piasecki in his memoirs, "of editing a secret paper, one of the worst accusations possible especially since there was the evidence. A legend is bandied about in the 6th division that the commander of the prison, driven by some mysterious sympathy, took care of him—let's say, he protected Piasecki from actual hunger, and from the bestialities of Sander and Burckle; more than that he could not do, even if he wanted to, in the Gestapo structure. In spite of all the real or apparent alleviations, the soul of this indefatigable warrior of the Polish underground must have suffered severely. He knew that because of his activities the enemy had imprisoned his wife also, but left the little two-year old daughter free. He had no illusions about his own fate. They say that he went to his execution quietly with a prayer on his lips."

I often think that if Stanley went like that to his death it was due to his meeting with Fr. Maximilian.

On May 26 boxcars securely locked, filled to overflowing with humanity, were standing in the station at Oswiecim. Auschwitz! That distorted Germanized Oswiecim became one of the most abominable places in the world. Millions of people died there, the most cruel, most painful death imaginable. What is the Roman Colosseum, drenched with the blood of a few hundred martyrs, compared with the Apell-Platz of Auschwitz, where millions died? However the difference is very great: not every torture is a martyrdom. In the Colosseum all the people were giving up their life for their faith; in Auschwitz the blood of martyrs is mixed with the blood of those who greeted death with blasphemy, with words of hatred; who were breaking down, falling into despair, cheating and robbing fellow prisoners, snatching their bread, tramping upon them with their feet in order to save themselves, a fallow earth where rarely does an ear of grain grow in the sea of weeds.

When, from the boxcar the crowd of newly arrived people fell out, almost unconscious from the foul air, pressure and hunger, there fell upon them a shower of blows from sticks and cowhides. They had to run the lane between the striking guards, foremen and blockwardens. These last struck in fear that if they did not strike enough, they themselves would be beaten. Human dignity immediately dishonored, they wallowed in the mud. Then to the dressing room, real tortures—tearing the hair with a dull clipper. A shower bath amid the roars of the guards and the ceaseless beatings ... Laufschrifft. From now on, it would always be on the run unless one stopped next to a SS man who says: "Mutze ab!" and "parade Marsch." And if anyone appeared, clumsy commands like these follow: "hipfen, rollen, tanzen, hinlegen!"

Instead of his Franciscan habit, a striped, drenched with blood and sweat, gown—Zebrazeug! Instead of a name, a number on a red square—16670 (an early number—afterwards they went up into hundreds of thousands). Instead of a cell, a tiny hall on the block filled beyond capacity, in which people lie in windrow fashion, bitten by lice, falling exhausted from fatigue and hunger. A frightening hunger twisted the vital organs, which deprived one of reasoning power, of peace and sleep, makes one think only of food and dream about eating. When at a common meeting at Apell-Platz the question arises: "Pfaffe?" Immediately there is a loud burst of raucous laughter, and the stripes and strikes fall again with the command: "Laufschritt!"

On the run, always on the run. After only a few days, Fr. Maximilian looked like a shadow. He breathed heavily and had a fever. He was transferred to the company "Babice," the very worst detail, a penal colony, a raging beast in human form, the infuriated barber from Berlin, Ernst Krankemann. Here the role was filled by the gloomy, bloody Krott, a sadist and pervert. He got a group of people, a few priests among them with the observation: "Listen, Krott; teach them how to work." With a snear he answered: "I will certainly teach them."

This teaching began: Laufschritt! The stick whistled, people fell under its strokes. Chunks of wood they had to carry had the weight of the Cross. Fr. Maximilian fell time and again under the weight of them. Krott felt a certain strange "predilection" for this friar with his expressive eyes, a predilection that can be satisfied only by inflicting pain. "I will finish you off!" he predicted. Greater burdens and heavier strikes! He himself made sure that this priest would run faster. Laufschritt! the insistent shriek in his ear! Schnell! At the intermission, when the rest were relaxing, Krott inflicted 50 strikes with his stick upon Fr. Maximilian as a punishment. After this bastinado the friar lay unconscious. Krott stood over him, kicked him and continued to apply his stick. Father Maximilian did not move. With another kick Krott shoved the body into a puddle. Let him lie there.

Dragged back into the camp, Fr. Maximilian still lived on.

They took him to the "infirmary," full of flies, foul air, and bad odor. On the three floors of plank beds the dying were eaten alive by vermin. No other help was given here beyond the release from work. Fr. Maximilian was laid on the lowest floor. It was dirty, dark, and suffocating beyond endurance. His makeshift bed was completely rotted. Although there was a chance to be taken to a higher "floor," Fr. Maximilian objected. He would remain below. "Put the others there," he said. "I am all right here. I can pray for those that are dying." His comrades from the block brought him a piece of "organized" bread, he shared it with others. Someone complained loudly, "I am so hungry!" He gave him his soup and his bread . . . the most treasured things in the camp, and smiling, said, "They need it more."

He knew that he would die . . . but he did not call death in. If he gave his portion away to another he did this not to shorten his own sufferings, but to help a suffering person. There was in him not the slightest trace of a despairing philosophy of death. He comforted and strengthened his companions saying, "Persevere! Try to hold out!" He prayed together with them, heard their confession.

He said on occasion, "Everything will come to an end, and the sufferings will end too. The way to glory is the way of the Cross. The Immaculate Virgin is with us, She will always help us. It only is necessary to give oneself to her like a child, with eyes closed."

It is hard to believe that in this camp of hunger, misery, torture, and death, Fr. Maximilian not only preserved his serenity of spirit but mustered enough vitality of mental alertness to formulate for the last time the doctrine of his own life.

It was Sunday in the camp. The sun was shining. A row of living skeletons was lying in the sunlight beneath the wall of Block 15. Opposite these on a wheelbarrow sat Fr. Maximilian. He spoke and they listened to his words.

He repeated what he had said more than once in his talks with the brothers at Niepokalanów about the high standing of Mary in regard to the Most Blessed Trinity. This is what those who heard him at that time related from memory:

"The Immaculate Virgin through her conception of and bringing to birth of the Son of God entered into a spiritual relationship with the three persons of the Holy Trinity.

"With respect to the Father, She is his child, first-born and only-begotten daughter of God. All the faithful are children of God by grace, but the Immaculate Virgin because of another title and in a higher degree. She would have been so, even if Christ had not extended this grace to all the people.

"In regard to the Son of God, She is his real Mother. The dogma of the hypostatic union says that the human nature of Jesus Christ from the first moment of his conception was united with his Divine Person without which it could not exist. Therefore, Mary gave birth to God and Man. That is an infinite dignity which surpasses all creatures in heaven and on earth. In virtue of this maternity, Mary has the fullness of grace, is gifted with every privilege, and takes an active part in the Redemption. Consequently, she distributes all graces, having become for all of us the Mediatrix. She who gave birth to the 'only begotten Son of the Father full of grace and truth' has received, as St. Thomas says, higher privileges than anyone else.

"In respect to the Holy Spirit, she is his Spouse because she conceived by Him."

In the year 1937, he explained this matter in an unusual and original way, "In God the Father, there is one nature and one person; in the Son of God there is one person and two natures; and in the Holy Spirit, the Blessed Mother is most intimately united with the Most Holy Spirit. . . .

"What kind of union is this? It is first of all an intimate union of her person with the person of the Most Holy Spirit. The Most Holy Spirit resides in Her, lives in Her. On what does that life of His in Her rest? He Himself is love in Her, that love of the Father and the Son with which God loves Himself. . . . the union of the Holy Spirit with Her: not only does love unite these two persons but one of them is the whole love of the Most Blessed

Trinity and the second—the whole love of the creature, and so in this union heaven and earth are united."

Finally, a day in July, a tragic day. Somebody runs away from the camp. The sirens blast and roar. The commanders run together breathlessly to the Apell-Platz, a roll call is taken. It shows that in block 14, Fr. Maximilian's block, a man is missing. The guards go out in search of him. In the meantime, the crowd of prisoners stands in rows full of fear. They all tremble for they know with what this escape threatens them. The commander of the camp had told them: "If anyone runs away—for every escapee 20 of you will go to death by starvation." In Auschwitz where one always dies in a painful manner, death by starvation in the cellar means the most horrible death of all.

The search was prolonged... The runaway was not found. It was getting dark, and the people were still standing in the courtyard. At last they were permitted to return to their barracks. But the affair was not finished. There was no supper. The prisoners did not dare lie down to sleep. In the barracks fearful whispers could be heard. A young boy murmurs, "I'm afraid." "Don't be afraid of death," says Fr. Maximilian.

No doubt he heard confessions that night. Although he was threatened with the severest penalties for hearing confessions, he was always ready. He never refused.

In this same block, the block of the convalescents, is Francis Gojowniczek, a sergeant of the 36th division of the infantry. A sturdy, fearless man, he ran away from the P.O.W. camp once, but was caught when he was secretly crossing through Slovakia into Austria, intending to go to England. He was brought to Zakopane and from there in the company of 1,500 mountaineers to Auschwitz. In a few months there were only 40 left of the 1,500 strong Podhalan. Barely two or three of this group outlived the war.

Fr. Maximilian did not know Gajowniczek. Acquaintanceship at Auschwitz was limited most frequently to the people in the same house. Furthermore there were others besides Poles.

In the morning there is another assembly. Yells, beatings, commands, count offs! Then comes a coveted moment of respite. . . . the comandos march off to work with their people. But block 14 remains. They stand in deathly fear of the danger threatening them.

Noon comes and goes; . . . they are still standing. They had no breakfast; they will get no dinner. The commandos return from work. The Platz, really only a wide street between the barracks, is being filled with thousands of people. What now?

Surrounded by the SS men, Lagerfuhrer Fritsch, the right hand man of Hess, is approaching slowly. Short, lean, with a drawn face, his evil eyes glower from beneath the rim of his cap drawn down low on his brow. He walks deliberately swinging his hips. It delights him to see fear in the people waiting for his coming. He stops suddenly. He says nothing, only looks. Like a snake he hypnotizes with his stare. Finally, he begins to speak. He throws his words out quickly, hoarsely. The interpreter obediently translates his words:

"Running away? But you do not want to work. If you would work better there would be more food. But since you run away, I will show you. I promised you: twenty for one. Today only ten will go . . . as a warning."

Deathly silence pervades the atmosphere of the place. The people turn pale and feverishly breathe in the air with open lips.

Fritsch approaches the first row. He walks along the standing line and looks into their faces. They dare not look him in the eye; . . it is forbidden to lower your gaze. He raises his hand and points with his finger: this one; . . this one. He goes on. In the deadly quiet only the creaking of his boots is heard. Now he inspects the second row. Again: this one.

At last he has ten . . . condemned to a slow death by starvation in the underground bunker of one of the blocks. Not to a merciful gunfire, but to torments about which news that froze the blood in one's veins circled around the camp.

One of those chosen was Gajowniczek. This rugged man

breaks down. He sees his wife and two sons before his eyes. He is strong enough to withstand the camp, but the perspective of a starvation death is too much for him. He bursts forth in tears crying something about his love for his wife and children.

And then, in the presence of the ten rows of prisoners, there suddenly edges out a frail human figure in striped clothing. The head is bent slightly toward the left shoulder. An unheard of thing, a prisoner unsummoned steps out of ranks! Fritsch impulsively grabs his pistol. What is this? A coup d'etat?

"Steh! Was ist los?" he shouts to the oncoming prisoner. The man stops, says something.

"Was wunscht dieses polnische Schwein?" asks Fritsch. Fr. Maximilian speaks softly, but in perfect German which he knew well and even gave lessons in conversation in Japan.

"Please, sir, permit me to die in place of one of the condemned."

"Are you out of your mind?"

"No. Please permit me...."

Fritsch is silent for awhile. His face twists like that of a dog about to bite. He had never heard anything like this. He does not look at Fr. Maximilian. The other SS men when they met the friar's look would shout, "Look at the ground, not at us!" Suddenly he asks, using the polite "sir" for the familiar form: "Who are you, sir?"

"A Catholic priest."

"In whose place do you want to go?"

"His," and Fr. Maximilian pointed with his finger at Gajowniczek.

"Why?"

"I am an old and single man. This man is young and has a family...."

That is true, Gajowniczek had a family. But it is also true that he will not have it after he survives the war and returns home. His sons will die heroically in the battle of the occupation. And yet there is a mysterious sense in this choice.

Fritsch gives a sign that he agrees, turns on his heel and immediately departs.

The guards lead the condemned men to a windowless cellar in the block bearing the number 11. They command them to disrobe completely. From now on they will get nothing to eat or drink, but they will have their morning exercises under supervision by one of the guards. Ordinarily, when condemned prisoners are found in the cellar, others can hear their howls, shrieks, and curses. But this time....

In 1966 Sophia Kossak wrote a brief scenic playlet. This is one of the scenes:

SS man I: "Someone singing?"

SS man II: "The men in the bunker...."

SS man I: "Unheard of!. It's already the fourth day they are sitting there. Usually they howl, curse and now look: they are singing. What happened?"

SS man II: "Maybe the priest changed them ... the one who went instead of another."

SS man I: "He must be a very extraordinary man...."

This time the condemned men really sang pious humns. The guards listened full of astonishment. Someone said: "This priest is indeed one outstanding man. Such a one we have never had here before...."

On August 14, the vigil of the feast of the Assumption, when the SS men entered the bunker, only Fr. Maximilian was living. He was done to death by an injection of carbolic acid.

He died the day before the feast of his Queen, a faithful knight.

Years before, when the brother of Fr. Maximilian died, Father Alphonse, the guardian of Niepokalanów and the news came to Japan, Fr. Maximilian wrote, "After the first reaction, a great joy entered my heart because the letter was dated on the anticipated vigil of the Immaculate Conception and at the 16th hour, so no doubt on the day of his death ... and that took place on the vigil of the Immaculate Conception. The funeral perhaps on the feast itself.... How can one be sad? Evidently, the Immaculate Virgin took him herself....

The saint

In August 1946, upon an invitation from the brothers of Niepokalanów, I went to the monastery to write a book about Fr. Maximilian. The motorcycle on which I was riding met with a catastrophe. The basket in which I was sitting broke away during the ride, but nothing happened to me.

Then I wrote the first version of "God's Miser." At that time I said, "There's a saint somewhere around the wooden huts of Niepokalanów. Maybe he is living, and maybe he is no longer living. I know, we are not allowed to call him this prematurely, not even the one whom we judge to be one. But should one be surprised that human thoughts look for holiness above all in a man who was the creator and founder of Niepokalanów, who lived by the ideal of Niepokalanów, who worked for the aims of Niepokalanów and who finally died voluntarily for its ideal?"

Today we can already say of Fr. Maximilian... the saint...

In 1943 the first booklet about him appeared in Italy. It was written by Professor Chiminelle. In 1946 "God's Miser" appeared in Poland. The publication of my booklet coincided with the permission given by the Apostolic See to initiate the informational process for the cause of beatification. The first bishop to mention beatification of Fr. Maximilian to the Pope already in 1948 was Bishop Yamaguchi, ordinary of the diocese of Nagasaki. The same year the process of beatification was begun in Padua. In 1961, the Apostolic process.... In 1965 the Apostolic See permitted the introduction of the discussion of the heroicity of the virtues of Fr. Maximilian, in spite of the fact that the 50 years required by canon law had not yet elapsed.

On January 30, 1969 the general session of the Congregation of Rites conferring under the leadership of the Holy Father Paul VI declared that Fr. Maximilian reached the degree of heroism in his theological and moral virtues.

On October 17, 1971, Pope Paul VI solemnly beatified Fr. Maximilian Kolbe. In his breve issued for that day he wrote:

"Maximilian Maria was born in Zdunska Wola in Poland. On April 28, 1918, his fervent desire was fulfilled when he was ordained a priest in the Roman church of St. Andrew della Valle. In the first days of his priesthood, words were written in the little daily missal expressing most clearly the prediction of what was to happen in the future. He offered the Holy Mass "for the conversion of sinners," and "for the grace of apostolic zeal and martyrdom."

The Holy Father recalled that "released from the camp in December 1939, for 14 months he made every effort to nurse the wounded, to house the displaced and to care for the Jews, about 2,000 in number. However, in February 1941 he was seized a second time and taken to the Pawiak prison in Warsaw, and from there to the extermination camp in Auschwitz. In the Pawiak jail he was frequently insulted, beaten, and physically injured only because he dearly and faithfully loved the Crucified One whose image he carried suspended from the rosary at the belt of his Franciscan habit. He suffered much also in Auschwitz in defense of the Lord Jesus Christ; there, no occasion was omitted to cause him bodily harm or moral indignity. With all that, he found enough strength to comfort the cruelly mistreated coprisoners, directing their minds to thoughts of eternity. More than that, not infrequently, he gave his daily portion of bread to the younger people tormented by hunger; and more than once he took their guilt upon himself, thus bearing his neighbor's burden. At night he would often crawl on all fours to the needy with help and console them as best he could with the administration of the holy sacraments...."

"The piety of Maximilian Maria was firmly rooted in his faith in the Most Holy Trinity. Likewise a great love for Christ hidden in the Most Holy Sacrament urged him on. Therefore, in Niepokalanów he introduced perpetual adoration. He looked upon Mary as his sweetest mother ... honored her above all for her undefiled purity which he imitated in particular.... His whole life is witness to his intense love of God and neighbor.... Worthy of praise is his prudence in dealing with everybody, be he Protestant, or Jew, or Buddhist. Before the Church even began to promote the ecumenical movement Maximilian Maria was already developing it...."

And the formula of beatification, "Fulfilling the wishes of many brothers... after beseeching light from on high, with our apostolic power and authority we enroll the Venerable Servant of God Maximilian Maria Kolbe, among the Blessed with the approval that his feast be celebrated on the day of his birth for heaven... the 14th of August..."

We shall pray that the act of beatification be speedily completed by the act of canonization.

In the 1970s there appeared in Assisi a book entitled: "I knew Blessed Maximilian," by Bro. Juventyn Mlodozeniec, a former companion of Fr. Kolbe. It was soon translated into several languages.

In August of 1975 I took to writing the life of Fr. Maximilian for the second time. Happily, I could now profit by the wealth of material available. Certain phases of his life, especially the most interesting one: his sojourn in Japan, are so rich that I think I will return to them again, especially if I am fortunate enough to get to Japan.

In my writing, I tried to keep to the framework of the old *Miser of God*. I broadened and reworked certain pages, canceled others, especially where there was more of my publicizing than words of the Blessed Father. Thus this is once more *God's Miser* and at the same time something new.

I would like to see this work of mine as a contribution to the process of canonization of a Man who belonged to my generation and whose influence on me I felt all my life. I used to write for the *Little Journal* and for the *Knight of the Immaculata*. I could have been together with Fr. Maximilian in Auschwitz and it seems to me at times that he gave up his life for me also as he did for Gajowniczek and others.

Blessed Maximilian, patron of those dreadful times, pray for us!

August 1946–August 1975